Essential Acting

How do actors fuse thought, emotion and action within their creative process?

Essential Acting is an inspired and reliable toolbox for actors and teachers in the classroom, the rehearsal room and the workshop. RADA's Brigid Panet has distilled 50 years of acting, directing and actor training into a unique recipe which brilliantly combines the teachings of Stanislavski and Laban into an invaluable practical resource.

These exercises are built around the need for simple, achievable techniques that can be applied by actors, teachers and directors to answer the myriad requirements of actor training. The goal is to produce a continuous level of achievement, addressing:

- How to rehearse
- How to work with a text
- How to audition for drama school
- How to access the *truth* of feelings and actions

Essential Acting will be a must-have purchase for anyone looking for a comprehensive study guide to the necessary work of the actor.

Brigid Panet's teaching and directing career includes productions for the Royal National Theatre, Rio de Janeiro, Montreal, Boston and major English drama schools including LAMDA and RADA.

I first heard about Brigid Panet's work when, as a young director about to do my first teaching job, I was handed some notes by a friend who had attended one of Brigid's 'how to run a workshop' workshops at the National Theatre Studio. Ideas and exercises from those (now rather dog-eared) notes have remained with me ever since and are as essential a part of my teaching today as they were then. The title of the book is spot on, because there is something 'essential' about Brigid's work; it gets to the essence of things, and the number of students and young actors who have benefited from that essential rigour over the years is legion. I was delighted when I took over at RADA to find that she was one of the regular teachers at the Academy and I am every bit as thrilled and every bit as delighted that this treasure trove of teaching is now available to those of us who have only ever benefitted from her work second-hand, through the skill and attitude of actors she has taught. Some of these exercises I knew well, but so many others are new to me that reading this book leaves me eager to get back into a rehearsal room to try them out.

Ed Kemp, Artistic Director, RADA

Brigid Panet manages to bring together a dancer's understanding of movement and body language, with an actor's sensitivity to text and the spoken word. The result is enlightening, fun and liberating. I think this book should be compulsory reading for every Drama teacher in the country: it is a simple, concise, no-nonsense approach to learning the complicated art of acting.

Adrian Lester

Essential Acting

A Practical Handbook for Actors, Teachers and Directors

Brigid Panet

with Fiona McHardy

All author royalties from this book will be donated to Sightsavers International

Routledge
Taylor & Francis Group

LONDON AND NEW YORK

First published 2009
by Routledge
2 Park Square, Milton Park, Abingdon, Oxon OX14 4RN

Simultaneously published in the USA and Canada
by Routledge
270 Madison Ave, New York, NY 10016

Routledge is an imprint of the Taylor & Francis Group, an informa business

© 2009 Brigid Panet

Typeset in Janson by
Keystroke, 28 High Street, Tettenhall, Wolverhampton

Printed and bound in Great Britain by
TJ International, Padstow, Cornwall

British Library Cataloguing in Publication Data
A catalogue record for this book is available from the British Library
Library of Congress Cataloging-in-Publication Data
Panet, Brigid, 1948-
    Essential acting: a practical handbook for actors, teachers and directors/
Brigid Panet.
        p. cm.
    Includes bibliographical references and index.
    1. Acting—Handbooks, manuals, etc. I. Title.
    PN2061.P27 2009
    792.02′8—dc22   2008029201

ISBN10: 0–415–47677–1 (hbk)
ISBN10: 0–415–47678–X (pbk)
ISBN10: 0–203–88238–5 (ebk)

ISBN13: 978–0–415–47677–5 (hbk)
ISBN13: 978–0–415–47678–2 (pbk)
ISBN13: 978–0–203–88238–2 (ebk)

To Lorna –
with love & admiration –
Tsipw

This book is for my son and daughter, Dominic and Lucy, and their children: Reuben, Benjamin and Alice, with my love, and for Teresa Cristina Fournier and all the dear actors who have been my best teachers and friends, encouraging me to write this book at last.

Remembering with love my parents Brigadier Henri de Lotbinière Panet and Truda Panet, Sylvia Barter, Alex Hall, John Gulliver, John Foxen and Michael Joyce.

The art of theatre is the art of acting, first, last and every time.
(Harley Granville-Barker)

Contents

Art itself may be defined as a single-minded attempt to render the highest kind of justice to the visible universe; by bringing to light the truth, manifold and one, underlying its every aspect

(Joseph Conrad)[1]

There is a vitality
a life force
an energy
a quickening that is translated by you into action,
and because there is only one of you in all time
this expression is unique
and if you block it
it will never exist through any other medium and will be lost;
the world will not have it.

It is not your business to determine how good it is,
nor how valuable,
nor how it compares with other expressions.
It is your business to keep it yours
clearly and directly,
to keep the channel open.

You do not even have to believe
in yourself or your work.
You have to keep
open
and
aware directly
to the urges that motivate you.
Keep the channel open.

(Martha Graham to Agnes de Mille)[2]

Introduction

This book offers simple, practical and effective teaching in the basics of acting and rehearsing a play. I wrote it in response to the requests – demands, even – of the many students and actors I have worked with over the years who have wanted to enjoy our rehearsals and classes without the bother of taking notes and trying to remember the details of an exercise or technique. I developed the ideas and the exercises that illustrate them in the energy of class and rehearsal, to solve problems in acting as they arose. They have proven consistently useful, facilitating the learning of basic theory through direct, active experience.

The teaching uses as its base the Method of Physical Action developed by the Russian actor, director and teacher Konstantin Stanislavski (1863–1938). My approach joins this, his final and most useful approach to acting, with the practical analysis of rhythm and movement developed by Rudolf von Laban (1879–1958), the Hungarian dancer and teacher whose theories of choreography and movement helped to create the central foundations of modern European dance.

> You cannot master the method of physical action if you do not master rhythm. Each physical action is inseparably linked to the rhythm that characterises it.[1]

Stanislavski's previous 'systems' relied on the rigorous planning of each character's emotions and on the actor using willpower and imaginative force to summon belief in his character and the Given Circumstances of a scene. But in the last five years of his life, when he was too ill to act or direct, he turned instead to a simple, practical method where truth of expression is found in the through-line of a role's physical actions. Stanislavski put physical action *before* emotion as a technical strategy, because, as he said, 'You cannot set feeling, you can only set action.'

In practice, every action has its unique emotional twin – maybe if we could express the effect of this strategy in two words at once, we would say action/emotion: action comes first, then spontaneous feeling arises effortlessly. The word 'feeling' combines the physical sensation perceived by the five senses with the emotional response that ripples through the body, changing breathing, muscle tone, heartbeat and even the flow of blood (causing the actor to blush or grow pale). This is acting as direct experience. This approach frees the actor from searching for feelings within himself and directs his attention outwards towards the task of the character and his partners in the scene.

In developing his Method of Physical Action, Stanislavski searched in vain for a reliable, systematic breakdown of behavioural movement and rhythm; I think he would have found what he was looking for in Laban's analysis of action – the combination of the two provides, in my experience, all that the actor needs to be confident, to have a sustained feeling of truth in his acting, and to increase his ability to practise and improve his craft.

* * *

Recently, I gave a short workshop to young would-be actors with the title 'What is acting and how do you do it?' I gave the actors some big sheets of paper and asked them, in small groups, to write down the answers to the first question, 'What is acting?' The papers came back filled with big statements such as, 'it is being somebody else'; 'it gives me the chance to become another person'; 'it is leaving myself and being someone new', and so on. And what worried me was the verb 'to be': you can't be another person and if that was what people thought acting was they were trying for the impossible, and wasting their efforts and dreams. But if we eliminate the infinitive 'to be' and add the magic 'if', followed by the subjunctive (which expresses a wish or a possibility), then the job description of acting becomes reasonable and attainable. So now we have 'Acting is behaving as if . . .' The word 'behaving' gives us the physical action and the 'as if' gives the imagined situation, including the character.

> If it is not being somebody else, what is it?
> It is as if somebody else is being you.

It is the direct experience that you are having as the imagined character in the imagined situation. Your job is to allow that situation, in those Given Circumstances, to matter as much to you at that moment as it would to the character.

Faced with any play, your job as an actor is to answer and then convey the Three Essential Questions about your character's situation in the world of the play. The first question is: what is your character's Aim? What is it that he seeks to achieve? The second is what Obstacles must your character overcome if he is to achieve his Aim? The third is what series of Strategies does your character use to overcome those Obstacles? Through a series of improvisation techniques and exercises, this book encourages you to experience these three essential questions and then to transfer this knowledge to the more difficult task of behaving naturally in public as an imagined character in an imagined situation.

* * *

Looking back at my own acting training at the Central School of Speech and Drama in London, between 1954 and 1957, I can't remember having any lessons in acting; after the first term of mime we started to work on plays and were expected to learn through doing. This was fine in some ways, but I'm not sure how we were expected to improve, if the only coaching we got were the (excellent) voice classes with Cicely Berry, some practice in the technicalities of rehearsal and our few performances in front of staff and our peers.[2]

Some of our small group, such as Judi Dench and Vanessa Redgrave, were exceptionally talented and had had some experience, but I was only 16 when I joined the school, coming straight from a ballet training. (I didn't even want to be there! My anxious parents had suggested an acting career as I was not physically strong enough to continue as a dancer.) Each individual talent has its own rhythm; I think that mine is largely instinctive and that in rehearsal I tended to muddle and fudge the useful 'first response', because I did not have a firm understanding of what the jobs of rehearsing and the actor's homework were.[3] This is a key reason for my urge to offer any help I can to younger artists.

Leaving Central to go into weekly rep – the system of the time where regional theatre companies presented a different play each week – suited me well and I was very happy working in those years before every home had a TV and people would go regularly to their local theatre to see the latest West End hits or plays that reflected their own society. When you have to learn up to 30 pages of dialogue overnight and are rehearsing one play each morning while performing another at night there is no time to worry about 'what acting is' and I was lucky in that many older, experienced actors led those companies and I could learn by example from them. (It is a pity that young actors now have no chance of working with the 'mother elephants' who carry on the traditions of good theatre and support and teach in the best way, by unobtrusive example.)

Some years later, when my children were growing up and I had stopped acting in order to take care of them, I started to teach and direct plays in drama schools, and that was when my real training in 'how you do acting' began. Teaching is the best way of learning, which is why I love doing it and never get bored! For the first time, I had to clarify and structure what I thought acting was and to find practical ways to teach it. This was where the exercises and approaches to rehearsal in this book started: they were all invented in the urgency of the moment, to solve particular problems through action.

From my ballet training I had grown up with firm, trustworthy physical groundwork that I could rely on practice to improve; there were exercises that extended the stretch of the legs, or enabled me to turn twice round in pirouettes, etc.; if I practised them correctly I could then achieve a specific result. Acting, however, seemed to have no such logic; it was all misty and relative – one person could say you had been truthful and expressive while another called your performance wooden and unconvincing. When you felt that you had done well, you could be scolded for bad work, and when you felt that you had failed, a director or teacher would suddenly congratulate you, 'At last, you have got it!' This could be painful and frustrating and, as I taught, I wanted so much to save other young actors from confusion like this.

* * *

As a distillation of my 50 years' work acting and training actors, the book contains 'recipes' and ideas for the actor, teacher and director: exercises in the basics of acting; work on status, eye-gaze and poise; a guide for a creative rehearsal process; a collection of useful techniques for the actor and director; an introduction to playing Shakespeare; and my adaptation for actors of Laban's analysis of physical and emotional action. I have found that actors experience difficulty in practising their craft on their own, out of class or rehearsal. Individual practice in the Laban exercises allows the actor to develop and refine his work on rhythm. This gives him a vocabulary of action, which he can use to record his observations, so as to be able to incorporate them into his work on text and character.

My aim is for actors, teachers and directors to enjoy a continuous feeling of achievement, the experience that Stanislavski described as the sensation of successful actors: that feeling of 'I am solving this problem.' The actor sustains his positive outlook as a worker and, as the imagined character he is playing, he sustains it in the imagined situation of the scene, enjoying the two levels of consciousness.

Brecht, who saw actors as 'scientists' of human behaviour, quoted with approval Charles Laughton's reply to the question of why he wanted to be an actor: 'Because people don't know what they're like and I think I can show them.'[4]

* * *

Author's note: Acting, unlike dance and music, has a limited vocabulary to help study; so I have used capital letters to denote technical terms, such as Given Circumstances, Aims, Obstacles and so on.

Editions of Shakespeare can vary greatly: not only words, spellings and punctuation but also line numbers, so I have given only the Act and Scene numbers when discussing Shakespeare's language. In Part Five I have changed capital letters at the beginning of lines to lower case, because it is important to look at the text in terms of sentences and sense rather than cutting it up at the line endings.

* * *

I am the vessel through which 'the Rite' passes.

(Igor Stravinsky)[5]

Acknowledgements

Grateful thanks to Fiona McHardy, without whose help and enthusiasm this book would never have been finished, and to Louise Burns of Andrew Mann Ltd and Talia Rodgers of Routledge for their work and support.

Part One Acting exercises

1   Introduction

To behave as if you were living unobserved in a private space, when you are actually in a brightly lit public space with many people looking at you, is difficult. To speak someone else's words as if they were your own, while behaving in a way that is foreign to you, in a situation that is purely imagined, is not easy. Talent is not enough to make it consistently possible.

Actors work in three functional areas: they exercise, rehearse and perform. It is useful to be clear about which area you are in: when you are exercising you are neither rehearsing nor performing, when rehearsing you are neither exercising nor performing, and when performing neither exercising nor rehearsing. But in all of those functions you are playing and the important thing is to take this conscious decision to play, to start to take action at once and to stay in the world of imagination until it is time to finish. If you do that, the work is not tiring and the fun leaves no room for fear.

To clarify the shift from the actor's daily life to his creative life, I use this analogy: my right arm represents my daily life (note that I have not called this my 'real' life, because both aspects of my life are real). My left arm, nearer my heart, represents the life of the imagination, which I use for acting. Both arms connect through the centre of my body and at times can work together, though usually one is more active than the other. When I decide to move from one function to another, from my daily life to the life of the character in the scene, it is a natural change of focus from, as it were, the right arm to the left; then, when the exercise or scene ends, I change back again.

NOTES FOR THE TEACHER OF THE ACTING EXERCISES

It is not always easy to sense how long an exercise should last. I have suggested an average duration for each one listed below; this includes time for feedback. I have found that in any game the group's energy will drop after a fairly short time of playing. In an inexperienced group this drop will usually happen quite soon. The teacher will probably feel that this is the moment to stop and maybe go on to another activity, but if he has the courage to let the group continue to play on through those 'dead' moments, he will nearly always find that the energy rises again, this time with a new and fresher impetus, more invention, more team-playing and a sense that the activity now belongs to the group and will now continue until players are tired or till it comes to a natural conclusion. These exercises can be used more than once with a group. Once players know the rules they can become more skilful, have more fun and maybe invent new variations.

Many games involve working in pairs, but, if there is an uneven number in the group, three players can work together; in this case, the teacher may need to give the group of three a slightly different change-over signal, earlier than the signal for pairs, so that each player in the group of three can have a turn. If the exercise continues with new pairs a new group of three should be formed.

It is often useful to have time for feedback after an exercise; this gives the group a rest if they have been working hard and an opportunity to consider the purposes of the experience that they have just shared. I tell players that their effortless achievement in these exercises takes away all future excuses; that if they can do this then they can play the character in the scene.

Never tell people how to do things; tell them what to do and they will surprise you with their ingenuity.

(General Patton)

2 Making a good start

FREE DRAWING

A quiet exercise. Most useful as a start to a class or rehearsal, also useful as a means to explore characters and relationships in a play. Works well with new groups and does not lose its power however many times it is experienced.

Recently, a student who works at a shoe shop each weekend in order to pay for her course told me that she had introduced free drawing to her fellow shop-assistants during a long afternoon with no customers. The girls enjoyed the game so much that they now turn to it whenever they have a free moment; it seems that the need to express feelings non-verbally and to allow oneself to play without aiming for a result can be satisfied with this simple exercise.

Focus: To naturally direct attention into creative action.

Space, time and numbers: Room for all players to sit and draw with their paper on the floor; can be brief, around 5 to 7 minutes, but can be extended; any number.

What you need: A sheet of paper, at least A4 size, for each player and plenty of colouring pens, crayons or pencils. A bin for the drawings that are torn up.

I find this exercise so valuable that I now start every class or rehearsal with 5 minutes of free drawing. Almost every group, no matter what age or stage they are at, enjoys it, finds it helpful and wishes to do it as a starter to every session. Quietly doodling / scribbling / drawing allows people to become calm, to arrive more completely in the room and to express their feelings at that moment. I have been surprised and delighted to find that the quality of the work and the atmosphere within the group are so much better after this brief experience. For myself, when I need to move from working with one group to working with another, or from my life outside the rehearsal room to the world of the scene, the 5 minutes of quiet focus with everyone in the group give me the clarity and presence I need to do good work.

On her way to one of my classes, a student had had angry words with a taxi driver. As she settled to draw, she had time to understand her hidden upset, to express it by scribbling black lines on paper and so to get rid of those unpleasant tensions, which enabled her to work freely and happily in the group.

For a different class I gave – a one-off workshop with young students, one group aged 8–11 and the other aged 12–18 – I had planned to do the drawing for around 5 to 10 minutes as usual, but once the kids had started to draw, it was clear that this was giving them a chance to express themselves and in the end the drawing continued for almost the whole 2-hour session. In this case the children wanted to show and explain their drawings to me, and that added to the time we spent on that one exercise. It was also important to tell them – and all groups – that they could tear up their drawings if they wished to. Young girls, drawing pictures and images of people who bullied them at school, needed then to destroy those images. With one group we all tore up our pictures, throwing the tiny pieces of paper up so that they fell like snow all over the floor. (Then, of course, we cleared them up together and put them in a bin!) In another group, a boy, rather small for his age, found it hard to start drawing; it was difficult for him to feel safe about expressing himself, so he needed to work privately and to be able to hide his first drawing after showing it to me; after this one, where he had drawn himself trapped behind prison bars, he went on to do many more, ending with several that showed him as a mountain.

When I started the work I experimented with the time limits, asking groups which suited them best: 5, 6, 7 minutes . . . up to 20 minutes. The consensus was that 7 was best for them. (This was with two separate groups of American actors doing a class on Shakespeare's sonnets.) If the free drawing is used as a starting exercise it is best, I think, for the teacher to say '5 minutes', then, at 5 minutes, to start to collect the pens and let people stop drawing within the next 2 or 3 minutes. Alternatively, the exercise can run as long as the energy lasts.

To introduce the idea, I do a 2-minute drawing myself, explaining as I go along and being truthful about what matters to me at that moment. So, I usually start with an image of the group and myself – maybe a circle with bright lines radiating out of it – then I could go on to scribbles of my home; absent family members who I am thinking of; my garden, if I want to be working in it after class; possibly money if I am concerned about that, etc. Each time is different and cannot be prepared. I use words too, if I want to.

Using free drawing in rehearsal

You can develop the exercise to explore characters' backgrounds and their situations within the play. When I did this with a cast rehearsing *Macbeth*, the actor playing Macbeth drew a picture of his character, as he saw him, full of images from the play. We then began to draw other characters and, from there, to draw one character from the point of view of another, so 'Macbeth' drew 'Duncan'; 'Lady M' drew her husband; 'Duncan' drew 'Lady M' and so on. We found this fun and useful and that it could be used as a practical way to build a character, using images found in the text. If you make time during rehearsals for quiet creative work like drawing you will find it a release from anxiety, a welcome change of rhythm and a gentle means of drawing your concentration in to the world of your character, which will provide the foundation of belief when you get up to play your scene. The drawing seems to release an inner understanding, free of judgement, enabling us to drop a bucket into what Stanislavski calls the 'creative subconscious'. This is the sense of play that we need and enjoy as actors.

YES, AND . . .

Focus: To explore problems of approach and shared energy in acting.

Space, time and numbers: Anywhere; about 15 minutes; any number can play as long as people are working in pairs; players should change partners at each of the three stages so that they work with three different partners. Allow time after each stage for feedback.

This very helpful game comes via the work of Keith Johnstone,[1] who found it in Viola Spolin's *Improvisation for the Theater*.[2] The uses of this simple game extend far beyond the first playing of it: many blocks and problems in acting and life can be recognised and dealt with by remembering how you felt during the two first stages of saying 'no' and 'yes, but . . .' before moving onto the freedom of 'yes, and . . .' The psychologist Raj Persaud calls these mental blockages ANTS: Automatic Negative Thoughts – a useful description.

Some time ago I made one New Year's resolution which I have kept: I will not do anything which is not fun to do. Writing this is fun as I write it; when it stops being fun I will stop and play another game . . . maybe I'll do the washing-up or read a book. If I can sustain my recognition of the autonomy I have, that is, know that I have the power to choose and take responsibility for my choices, then whatever I decide to do has that bubble of fun inside it. Are you already thinking of situations where the person has no choice? I heard a true story the other day about a Palestinian man held up at a border-crossing by an Israeli soldier who told him to strip to be searched. The Palestinian had a choice, although there was a gun pointing at him. He chose to refuse to strip and eventually the soldier let him pass. Both men made a free choice of action. We, in our relatively free society, have the daily privilege of choice: what to wear, where we live, what we eat, what we say and do; there is no excuse for us to hide behind the 'mind-forged manacles' as Blake calls them, of 'I have to'; 'it makes me feel like . . .'; 'I can't help it' and so on.

Stage one: Saying 'No'

A makes offers to B that she hopes B will find hard to refuse; B just says 'No' to every offer made. This 'No' needs to be simple and unequivocal, just a calm, firm block to every suggestion from A.

Example:
A: would you like to star in a play at the National Theatre? B: No.
A: What about a holiday on a beautiful island, all expenses paid? B: No.
A: Would you like some chocolate? B: No.
A: A cup of coffee? B: No.
A: A million pounds? B: No.
And so on.

The players then reverse roles, with B making the offers and A refusing them. This stage illustrates the frustration and deadening negativity of the actor who will not respond to her partner; it is not a problem that often appears openly but it can be used as protection or concealed attack, usually due to fear.

Stage two: Saying 'Yes, but . . .'

This excuse is used when 'the native hue of resolution is sicklied over with the pale cast of thought, and enterprises of great pitch and moment . . . lose the name of action' (*Hamlet*, Act 3, Sc. 1). If we are honest we can all remember times when we have wriggled out of taking action with a clever excuse; in fact, people can be quite creative with their 'Yes, buts . . .' A feeble avoidance of the creative state – what I call 'nesting in the Obstacle' – can often be seen in actors and needs to be recognised and challenged.

Example:
(The players now have new partners.)
A: I'd like you to star in my new film.
B: Yes, but I would want 3 million dollars for the job.
A: I'd be so happy to give you 4 or 5 million.
B: Yes, but I've got everything I want already, so I don't need the money.

A: Well, would you like a glass of champagne?
B: Yes, but it might give me a headache.
And so on.

Players now understand how draining this avoidance and concealed refusal of response can be and how the active offerer feels baffled by it. Acting is no fun when one person plays 'yes, but . . .'

Stage three: Saying 'Yes, and . . .'

This stage is fun and easy. The players have changed partners and this time there is no division between A and B; they just bounce off each other, taking up the first offer and then flying together with it.

Example:
A: Let's form a new theatre company.
B: Yes, and we can do all the plays we like best.
A: Yes, and we can write our own plays too.
B: Yes, and we can work all over the world and be rich and famous.
A: Yes, and we can start a theatre on the moon.
B: Yes, and we can have spaceships to bring our audience up there . . .
And so on.

The energy in the room will have risen right up and the players will be reluctant to stop this mutual creative flow. This is the ideal approach to acting, full of life and enjoyment.

COUNTING TO 10

A quiet game of attention.

Focus: The exercise gives practice in listening, being aware of others, surrendering to the group aim and understanding one's own physical reactions to the stresses of wishing to succeed.

Space, time and numbers: Any size space (I have used this game when stuck in a small, crowded space with a group while waiting for our large space to be available). The time required can be from 3 to 20 minutes, so the game is also a useful 'filler' for ending a class. Any number of more than eight can play. The game can also work as a starter exercise for a new group. In a large group, there can be two or more sub-groups working at the same time and in competition with each other; for this, you need a reliable leader in each group, to prevent any cheating.

Sitting in a circle, preferably on the floor, the group's Aim is to count to 10, each person saying one number at a time and taking random turns (i.e. not counting in sequence around the circle). The Obstacle is that if any two or more players speak at the same time, the group has to return to number 1 and start again. So, A says '1' and, after a pause, B says '2'. Quickly, C and D both say '3' and so the counting has to start from '1' again.

Once the group has counted to '10', you can count back down again to '1'. With practice, you will get skilled and the target number can be increased to 20 or even more.

The person running the game must ensure that players don't cheat by signalling to each other or keeping the same number each time. As an actor, it is useful for you to check how your body reacts to the stress of preparing to speak and 'making a mistake'; this stress can increase as the stakes get higher, when the game is going well.

Once players have checked on weight withheld from the support of the floor and consequent held breathing and muscular tensions they can play again with their attention on the releasing of these habits (see Chapter 9, p. 87). Allow time after the game to discuss the differences in the process. See if the actors can relate it to the stresses of performance. The game can also be played with closed eyes, a pleasant experience for the group, which often leads to a more successful result because of the mutual trust and easy empathy this engenders.

SHOWING, TRYING AND SIMPLY DOING

A short exercise to illustrate some common problems in acting.

Focus: To expose two mistaken approaches and one satisfactory approach to acting.

Space, time and numbers: Anywhere; allow at least 3 minutes per player over all three stages; any number above two players.

Choose a simple physical action that can be repeated for each of the three stages of this exercise; for instance, a large circling movement of the arms, joined with a knee bend, or a walk across the room, ending with sitting in a chair. One or more players demonstrate the movement at each stage to the rest of the group.

Stage one: Showing

Actors show what they are doing when they are unsure of themselves, not trusting the power of simple action. Showing involves distracting effort and a split focus, because the actor is considering the effect he is having on the spectators, wishing to succeed and to please. In Stanislavski's words, he is in the 'actor's state' rather than the 'creative state'.

Actor's state =   I am trying to play this scene
                I am trying to get it right
                I am trying to feel the 'emotional state' of the character

Creative state =   I am solving this problem
                I am in the situation of the character in this scene
                Active communication is my priority

Stage two: Trying

Trying is also a common fault. It is another form of Showing, and arises from anxiety and a fear of failure. The actor indicates as he performs the action that he is attempting to do something very difficult and that he is doomed to fail; this victim role can be a habitual refuge, so it is useful to expose this protective strategy, as it destroys creative energy.

Stage three: Simply Doing

This approach is the answer to problems of acting; the required action is performed with a complete, trustful attention on the sensations of the moment.

Guess which approach?

Choose which of the three approaches you are going to use. The rest of the group has to guess which it is. Perform a specific movement or action, such as picking up a book and reading it silently, drinking a cup of water, or any other simple, everyday activity. This exercise is useful for you to learn to recognise these faults and hopefully avoid them in all future work.

You can be 95 per cent in the creative state of the character, while keeping 5 per cent of your awareness on the actual physical conditions of the performance, so that you and your scene partners are safe, you can ride laughs or coughs from the audience and manage any unforeseen problems in a professional way; you must always retain that sense of reality. The actress Fanny Kemble in the 1800s remarked that while tears were pouring down her face in a tragic scene, she managed at the same time to keep them from falling on her silk dress, so as not to stain it. Shakespeare, too, was fascinated by this double awareness in acting.

TWO CHAIRS

Focus: To examine a common problem in acting: that of functioning in the wrong time zone.

Space, time and numbers: A large, clear space; allow at least 5 minutes for the sequence; at least four players – two players and their audience.

What you need: Two upright chairs.

Place the chairs facing each other, as far apart as possible. Player A sits in chair A and Player B in chair B. Player A is the active partner and B co-operates with her. The idea of the exercise is to illustrate action in three time zones: that of the past, the future and the present moment. In all three stages Player A goes over to Player B, who is sitting in chair B, and leads him over to chair A, where she seats him; Player A then returns to sit in chair B. They do this silently.

Stage one: Working in the past tense

Player A: Think of a past event in your life (avoiding any sad or traumatic event) or a play, film or book you have seen and continue to think of that all through the exercise, as you move Player B. At the end of this stage you will both have a chance to say how you felt. A: How much notice did you take of your scene partner? Did you have time or attention to spare to connect with him?

Stage two: Working in the future tense

Player A: Now move Player B into his chair as quickly as possible, thinking of nothing but the result of your actions, not of their process.

SAFETY NOTE: It is important to ask two other people to stand behind both chairs, holding them firmly so that they don't tip over when the players land in them.

How did you feel this time? In the rush of achieving the Aim, was the process or means whereby the action happens forgotten? Does the end justify the means when the means have so little meaning?

Stage three: Working in the present moment

This is the pleasant one. Player A: Simply move B with your complete attention on him and your actions. What a relief and how easy this is; there is an effortless connection between the players, a storyline seems to invent itself and, however many times you might repeat this stage, it is always fresh and interesting to play and to watch.

3 Experiencing the Three Essentials

TOUCH THE SMALL-OF-THE-BACK TAG

Focus: Playing a physical Aim and finding strategies to overcome a clear Obstacle, with outward attention focused on the partner.

Space, time and numbers: The game needs a large clear space with a non-slip floor. If the floor is slippery, players should be barefoot or wearing non-slip shoes (not socks). Lasts about 10 minutes. Any number of people can play, in pairs, depending on the size of the room.

This is a tag game. Make a pair with another player. The Aim for both players in the pair is to touch the small of their partner's back. Each player keeps one hand behind his back; as they play, Player A tries to touch Player B's hidden hand, while preventing B from touching her, A's, hand behind her own back. Meanwhile, Player B is trying to do the same to his partner A.

After a while, change the partners, so that B is now playing with C and A is with D; three changes of partner are usually enough, as the game is so energetic.

Version 2: No-smiling tag

While acting, many players unconsciously paste the mask of a slight but permanent smile over their faces. This is part of the strong desire for acceptance and approval shared by all of us. However, this smile means that the actor is standing in the way of the character and unable to inhabit the scene (I call this 'interfearance'). To move from the fun of the normal energetic warm-up tag game into playing it without smiling will give you a useful experience of action in a serious, almost dangerous, situation.

The contest is dark and intense. Most players find that the times when it is most difficult to keep to the 'no-smiling' rule are the moments when you get a 'hit' and succeed in touching your partner's hand, and the moments when you change partners without stopping the game, as it is so natural to smile when contacting a new partner. It is worth practising this exercise till you can achieve it to a full and truthful extent, as it is an excellent test of an actor's ability to stay in the Given Circumstances of a scene.

> **Mercury the messenger:** The actor needs a sort of mercurial energy, which is wonderful to behold. A limitless pool of spirited energy that can be honed and disciplined so that it can take the actor where the story needs him to go.

TWO'S COMPANY (THREE'S A CROWD)

> **Focus:** To give experience in playing the Three Essentials. This game demonstrates the techniques of making and accepting offers, playing a clear physical Aim and being willing to change strategies and rhythms in order to achieve this aim. It also rewards a 'Yes, and . . .' approach in the players and explores their willingness to change.
>
> **Space, time and numbers:** This is an active game for three players at a time within a group; any number of more than eight

> can play. You will need a large clear space, with the big playing space in the centre and the other players sitting around the edge or against the walls of the room. Allow enough time for everyone to have a turn of roughly 3 minutes.

I invented this game years ago when I was rehearsing *A Midsummer Night's Dream*, to illustrate the situation of the three bewildered lovers in the magic wood. The Aim is to be part of a pair, and the Obstacle, which gives energy to the action, is that there are three people in the situation. Two's Company is close to a playground game and, because no one enjoys being left out, it is important to remember that if you are the third player (the person not at that moment in a pair) you are actually the player with the power to change the situation, to be inventive and to solve the playful problem.

The game has no props, real or unreal, so no mime is allowed. It is played without speech, though at times vocal sound can be used as long as it doesn't take the place of speech.

> The game starts with two players in a pair; it is helpful for an experienced player to be the third player in the game at this time, as she can demonstrate the possibilities of playing with rhythms and simple activities. The teacher can pick two players to be A and B; they can simply walk around the room, or stand closely together: the important thing is that they share each other's rhythms and movements. Player C, the person with no partner, now needs to 'make an offer' to attract one player of the current pair to join her. This simple, active offer could be clapping her hands, running around the pair of A and B, lying on the floor, or any action that either joins or offers a distinct opposition of rhythm to that of the pair. If C's offer is refused, she tries another strategy.

Now, A and B could, of course, just refuse to change; they have got their Aim, so why should they risk losing it? *But* the instinct for playing – the strongest need for the actor – will allow them to take a chance, to be willing to betray their present partner in order to find a new one.

> As the game progresses the teacher needs to pull the player who is not at that moment part of a pair out of the game and put in a new player from the group. In this way all players have a turn without breaking the rhythm of the game, because it is important to keep it flowing along. I ask each player to return to their previous place sitting around the edge of the room, so that I can be sure not to leave anyone out.

The exercise makes clear the idea of making, accepting and refusing offers, which is a useful way of looking at the action of a scene. It also gives confidence in trusting the power of rhythm in action and in the enjoyment of change for its own sake. Once the Laban vocabulary has been learned (see Chapter 23), the choice and control of rhythms will be an integral part of your technique and skill.

> After everyone has had a turn, the game can be played again with a free choice of any member of the group coming in or out of the three active players, like a constantly changing tag game. It is useful to have time for feedback after the game: for players to comment on how free and unselfconscious they felt while playing; how at first the sensation of being the 'odd one out' was rather distressing, until they understood that at that time they are really in charge of the game; and how the audience were constantly interested and entertained by the action of the story so clearly played in front of them.

Two's Company improvisation

Two's Company can be adapted for an improvised scene with groups of three players. The important thing is that each player in the group of three connects with both the other two players, as in this example (Player A connects with B, while C is left out; then B connects with C, ignoring A; then C connects with A, ignoring B).

The game can continue with many changes of focus between the three players; it could then expand to join other groups of three, where there is more choice of pair partners, maybe eventually involving the entire company of players. The experience is useful for clear playing of group scenes in a play, such as the coffee scene in Act 1 of *The Cherry Orchard* and the play scene in *Hamlet*.

Example:

A (to B): I want to give a party for your birthday tomorrow.

B: Thanks! That's so nice of you. Let's invite all our friends.

A: I've already done that and they're all bringing presents for you.

C (to B): My present is two tickets tomorrow night for that play you so wanted to see.

B: That's exactly what I wanted most!

C: Yes, and we can meet the star afterwards; she's a great friend of mine.

A (to C): Didn't you know she's ill and the understudy will be playing tomorrow?

C: Well, actually, I did know; she's not really ill, she's just taking a night off to come to a small, private dinner with me and just one special friend of mine to talk about a film we're casting – there's one part that would suit you.

A: I'd love that, thanks! The birthday party's not important; I'll just cancel all the invitations.

Then B can claim some attention and the game continues.

SIMPLE SIMON

Focus: This game forces the actor to stick to the Given Circumstances of a scene, no matter how difficult these are. Actors need to be able to do this to prove they can act. The exercise is connected to the work on status (see pp. 75).

Space, time and numbers: Anywhere; allow at least 30 minutes; requires at least six players but can involve the whole group. What you need: A bunch of keys.

The exercise, an extended improv, is based on the nursery rhyme of Simple Simon and the Pieman. The exercise runs in a series of two-handed scenes and shows how a character changes from high to low status according to his financial circumstances. (For this reason, it can be useful when working on Brecht.)

Scene one

Simon wishes to get a pie from the Pieman but fails, because he hasn't got a penny. That is the story of the scene. The Given Circumstances are that the Pieman will not sell a pie unless he gets a penny and that Simon has no means of getting money. Don't fudge this or try to get round the Circumstances; you must bring the action back to the story. Most players do try to compromise here – I have found that the only players who can always be relied upon to keep to the Circumstances are young children or experienced, confident and talented actors.

Scene two

Mr Pieman comes home to his wife. As he has sold no pies today he has not got the penny needed to pay the rent, which is two weeks overdue. If the rent is not there at 6pm (in 5 minutes' time) the Pieman family will be turned out into the snow. So we see the previously strong and relentless Pieman helpless before the reproaches of his wife. Remember that the Circumstances are that the family has no assets and no way of getting any money. It also helps to have the crisis of 'This scene must finish in 5 minutes.' This will force you to keep to the story.

Scene three

The Rent-collector arrives. Mrs Pieman, abandoned by her husband, pleads to stay in her home, but as she cannot pay the rent she and her family are turned out into the snow. (Here I have found it useful to use a bunch of keys as a prop, to represent the ownership of the house; Mrs Pieman has to hand over the keys to the Rent-collector as she leaves the house. Actors often find it extremely difficult to do this!)

Scene four

The Rent-collector goes to the Property Owner. He has failed to collect the Pieman's rent so he in turn must forfeit his house to the Owner, giving her his keys, which now represent all of *his* possessions, and then be turned out into the snow. His previous hardness with Mrs Pieman, 'I'm just doing my job'; 'You got yourself into this mess'; 'It's your problem, not mine' etc., are now turned on him. He is visibly the same man but he is behaving in a completely different way to when we last saw him. ('The continuity of the ego is a myth,' says Brecht.[1])

Scene five and following scenes

The Property Owner meets the Bank Manager who turns her out of her house; the Bank Manager then meets the Managing Director of the bank and so on. An elegant ending is provided if Simple Simon reappears, having in some way become a multimillionaire, as the last and most powerful figure in the chain of capitalists!

This is a testing exercise which should be practised until it can be played accurately. If an actor is not prepared to 'behave as if' as required by the Given Circumstances he should think again about his vocation.

THE CHALK CIRCLE GAME

Focus: Practise in playing a strong physical Aim and working within Given Circumstances. The initial game leads onto work on physical memory and finding spontaneity within a rehearsed sequence. It is also useful as a rehearsal tool. A variant can be found in the Status section (p. 57).

Space, time and numbers: This energetic exercise needs a large, clear space with a non-slip floor. It is played in pairs and any number can play, but they may have to take it in turns, as the game requires so much space. (Anyway, it's really good to watch.) Allow at least 10 minutes per pair. For each pair, a square or circular space (the shape is not important), about 4 or 5 feet across, needs to be marked out, in chalk or masking tape. These circles need to be placed as far apart from each other as possible and away from walls and furniture.

What you need: Chalk or masking tape; several pieces of strong material in different colours.

The Given Circumstance of the game is that Player A is trapped inside the chalk circle and can only escape when she manages to grab the cloth held by Player B, who is outside the circle. When A gets the scarf the players change places, so that B is then imprisoned and A is free and so on.

SAFETY NOTE: Players must be warned never to hold this scarf close to their faces, as the game is very energetic and their partner could hurt them accidentally when trying to grab the cloth. The teacher should watch for this right through the game and continue to remind players to be careful. Also, it is best to play in bare feet, as shoes and socks can be slippery.

Stage one

Player As stand inside your circles, with Player Bs outside, holding the cloth. A useful start to the game is for both players to state your Aims. Good acting is specific, bad acting is generalised, so choosing a specific Aim sentence is a reliable way to begin work. Player A's immediate Aim can be stated as 'I want to get the cloth in order to leave the circle.' Player B's can be 'I want to tease A with the cloth.' Player B needs to consider the statement of his Aim: if he says, 'I want to keep the cloth away from A', then his logical action would be to keep so far away from A in her circle that there is no chance at all of her getting the cloth from him, and so the game is blocked from the beginning. An Aim is best stated in a simple, positive sentence: 'I want . . .' followed by an active verb ('to play'; 'to get'; 'to tease') completed by an object ('this game';

'the cloth'; 'A'). The simpler and more precise the Aim statement, the easier and more fun it is to play. Be aware that it is not possible to play a negative aim: for truthful, lively acting, change 'I don't want to stay here' to 'I want to leave here.' And a non-specific Aim such as 'I want to be happy' is also useless, leading to generalised 'mood' playing.

Because the game is so simple and the Aims are so clear you will find that you become endlessly inventive as you play the Chalk Circle game. Use words – if you get puffed, just play more quietly. After a while, changing partners is fun; you will find that the game is quite a different experience with a new person.

Stage two

Henry Irving said that 'the secret of good acting is its apparent spontaneity'. This stage of the game gives practice in that skill, which can be summed up in these five words: *this has never happened before*. Because, however many times one plays a scene, each time is always the first time. Now, to test this capacity for finding spontaneity in a rehearsed action, in your pairs work out a brief sequence of the Chalk Circle game (lasting about a minute), based on your improvised playing of it. Rehearse this, including any words, laughter and 'mistakes' that occur – it is like writing and actioning a short scene. When you have thoroughly learned every move and spent as much time as you need rehearsing your 'scene' you can have a final rehearsal in which you run your sequence through twice without a break.

Note: If during your sequence A gets the scarf from B, leading to you swapping places, then you will both need to improvise a change-over to link the first and second runs of your rehearsed 'scene', as the second run will need to begin with A back in the circle. This is to practise the skill of making a 'seamless join' in acting, so that if lines or actions are missed in a play, you will have the confidence to make a logical restoration to the scene.

When your pair finishes the second run-through of your double sequence, sit down and wait until the other pairs have finished rehearsing. Then each pair performs their sequence, played through twice without a break, to the rest of the group. In order to test you further, the teacher can ask your pair to begin with a short unprepared burst of the game and then to slide smoothly into your rehearsed sequence.

This acts as a warm-up for you and a test for the audience, to see if they notice any difference between the truly spontaneous playing of the game and the performance of a rehearsed sequence.

In the unrehearsed section of the game, the Who, What, Where, When and Why of the scene are usually the same, but how it happens is always new and unpredictable (for the five 'Wh' questions see Chapter 10, p. 95). However, the rehearsed sequence tends to lose this unpredictability. This stage of the game illustrates two common problems in playing a rehearsed scene – both problems come from ignoring the full force of the Given Circumstances and Obstacles:

1   *Making it easy for each other*
    You become more concerned with co-operating with each other as colleagues than with the conflict of the scene, which then loses energy and purpose because the Aims of your characters are not being played.
2   *Preparing to lose*
    Another danger is that you stop trying to win, because you know in advance that you will lose the game . . . you reach half-heartedly for the cloth or you are careful NOT to catch it, when, if the game were happening for the first time, you might well be able to grab it. The moment you lose the truth of the situation like this, you and your audience will lose belief. The answer in this game and in playing a scene is to play the Aim with full strength, trusting your partner to stop or outwit you when the scene demands it. Have you ever played a game with a partner who helped you to win? Maybe you can remember the frustration of playing a game when you were younger with a doting adult who would not try hard enough. That game is not a real game. A scene where the actors are not trying as hard as they can to achieve their Aims is not a real scene because it is not like life; energy leaks and the fun fades.

Chalk Circle improvisations

1   The Chalk Circle game can be played sitting at a job interview with the employer holding the cloth and the applicant wanting to snatch it. In this version, the cloth acts as the 'hidden agenda' of the scene and the top line of action, the job interview, continues regardless.

This can be used also as an illustration of a scene in which there is a strong 'subtext' Aim (see also Doing, Saying and Meaning, pp. 44–6).

2 Playing the central Aim of two characters: The game is really useful applied to problems of acting a scene. The cloth represents your character's Aim and the chalk circle stands for the Obstacle that must be overcome. Taking *Macbeth* Act 1, Scene 1, as an example, Macbeth might be inside the circle and Lady Macbeth outside with the cloth. You need time to decide what Aim the cloth represents to your character at a particular moment of the play. Let's say that this moment is just before the murder of Duncan: Lady Macbeth might find an Aim statement like 'I want Macbeth to kill the King so that we can rule.' The Obstacle that she needs to overcome, represented by the chalk circle, could be the integrity (that she sees as weakness) in Macbeth's character. Macbeth's Aim statement could be: 'I want my wife to love me no matter what I choose to do' and his Obstacle is his integrity and loyalty to Duncan. If Macbeth gets the cloth he gets his wife's unconditional love and if, when she is in the circle, Lady Macbeth gets the cloth, then she gets her desire.

You can improvise the scene as you play, using the abrupt changes of power as, in turn, one or the other of you achieves your Aim, represented by the cloth.

3 You can also play this game using the text of the scene. This can enliven a scene that has become stale or over-careful. In this case, players have to adapt to the unexpected changes of power as the cloth changes hands. The text used can be the whole scene or some lines that have been learned from it, for instance lines 59–60: Macbeth: 'If we should fail?' Lady Macbeth: 'We fail.'

CHRISTMAS DAY

Another way of giving full value to the Obstacle faced by a character is to play the Christmas Day game. I invented this in a rehearsal of *The Cherry Orchard* during the scene where Lopakhin fails to ask Varya to marry him; it was getting bogged down by their anticipation of his failure and a consequent leaking of energy from both actors. The premise – and we all wish it was true – is that we get exactly the present we want most on Christmas Day. The shock of unexpectedly hearing his dreams coming true and having his problem solved brings an actor back to his real Aim of playing to succeed, so that he can allow the failure to hit him as a surprise. It is a useful device whenever a scene is losing its momentum, which can easily happen when repetition makes the urgent situation stale.

So, in a short improvisation, to be used when an Aim loses energy and the actor is skating over a big Obstacle that might well defeat him in the situation of the scene, the director can take one of the other players aside and quickly set up this improv without the knowledge of the blocked actor. The next time the scene is played, the blocked actor plays the scene according to the script as usual, but when he reaches the crucial moment – usually where his character fails to achieve his Aim – his prepared partner switches to improvised speech and gives him the surprise of granting his dearest wish. The astonished joy felt by the blocked actor shows him how much that Aim means to the character and what a painful shock it would feel to have that wish disappointed; so the peaks and troughs of the scene are restored and the situation once more matters as much to the actor as it would to the character at that moment. (Another example where this game could be played would be for Duke Theseus, in the first scene of *A Midsummer Night's Dream*, to allow Hermia to marry her Lysander.)

4 The Magic 'If'

TYING THE SHOELACE

Much virtue in if.

(Touchstone, *As You Like It*, Act 5, Sc. 4)

Stanislavski warned against 'losing yourself' in a role; rather, you should find the role in yourself. The use of the Magic 'If' is to understand that 'the Given Circumstances of the play are not true in the terms of my real life, but IF they were true, IF I were that particular person in that unique situation, what would I do?'

I was once teaching an earnest actor who challenged this idea of our not being able to change into another person; he told me firmly that he could change himself completely and that this was what he felt an actor must do. After some discussion I asked him whether, if he were playing the part of a tree, he would actually change himself into one. He said he would. The class had by then reached tea-break time, so we decided to take 10 minutes off, leaving the 'tree' to himself, as trees do not have tea breaks . . . it was not long before he joined us.

Focus: A quiet exercise showing the power of the Magic 'If' and the ease and naturalness of the imagination in action.

Space, time and numbers: Any space (a clean floor!); 10 minutes; any even number over two players.

What you need: One lace-up shoe between each pair of players.

The game is played in pairs sitting on the floor. The Aim for the game is for A to show B how to tie the shoelaces in a knot, then a bow; the Given Circumstances are that B does not know how to do this and wishes to learn from A.

Sitting comfortably on the floor, talking to each other when necessary but probably using more actions than words, work gently and co-operatively with your partner.

Do not finish until B can tie a lace by himself; each person will take a different time over this task. When this has happened, A and B change roles, with B now teaching and A learning. If you have finished both stages of the exercise while other pairs are still working, then go quietly to observe the working pairs. This is good practice for all players: the working pair will find their small circle of attention increased by the wider circle of attention of their audience.

I find that everyone enjoys this quiet game, finding it effortless in both their roles; the experience takes away any doubts or excuses players may have about their ability to believe and immediately act upon the Given Circumstances of a scene. The easy change-over of roles, from teacher to learner, is also useful practice for actors.

Not only the physical rhythms change, but thoughts, vocabulary, the inner sensation of identity and the balance of the relationship between the two players alter radically with the swapping of roles.

It is useful to discuss this game once it is over, relating the experience of the game to the task of the actor.

THE THIEF AND THE KEYS

Focus: This game gives practice in sustained action within strongly imagined Given Circumstances.

Space, time and numbers: You will need a large clear space, as large as possible. The game has two stages and so needs plenty of time to play through both, giving all players a turn at each stage – allow an hour. This game can be played with a group of 10 or more players.

What you need: A set of several keys on a ring or a chain and two or three soft cloths for blindfolds.

Choose two players to be the Thief and the Guard. The rest of the group forms a circle or square by holding hands at the fullest extent of their stretch, then sitting down on the floor at the same distance apart from each other. This group forms the 'walls' of the playing space in which the Thief and the Guard will be acting; the function of the group is to form a safety barrier, because the two players in the scene will be blindfolded. If, during the game, either actor approaches the 'walls' of the space, then the person nearest to them touches them gently on the shin to warn them that they are too close to the perimeter. Safety is always the first consideration in these acting games.

Stage one

Once everyone is aware of the safety rule, the Thief and the Guard are blindfolded and gently turned about so that they don't know where they are in the space. Meanwhile, the bunch of keys is placed silently on the floor somewhere within the playing space. Once this is done and all members of the group are sitting in place ready to be the protective walls of the room, the Thief and the Guard can start their scene, which is played in complete silence.

The Aim of the Thief is to find the keys while avoiding the Guard and the Aim of the Guard is to find the keys and catch the Thief. The Given Circumstances are that the room is in total darkness; this is what is experienced by the blindfolded players. After the first two players have either found the keys or each other, or after a reasonable time without a result, the game is stopped and two other players take their turn until everyone has played the blindfolded stage.

Stage two

The game is played in exactly the same way except that this time no blindfolds are used and the Thief and the Guard play with their eyes open; the 'darkness' is now only imagined. The people around the edge of the room must also join in this imagined problem. This gives a useful experience of the power of the imagination and in sustaining that 'willing suspension of disbelief' while actively solving the problem of the two characters with their conflicting Aims.

It is good to allow some time for discussion after the game, or after each pair has played, if people want to talk. One interesting problem is that sometimes players are nervous about 'succeeding' – finding the keys – in this stage of the game, being concerned that people might think they were not having enough difficulty with the search. But finding the keys quickly can happen, just by accident, even when players are blindfolded, and if the scene leads players that way, they should go with it, without anxiety.

5 Exercises in immediate response

BETTY PLUM

Focus: The technique being practised here is that of responding instantly and instinctively. The artist needs to be encouraged to trust in the immediate response and to become free of the 'inner policeman' who tells him to be wary and never to risk a 'mistake' in case he looks foolish. Pauses and hesitations before the response to a question indicate that the player is 'censoring' his imagination – which is a pity because it is impossible in this game to 'get it wrong'.

Space, time and numbers: Betty Plum may be played with any number of players, with one as a leader or questioner, and can be played in any space. Allow 30 minutes.

I call this game Betty Plum because that was the name of the first imaginary character invented by the first player to take a turn when I invented the game as a way to create the specific factual details of a character's back story. The questioner leads the exercise; if you wish to share the task of questioning, the role can be passed round players in the group, or the questions can be shared generally, as long as players understand the rules of the game.

In the first stage this is just a talking exercise but it can be expanded into an active improvisation, almost like an unrehearsed soap-opera, as an experiment in building a group narrative. If you wish to follow characters and relationships through to an acted story, it would be useful to record the work or to ask someone to take notes.

Turning to any member of the group, the questioner asks someone to give a first name, male or female, the first name that occurs to them. Names of people in the group are not allowed.

Example:

Questioner asks an actor at random:

What's your name?
Actor: Sam.
What's your surname?
Sam: Wilton.
When's your birthday?
Sam: August 8th.
What year were you born?
Sam: 1874.
Where were you born?
Sam: Southampton.
What was the address?
Sam: 6, London Street.
Was that your mother's house?
Sam: No, it was my aunt's house.

The questioner turns to another actor, who will now play the aunt:

What was your name?
Maryanne: Maryanne Morrison.
Your birthday?
Maryanne: June 8th.
What does the house look like?
Maryanne: Little, old, grey brick, blue paint on the front door, flaking with some brown showing through.
When did you move there?
Maryanne: Last year, my other house burned down.

The questioner turns to another player:

Did you see her house burn down?
Neighbour: Yes, I was her neighbour.
What's your name?
Georgina: Georgina Howell.

And so on, until everyone in the group has a character, with a factual background and all have a direct connection with at least one other person.

You can see that the answers, which must be immediate, were not madly original; the birthday date of the 8th was repeated, for instance. What mattered was the willingness of actors to be in a 'yes, and . . .' frame of mind, to listen to each other and to trust their first impulse for an immediate uncensored factual answer to the unexpected questions.

The skill of the questioner is to follow impulses to switch from one 'character' to another and to ask for specific information in the answers. If a player cannot provide this, because of anxiety, the question can quickly be turned over to another player, with no judgement of the 'blocked' player. As the game continues, a 'family' of imagined characters, each with their specific background of 'facts', will emerge and then characters can be allocated to players who can flesh out their stories in smaller groups and begin to interact in improvisation.

This is useful practice for an actor when creating the background of any character in a play; it gives confidence in quickly choosing factual information that can form the structure of an imagined previous life. Once a factual base has been formed the imagination is free to create the essential 'internal film' that gives reality to the character, based on those experiences and relationships in his past life that have made him who he is at the time of the scene (see pp. 122–4). See also the chart of 'invisible characters' for *The Cherry Orchard* (p. 118), as an example of how to flesh out the character's world from the information available in the text.

WHO WILL BE CHOSEN?

Focus: To explore and clarify the personal relationships of imagined characters. This improv game can be used as a development from Betty Plum or on its own, using characters in the play that is being rehearsed. It's also related to the Characters in a Circle: The Three Statements exercise in Chapter 11 (p. 117).

Space, time and numbers: Any space is fine; allow at least 20 minutes; requires a minimum of eight players arranged in a circle, with one player in the middle.

The Aim of the players around the circle is to persuade the player in the centre to choose them to spend time with today. The persuading must be done with no touching of the centre player. Each person has a turn to try to persuade the centre player to join him; relationships of family or other connections (such as lover, teacher, friend, boss) can be claimed by each speaker in turn, each using an invented name.

So, the first speaker may connect as a parent, the second as best friend, the third as sibling and so on; the centre player may respond if he wishes, so that each connection in turn can be a short improvised dialogue. After each player has had a turn, there can be a brief burst of everyone speaking at once to claim the attention of the centre person, then there must be a time of silence while the centre person chooses who to join; I remember a powerful example in this game when one player, having made his individual claim, remained silent in the middle of all the shouting and pleading from the others, just connecting with eyes and attention, and the centre player chose to be with this silent one at the end.

STORY IN A CIRCLE

Focus: Practice in listening, not preparing, being ready to adapt, being audible and keeping to the through-line of a narrative.

Space, time and numbers: Any size space; the game can take between 10 and 30 minutes, depending on the number of players; any number can play.

This is a quiet talking game in which you are inventing a collective story. Sit in a circle, preferably on the floor. In turn, each player says one word of the story that you are inventing together. This often begins with: A: 'Once' ... B: 'upon' ... C: 'a' ... D: 'time' ... E: 'there' ... F: 'was' ... and so on.

This simple game demands courage and attention. For some players it may give practice in speaking clearly and loudly enough for everyone to hear. Other people may feel nervous as their turn comes round and will miss their 'cue' word and so be unable to keep the story going. Others may feel the need to be 'interesting' or different and will put in a distracting word when a simple one is necessary to sustain the logic of the story. Practice in this game provides essential skills for actors – in confident cueing, in having the breath, together with the creative impulse, ready to contribute and in being alert and receptive to your partners. These can be summed up in two words: the skill of *outward attention*.

Once you are at ease with this story game, you could try a new tale beginning with the word 'I'. This device makes the story personal and I have found, working with groups of older students and allowing plenty of time, that it progressed inevitably through the subjects of parents, love, death and the after-life. I was amazed by this pattern, especially when I found it repeated with very different groups in exactly the same sequence!

HE STOOD THERE

Focus: Practice in specific visualisation, which can be used to work on text and character.

Space, time and numbers: As before.

This is a quiet question-and-answer exercise, played in pairs or in a group. There is always one 'responder', but she may have one or more questioners.

The responder begins the dialogue with the words 'He stood there.' (Or 'she', of course.) The questioners ask a variety of 'Wh' questions (Who, What, When, Where, Why – see Chapter 10, pp. 95–7). As soon as the responder gives her answer, the next question is asked in quick succession in order to prevent the responder pre-planning, because she needs to trust to her imagination to create the 'internal film'– that unbroken sequence of bright images which lies behind our words in life and so imaginatively in acting. If there are many gaps, the visualising player is probably feeling some strain, so she may need help and reassurance.

In this exercise you are answering the five 'Wh' questions in the same almost unconscious way in which you recall details of the events in your own life. If I ask you what you had for breakfast today, you will immediately 'see, hear and feel' what happened to you in your real life. So, when you play a character you 'hold the mirror up to nature' and allow your imagination instantly to provide those memories and sensations for the character you play.

Sample questions:
What is he wearing?
What can you see around him?
Is he alone?
Where is he standing?
What can you hear?
How long has he been there?
What is the weather?
What time is it?
Why is he there?
What does he want?
Where does he come from?
What is his name?
Where will he go next?
What colours can you see?
What plants or trees are there?
What buildings?
Are you there or are you looking at him?
And so on.

I found that my imagination was creating clear images as I quickly wrote those questions: my man was standing on the tow-path of a canal, in a town, on a grey morning in April at 12.30. It has been raining and he has been there for about 20 minutes, just standing looking at the water and at times along the path to his right; he seems to be waiting for something or someone and to need this time to pause and consider a serious choice in his life. He has not yet decided where to go next – probably he'll go to a familiar cafe to have a cup of tea; he is alone at the moment. He's wearing an old coat that belonged to his father; it is grey tweed with a belt at the back, worn open; he has a dark red jersey underneath, I can see the cuffs and a cheap gold-coloured watch on his right wrist; no gloves, no scarf, just the roll neck of the jersey; an odd dark brown knitted hood covers his head; his shoes look worn but quite expensive dark brown leather. My impression is that this man has little money and is rather dirty; maybe he has recently been made homeless. I can hear distant traffic and some sparrows twittering; then suddenly the hoot of a train in the distance. The colours I could see are all dim, brown, muddy green grass and weeds, pebbles on the path, an old brick wall behind him with an elder tree growing against it on his left side. I wasn't there myself; I was looking at him as a stranger from some distance. And of course I could have continued to allow this picture and its corresponding story to grow, because my imagination is always ready to create pictures and then to justify them.

SIMULTANEOUS MIRRORS

Focus: This is a valuable warm-up exercise that gives actors confidence and practice in noticing and reflecting everything their partner does.

Space, time and numbers: A large clear space; at least 15 minutes of playing time – though I have known the game to continue for 45 minutes; any number of more than six can play.

This is not a conventional mirror exercise where A copies B's movements. In Simultaneous Mirrors there is no leader: the idea is that each player reflects simultaneously, not initiating any actions of their own, but being led only by what they see happening in their partner's breathing rhythms, small balances, facial expressions and so on. The game can be played in pairs or standing in an evenly numbered circle, in which the player standing opposite you is your partner.

All players: turn round once quite gently; when you see each other again after the turn, your partner will be adjusting to the changes in your balance and breathing from the turn as you will be adjusting to what you see in him; these small natural actions are what you reflect.

Now, the essence of this game is to accept the simple physical movements as they are and not try to 'improve' them – the difficulty lies in having the courage to repeat, because of the infinitesimal time-lag between what you observe and your active reflection of it. For example, you may find that the person you are copying makes a slight movement of her arms. You copy that and she sees you copy that, so she copies that same movement *again* and so do you . . . You see that one small movement can continue on and on, because you are both content to 'be' each other, giving up your own will to partake of your partner's existence, breathing like them, shifting your position if they do (and they might well do that because they are copying *your* unconscious tiny shift of weight). The repeated movement continues until it changes *itself* – which it will. It will gradually develop into a new action, with new breathing and a new rhythm. Players are fully absorbed in the 'sensations of the moment', which is the essence of the Method of Physical Action.

There will be some sound with this movement: the sound of breathing, of course, maybe of a player laughing, coughing or saying something. Everything your partner does must be copied, nothing must be 'edited out' and any changes need to happen naturally, as they will when the repeated mutual reflecting of a gesture comes to its inevitable rhythmic development.

Being copied can seem threatening to some people, but this game is friendly and supportive, so the atmosphere stays creative and easy. This game can continue for a long time and does not have to stay as a pair game; players can be unobtrusively redirected to reflect any player in the group (who is himself absorbed in copying the person opposite him) so that the group can achieve a united rhythm. The use of sound is very important here: a cough or a laugh from one player builds into a rhythmic coughing or laughing sound from the group.

If a player gets tired and sits on the floor, then that is also copied by the group. The game can develop when players are asked to exaggerate the movement they are copying: this builds energy and good large movements and sounds. When facial expressions are used the game makes people laugh a lot, so this is useful for exercising the face.

Simultaneous Mirrors has many important lessons for actors, showing what can happen if players allow themselves to follow what is happening with no reservations and no anxiety about being 'interesting' or 'original'.[1]

FILMING THE POTTER

Focus: This exercise gives practice in clear focus on the imagined task, with freedom from 'end-gaining' or trying for a result. The flow of mutual attention gives valuable experience of 'being in the moment' and adapting to changing circumstances.

Space, time and numbers: A large, clear space so that each pair of players has their own circle of attention; plenty of time needed, at least 45 minutes, and more if possible; depending on the size of the room, any number of players.

This is a quiet game with a peaceful atmosphere. All the objects used in the game are imagined and mimed. Divide into pairs. A is the potter, with an imaginary pile of wet clay; B is the cameraman, making an imagined film of the potter's working.

The experience for the potter is one of calm concentration, not being disturbed by being watched and 'filmed' but using the attention of the imagined camera to strengthen her attention on her task; for the 'cameraman' the exercise heightens his visual awareness of how the light falls, how he can adapt to the changing movements of the potter, how he is using the space of the room, which may well include other pairs working on the game.

A: Begin your work on your imagined pile of clay, moulding it into whatever object you wish to create. Once your small 'circle of concentration' has been established, B can begin to 'film' you.

B: How will you begin your film? From close-up or from a distance? Taking in the whole room, then closing in slowly? From which angle will you approach the potter as she sits on the floor? How does the real light in the room hit her face and hands? How will you close the film with a strong image? Might you pull back from the potter to take in the whole room again, or end on a close-up of the hands?

At the end of the exercise you may well wish to talk about your experiences. A will probably have found that being watched actually increased her concentration, or, at least, did not disturb it at all. This is good practice for working on a part with a director or with a real camera. When watching, B may have found that his visual sense has been heightened and clarified; he has been entirely 'in the moment' as he worked and so could see the beauty and power of the simplest physical actions, the play of light in the room etc.

The game can then be played again with the roles reversed. Through this experience you will feel the pleasures of focused attention on your partner, or your activity, and how it feels to notice everything and to go with your immediate response to the changing situation. Maybe at a later stage of your training, being aware of your Laban rhythms will enable you to recreate the exercise. These skills of attention are basic to your work as an actor: having found them in an exercise, you can use them in a scene.

6 Acting skills, to be applied to rehearsal and performance

CONNECTING WITH OBJECTS

Any prop, large or small, solid or flexible – a chair, a glove, a coin, a flower, a piano, a sofa, a throne, a crown, a dagger, a letter, a ring, a bookcase (*The Cherry Orchard*), a portrait (*Hamlet*) – has power for the actor. Relationships with objects are an integral part of the connection or focus of your craft.

If you look around you now as you read this you will find that you have a 'relationship', or at the least an attitude of liking or dislike, to every little object that you can see or feel. Some objects of little monetary value may have an importance for you; memories and associations attached to them make them precious to you alone. You alone know their history and this affects the way you handle them and just looking at them or even remembering them when they are not with you arouses deep emotions and can lead to action.

> **Focus**: To practise precise observation and memory: necessary skills for actors.
>
> **What you need**: This is a quiet game, played in pairs, using the actors' personal objects.

Stage one: Observation and memory

In pairs, A and B: both select an object you own – a watch, ring, wallet, belt, or anything that has detail and some variety of shape, colour and texture. Swap objects. Take a few minutes to examine your partner's object thoroughly.

A: return B's object to him. B: holding it so that A cannot see it, question her about it, for example:

Did it have any numbers or writing on it?

What colours were there?

How many beads on the bracelet?

How many stones in the ring and what were they?

Describe the buckle and strap on the watch –

And so on.

When you have finished, hand the object back to A, who will have the chance to re-examine it with renewed interest. Now, A quiz B.

Stage two: The imagined story of an object

The game can then continue to an improvisation: in pairs again, A: give B an object. B: take a moment to look at the object, then begin an improv with something like, 'This is the last thing he gave me,' or, 'The first time I saw this was when I . . .' The connection with the object releases the imagination and eliminates self-consciousness because your focus is directed outwards and your Aim is to tell the imagined story of the object to your partner.

Sometimes you can use this exercise briefly during rehearsals as an impetus to emotional connection with the props, though there is a big difference between rehearsal props and furniture and those used in performance. Ideally, the real thing should be used throughout the process but often this is not possible. When the stage is set with the correct furniture, and when props and costumes finally arrive, you need to spend time and thought to make them your own and to understand the associations that each object has for your character. A good example of this is the old bookcase in Act 1 of *The Cherry Orchard*: Gaev makes a rather embarrassing speech about how the bookcase represents the tradition of family values, but everything else we see in that room that was once the nursery is also full of association, memory and power for the characters in the play. If your character lives in the room, then everything will have a history to him; if your character is a visitor, then everything must be noticed as new to you.

A useful exercise is to go round the set and to quietly talk through the imagined history of each object, so that they become a part of the background of your character. You could use the 5 'Wh' questions (p. 95) as a structure of enquiry. In this way, you will always have enough to do in a scene and won't feel lost. An actor with a little too much to do and to notice is a happy actor; it is like having a little bit 'too much' money in the bank: this gives a feeling of security and the possibility of pleasurable action, as opposed to the feeling of anxious poverty.

HIDDEN AGENDAS: DOING, SAYING AND MEANING

Focus: To give practice in playing Hidden Agendas or 'subtext'.

Space, time and numbers: Any space; allow about 6 minutes for each stage; the game needs at least two players (and an audience). Played at first in pairs, it can be expanded to a small group activity.

What you need: Real objects; mime is not useful for this work. The situation of each stage depends on what props and furniture are available – perhaps a table, a chair, some plates and cups etc., and some material to use as a tablecloth/dishcloth/duster. A collection of cards with different Aims written on them is also useful.

Sometimes an Aim can be hidden behind words and actions; occasionally a real Aim can even be unacknowledged by a character, who may be unwilling to face his own true feelings and wish to hide them even from himself, deceiving himself about his real motives and desires. The actor of this character needs to understand and to play the real Aim or need underneath its disguise, using the 'cover' as a strategy.

The game is in three stages; for each stage there is a shared activity between the two players. I suggest washing-up as a useful one; you could also use packing a suitcase, making a bed, laying the table – any common task that involves at least two people working in the same area of the room.

Stage one: Doing

Choose a task with your partner. Do it together silently, connecting naturally with each other without feeling the need for speech.

Stage two: Doing and saying

This stage has two parts:

1   Continue your task and talk, when you need to, only about what you are doing.
2   Continue to work, but this time talk about a subject unconnected with your activity, such as the weather, clothes, music or sport.

Stage three: Doing, saying and meaning

This stage also has two parts:

1   Both players continue to work at the task they have been given, while talking about a different subject, as in part 2 of Stage two, but Player A, you also have a hidden agenda. For instance, you might want Player B to leave the room but are not willing to tell him to go. Your real Aim is 'I want to make B want to leave the room.' If your Aim was simply to make B leave, you would tell him to go, or maybe give him a slight push, but absolutely no physical force or even contact must be used in this exercise. You need to formulate your underlying Aim clearly: maybe it is 'I want B to leave the room while still liking me.' Player B: Be alert to what Player A wants and be willing to go with it, as with the 'Yes, and . . .' exercise (p. 8). Don't be tempted to block A's intention with a 'No' or a 'Yes, but . . .' Sometimes you find that you may want to block the flow of the scene, so it can be helpful to stop and observe how the energy

is leaking all over the place, to consider what fear impulse led to that block and then cheerfully resume the scene.

We find what a character really wants by seeing what she does; this may be quite different from what she says, or even what she feels at any moment. For instance, if you are in the dentist's chair and the drill is approaching your sensitive teeth you may feel like leaving the room straightaway, but if your real Aim is to get your teeth repaired, you will stay in the chair in spite of the strong Obstacle of your nervousness.

2 Both players have a hidden agenda, while keeping to the rules of working at the common task and talking about an unrelated subject. Before starting, you should both write down your hidden Aim, so as to get it clear to yourself and to check afterwards if your partner guessed it correctly. This stage is over once one of you guesses and responds to the other's hidden agenda.

THE GHOST EXERCISE, WITH PRIMARY SOURCES

Focus: This exercise gives practice in speaking the words of someone else – in this case, the words of a real person taken from a transcript of an interview in a book or magazine – so that the actor can have the experience of another person. The importance of using a primary source, rather than a speech from a play, is that there can be no question of the reality of the experience; there must be respect and connection with the original speaker.

Space, time and numbers: Any space; allow 10 minutes for each script; the exercise is in groups of three – the Speaker, his Ghost and a Listener. The Speaker has not seen the speech in advance and has no idea of what he will be saying next; the 'script' is whispered into his ear by the Ghost. And because each speech we use has originally been spoken to an interviewer, the speaker in this exercise needs a Listener. It is good to rotate this game, so that everyone has a turn at ghosting, speaking and listening.

What you need: Carefully chosen and prepared scripts, about 10–15 lines long – see below for some samples. I like to use short excerpts from interviews, with a photo of the real person and maybe some information about them, if possible; these will be shown to the Speaker after she has had her turn. The excerpts do not have to be dramatic in content, though some of them may be about a crisis in the life of the subject. An excerpt can have a humorous aspect, be a story about an everyday incident, thoughts about life; they are very often memories of the far or recent past. The individual 'scripts' need to be typed out so that the Ghost has helpful clumps of words to whisper to the Speaker – each Speaker will have different needs in the accepting, remembering and use of the phrases whispered to her, so the Ghost must be willing to adapt and to be as clear as possible as he whispers to his Speaker.

The Speaker sits in a chair, the Listener sitting opposite at a comfortable distance, and the Ghost sitting at the Speaker's side, but with his chair facing away from the Listener, so that the whispering can be done more comfortably, the script is out of the eye-line of the Speaker and the Listener is not distracted by the Ghost. It doesn't matter at all if the Listener can hear what the Ghost is saying; what is important is that the Speaker should feel secure about what she is hearing, so that she can say the words aloud to her Listener.

Because the speech is necessarily interrupted by frequent pauses, while the next phrase is whispered to the Speaker, and because the Speaker's tone is often rather subdued – this tone is a response to the lack of inflection and low volume of the whispering – the speeches can seem to be quite solemn and sad; people notice this if there is a sequence of players trying the exercise; the rhythms of each excerpt have little variety. Do not be put off by this; the exercise has valuable results for the actor and it is useful to learn it so as to use it when learning lines and working on scenes from a play (p. 121). The quality of listening is remarkable and the transparency and simple force of the Speaker show the power of using words not one's own when fully supported by your Ghost and connected to your quiet, empathetic Listener. For players with dyslexia or those who find sight-reading difficult, the exercise can also be an experience of release and freedom from anxiety.

Sample primary source material for Ghost exercise

David
A lot of people don't know about me.
I'm courting a girl now and she's a lot younger than me.
I've known her for about four months.
She works at the same firm I work for.
I only told her about my past two weeks ago.
I thought it was only fair that she should know.
I said, 'I've got something to tell you, Gina, and I just hope you're not disappointed but I've got to tell you; you mean so much to me.'
I can't remember exactly how I put it but I told her I'd been in prison and that I'd killed my wife and how it came about and that it wasn't an intentional thing, just a spur-of-the-moment thing.
I told her all about it and she could decide.
And she decided.
She was pleased I'd told her and she didn't want to hear no more about it.
And I'm very pleased about that.

Alek (Female. Model.)
I grew up in a big family.
There were nine kids, my mum and dad.
I had a very happy childhood, but then when I was about seven the war in Sudan started.
One day the military came and knocked on the door.
The latch went click, click and they must have thought it was a gun.
The men started shooting at the door.
My mum said, 'Right, everyone, get under the bed.'
After that we had to leave, to go and live in a smaller village.
When we left we could see dead bodies where we used to get water.
It was very scary.

Peter (Aged 40. Businessman.)

I don't like it when women approach me . . . it doesn't feel right.

I like to make all the moves.

A bloke should keep the mystery going because women always want romantic surprises.

The physical side is much more important for men, and women should co-operate.

I expect my girlfriend to agree to sex whenever I want a bit, unless there is a bloody good reason.

Women need respect for the person they're having sex with, but men just need visual stimulation. So long as they've got their eyes closed and are thinking of Pamela Anderson, they'll have a good time.

I have slept with fifteen or sixteen women but I like my girlfriends to have slept with a maximum of two men, otherwise they're being a bit easy.

My new girlfriend, who I met on holiday last October, is having an effect on me, which is why I'm coming forward to confess in the hope that I can repent, but it's hard.

I do believe in monogamy once you've met the right woman.

But there's no harm in looking.

Margaret

I had this experience when I was giving birth to a child.

The delivery was very difficult and I had lost a lot of blood.

The doctor gave me up and told my relatives that I was dying.

However, I was very alert through the whole thing, and even as I heard him saying this I felt myself coming to.

As I did, I realised that all these people were there, almost in multitudes it seemed, hovering around the ceiling of the room.

They were all people I had known in my past life, but who had passed on before.

I recognised my grandmother and a girl I had known at school and many other relatives and friends.

It seems that I mainly saw their faces and felt their presence.

They all seemed pleased.

It was a very happy occasion, and I felt that they had come to protect or to guide me.

It was almost as if I were coming home and they were there to greet or welcome me.

All this time I had the feeling of everything light and beautiful.
It was a beautiful and glorious moment.

When you have had your turn as the Speaker you can at last see the
script (and it's interesting too if it is possible to include a photograph
of the original speaker). Give yourself time to consider honestly what
'interpretation' you would have put onto the speech if you had seen it
in advance and read it aloud in the usual way. This can be the big leap
of understanding for the actor: finding for yourself how you would,
with the best motives, have interfered with the direct communication.
We all feel the need to be 'interesting', to show that we understand the
character, above all, to inject 'feeling' into words and situations that are
not our own. Also, we are trained to read aloud with the eye travelling
always forward of the voice and this can mean that our thoughts also
run ahead of the word we are saying, so that we are never truly in the
moment of the word, as we are when we speak as ourselves, spontaneously. We need to recapture the sensation of not knowing what we
will say next, using words that are not our own, then transferring that
skill to a learned script. From this you can go on to the same truth in
the Pointing exercise (p. 110).

When, at the end of a long course of training, I ask student actors
to tell me what work has been most useful to them, I find that most
mention the Ghost exercise, both the introduction to the technique
using primary source material and the later application of it using a play
text (p. 121).

He who knows where he is going will not get very far.

(Napoleon Bonaparte)

WORKING WITH PHOTOGRAPHS AND PAINTINGS

Focus: For the actor to make a connection with the undisputed
reality of another person's experience.

Space, time and numbers: Requires a large, clear space; allow at least 10 minutes; at least eight players.

What you need: As many photos as you can find, usually from newspapers and magazines, of people who are not posed and who are unaware of or unconcerned about the photographer. Each picture needs to have a caption or description of what the picture is about.

I find that this exercise is most useful as a starting experience for a new group, as it shows how much an audience can gather from watching players and it also shows how the position and spatial relationships of a person can awake deep and true emotions effortlessly within the actor. It is an exercise that is always successful, so the players have a sense of accomplishment and confidence from playing it.

The teacher divides the group of players into several smaller sub-groups, based on the number of people needed for each photograph (as far as is possible; some images may need to be 'edited', focusing just on the main players), with one more student in each group as the director. Each group works in a different area of the room.

In your group, take time to examine your photo and read the caption. Your director will help you to copy the exact positions, expressions and spatial relationships of the original, embodying the photograph.

This exercise teaches the importance of correct and detailed observation right through the body, so that the positions of fingers, angle of a head, distribution of weight on the foot, spaces between bodies in a group can be precisely achieved. Present your completed 'picture' as a 'still' and hold it silently while the other groups watch and try to guess the situation. During the short space of time that the players can hold their positions in their picture, the teacher will ask the watching groups to give their immediate responses to questions such as:

Is this happening indoors or outdoors?
Where exactly are they?

Are these people rich or poor?
In which country is this happening?
Is it happening now or in the past? And if in the past, when is it?
Is it hot or cold?
What has just happened?
What will happen next?

Then the teacher could go to each frozen player and ask the watchers to say briefly what that person is thinking, in terms of 'I want to . . .' to give them practice in finding Aims.

What always amazes me (and the players) is how accurate and detailed the reactions of the audience are, with no advance information at all about what they are seeing; I remember playing this game once in Rio de Janeiro, using a favourite photo I have of two young couples going out on a Saturday night in the 1950s, and the Brazilians immediately 'knew' the correct date and that it was England, what time of day it was and what sort of people the characters were, as well as having an accurate awareness of the relationships within the group; also a group of Japanese actors in London 'knew' (by trusting their guesses) that they were seeing a protest march led by Martin Luther King in the 1960s; other 'audiences' have recognised a group of women after a Mafia assassination in Italy.

For young actors anxious about playing an aged character, it is most helpful to use photos of older people, as this immediately provides a truthful physicality for them. If there are some coats, bags, chairs in the room, these can of course be used to help the composition of the picture, but props are not necessary for the exercise.

Version 1: Working with paintings

This exercise can be useful when working on the background or social manners of a play, as well as being an experiment in imagining the story of an artfully represented fictional person. For instance, working on Chekhov's plays I find paintings by a group of Russian painters called 'the Itinerants' most useful, as they painted the life that was around them in spite of the severe censorship of the Tsarist regime, in this way sharing Chekhov's Aim to give us true pictures of their world. When directing my dramatisation of Dickens' *Dombey and Son*, I used

Victorian paintings; for Restoration and Noel Coward comedies, I used paintings and portraits of those times, to find out about how clothes were worn, typical attitudes of the hands and the spatial relationships of family groups.

I find that the players directly experience the situation of a group of invented characters in the Given Circumstances of the painted scene, and that their emotions are aroused and their imaginations stimulated by the physical changes that happen when they play the characters in the picture.

The method of playing is the same as with the first Photograph game. Small groups, each with a director, ask the 'audience' to give both their first impressions of the picture and to suggest the Aims of each figure. This exercise can act as a positive first introduction to the benefits of the Method of Physical Action.

Version 2: 'A scene from my life' – personal group photos

Choose a group of your peers to form a tableau or static picture of a scene from your own life. Choose a moment in your life that you wish the others to see, so that there is no invasion of privacy in the exercise. Then, without telling your friends what or who they are playing, arrange them in a group (this usually tends to be a family occasion), and put yourself in the 'picture' if you so choose. When the group is complete, ask the people watching to say what they see and ask the actors taking part in the picture to say what they are feeling and thinking and who they think they are.

This exercise, developed by the teacher and director Andrew Tidmarsh, is fascinating for the composer of the group and interesting for all taking part; it also gives members of a group an insight into the former or home background of their friends, and binds a new group closer together. It can also be used as the starter for an improvisation on the background of characters in a play.

Part Two Acting is behaving

7 Status

'Status' for actors is about how much power a person has within the space they occupy. It is best thought of as the power of an individual or group to change the space and the people in it. Status affects everything that we do and all our interactions with others; it can be used for good or ill and is in a constant state of flux, being affected not only by other people but also by clock-time, location, class (the accident of birth), money and other outside factors. Actors need to understand that they are already expert status players, because we all have to be in order to get along with others and gain our Objectives. These exercises expose the process, so that it can be refined and used accurately in acting.

Status work, as it is now understood in the theatre, started with Keith Johnstone's improvisation sessions at the Royal Court Theatre in the late 1950s. His inspiring book, *Impro: Improvisation and the Theatre* (republished by Methuen in 2007), is the source of my work on both status and eye-gaze in this chapter, as it is all for teachers and directors who use status as a basic tool for understanding human behaviour. Some of the following exercises are taken directly from his book and some are my adaptations, worked on over the years with many different groups of all ages: professional actors, students and teachers.

I was lucky enough to work for several years with the National Theatre Education Department, where I travelled to schools and colleges all over the UK to take practical workshops; the status games were always popular and exciting to watch. I remember one schoolteacher telling me that her relationship with her class had changed considerably for the better once she and her students understood the underlying dynamic of status in their group situation.

A good way to play with status is to use the status playing-card game. You will need a pack of playing cards with the aces, jokers and court cards left out. This leaves you with cards numbered 2 to 10. (The suits do not matter.) Your lowest number card is 2, your highest is 10 and these numbers represent the lowest and highest status of players in the game. Because the most usual and interesting status levels are in the middle range, I use only one card at 2 and 3 and only one at 9 and 10, and two cards each for 4, 5, 6, 7 and 8.

Spaces have status just as much as people and objects do. The actor always needs to know the status of the space he is in – the character's attitude to the space is one of the most telling things about him: if he is humble, he will feel the space to be better than he is; if proud, even a nice, well-furnished room or a beautiful garden may be felt to be below his worth. With a numerical tool to define status it is easy to discuss and experiment with the exchanges of power between people, spaces and objects.

A minimum of speech is used, because the exercise is being used to show the importance of body language relating to the space people are in. The space needs to be as neutral as possible, though one always has some sort of attitude towards a space or anything in it, so I call it 5½, in the middle of the scale, so that the player has a status that is always either above or below the status of the space. (This distinction between the player and his space is just for the purposes of this exercise; you could say that being at the same status as the space we occupy is often a cosy at-home feeling; we create externally the inner feeling of our worth; alternatively it could be a feeling of equal misery both within ourselves and in nature. The 'oceanic' feeling of unity between nature, the surrounding space and the individual, when all are merged and boundaries melt, can be seen as rising above all distinctions of status and comparison.)

The game begins at 2, the lowest status level (the number 1 is not used because of the status of the Ace in card games). Using only the three words, 'Hello, I'm [name]', the player enters the very edge of the space, introduces himself timidly and exits as quickly and unobtrusively as he can.

A low-status person feels unsafe in his surrounding space: the space above presses down on him, the floor below him feels treacherous and insecure; the space behind him and the space in front, including the audience to whom he is speaking, are terrifying. These physical shrinkings will give you the feeling of low status. You will find that your eye-gaze will be directed downwards, you will not be able to meet the eyes of the audience as you did when explaining the game to them a moment ago. Your voice will be low and faltering and you will be pretty much paralysed with shyness and timidity, feeling overwhelmed by the space and the people in it. (The lowest number of 2 can be hard to play correctly; a player may turn away from the audience, which feels 'right' to him but in fact gives an impression of rejection or arrogance to the watchers. In real life this can lead to people supposing that such shyness indicates pride.)

With status 3 there is a little more confidence, but the player still stays close to the edge of the space and leaves as soon as he can, after telling the audience his name. Maybe this time the eyes can lift more but they will still not be able to make contact with the eyes of the audience; they might be fixed above the audience's heads, or at their feet. The voice will be a bit stronger and the body slightly less shriv-elled against the power of the space, which is still 2½ points above the player.

At status number 4 the player can advance into the space; his timidity is no longer embarrassing, though he is clearly nervous and aware that his personal status is 1½ points below that of the space and the audience. The voice is stronger and the eyes can scan the faces of the audience, though direct eye-contact will not be possible yet. He is beginning to cope with his surrounding space, though still finding it difficult.

Do you see how valuable this precise relationship with the space is? How your internal and body-space react to the external space around you? Even in artificial situations such as auditions you will never be alone: you always have your 'silent friends' with you: the space, the floor, maybe a chair which you can relate to and use as support, both literally and figuratively. (See Chapter 9, p. 87.)

Continuing with the exercise, you have now got to status 5, only half a point below the status of the space, so you will now be behaving more normally. You will certainly get to the centre of the space. Your entrance, exit and the announcement of your name will now take more time; you expand into Time as well as into Space as you increase in power in the same way that you shrink when you lose power – when you have worked through the Laban exercises (Part Six, below) these changes will be familiar to you through the elements of action.

From status 6 upwards, your Time, Space and Force will increase in power. You will be able to meet the eyes of your audience; you will appear friendly and not aggressive in any way; the audience will feel that they could talk to you, that the time and space can be shared between you.

Number 7 is, I think, a good status to be in real life. It is quietly confident, yet ready to allow others to take a higher status if necessary.

Level 8 is where a teacher or director usually functions during work. A status 8 knows his job and what he wants but he will not dominate others unless absolutely necessary, when he will be able to rise to 9 or even 10 for a short while. An 8 commands respect but is not a bully.

In most of us status levels 9 and 10 are used only occasionally and then for short periods only. Those people who stay at 9 and 10 without allowing change, not letting themselves be lowered by anyone, not adapting to the rights or needs of others, are seen as arrogant tyrants. It is, of course, possible to be a 'good' 10, where the powerful person leads but also empowers those around him, but for the purposes of this exercise it is more useful to go for the 'bad' 10s. Many actors are frightened of 'behaving badly', maybe risking disapproval, even in an exercise; they prefer to retain their own self-image of being 'nice' rather than being true to the scene or the character, where the action is aggressive or nasty.

An actor needs the courage both to relinquish control, allowing himself to be defeated as a low-status person, and to domineer as a bad 10. He needs to remember the difference between play and his daily life. A status 10 (good or bad) will be still, keeping the spine and head straight and upright, will take his time, will ensure that everyone is paying total attention to him and will be easy with his position of command. His voice will probably be low in pitch and volume with an uninflected even tone. Shouting at people is not always a high-status activity; it can demonstrate uncertainty and defensiveness. A truly high-status player will need no defences; he will expect to be heard and obeyed and will show no effort in controlling the group. He is in control of the space and of the people in it. However, this control – the power to change the space and what people do in it, who is allowed in etc. – can only be maintained by the high-status person with the consent of the majority.

As with Laban, status work should be practised until you improve in skill and range of expression; it is easy to do at first on a rather facile level, but you should be able to move beyond the clichés, having experienced them a few times, to a more elegant and subtle handling of the status transactions in a scene.

GUESS THE STATUS NUMBER

Focus: The accurate observation of status.

Space, time and numbers: A clear empty space; one player at a time; allow 3 minutes for each player.

What you need: Playing cards – one card each of numbers 2, 3, 9, 10; two cards each of 4, 5, 6, 7 and 8.

Game 1, Stage one

First player: pick a card face down from the fanned pack and, looking at it but not letting anyone else see it, enter the playing space, introducing yourself to the group with the three words, 'Hello, I'm [name]', playing the status number on your card. The audience then guesses which number you were playing. (You must not help the guessers, because they are working as much as you, analysing how you use the space, your body language, voice etc.)

Truth and accuracy in playing the Given Circumstances must always be the priority. To play a 5 as an 8 is going against the Given Circumstances (the number on the card that you have drawn) of this exercise.

In a large group, you may move to Stage two after five or six have played Stage one, so that everyone gets a turn at one or other of the stages during the session.

Stage two

Two players, each with a card that they have drawn from the pack, the number known only to them, enter from opposite sides of the playing area, greet each other and then chat on some neutral subject such as the weather. Both players need to remember that they are now in the 'fourth wall' space (the audience being 'flies' on the wall); and that they are to stay in that 'private' space until the scene is stopped by the teacher. The audience can then guess which numbers are being played.

Now, this stage gives an extremely important lesson in acting, even though it looks so simple. The players do not know (as one can never know in acting or in life) *how* the little scene will happen. In this game they do not know their partner's status and must observe them with great attention to discover first of all if the partner is above or below them and then to adjust accordingly. All this happens very quickly; the first lightning impression is crucial and gives most of the necessary information, as it does in life. Stanislavski called this vital moment of mutual adjustment 'orientation' and complained that it was nearly always neglected by actors. He reminded his actors that a dog coming into a room would always check it out, no matter how familiar it was. (George Bernard Shaw said that his tailor was the only person who saw him realistically – he measured Shaw anew at every meeting.)

These status games, played in front of an audience of fellow actors, provide a useful lesson in the atmosphere and process of a creative rehearsal. The actor knows what message or story she wants to convey: in the status game this is her number; in the rehearsal it is the motives and situation of her character in the scene. She plays as clearly as possible but it may be that her story is not clear to the audience/director. In the game, she can then hear this request for more clarity without any sense of failure, like a director's note, using the criticism as a helpful clue and calmly tweaking her action so that her story is truthful to the scene. The usefulness of the game is in making obvious how each detail of action in space, rhythm, body language, vocal inflection, etc. gives information about character, relationships and situation.

It is like giving information to someone by writing a message on a blackboard: if your handwriting is too faint, cramped or even partially illegible the full message will not be conveyed to your scene partner or audience; you know exactly what it is that you wish to tell them and now you need to go back over the action one more time so they can see and understand you completely and at once.

Once this two-player stage has been played, three or even four players can play the game, extending it to a freer improvisation. Good situations for these improvs are people waiting for a job interview or an audition. (It is said that in auditions and job interviews the first few seconds decide the result . . .) It is best for players to enter one by one, so that orientation can be practised. The usefulness of having a status number is immediately apparent; even inexperienced actors can play well and truthfully because they always have a precise task or identity to occupy them and they experience status primarily as a physical activity, related to the space (at 5½) and its occupants.

However, any scene where actors stay stuck in only one status cannot be true to life . . .

STAYING AT LEVEL 6

Focus: To show that status is in a constant state of flux.

Space, time and numbers: A clear, empty space; 2 minutes per exchange; four players at a time.

Two players enter and talk about the weather. Their actor's Aim is to stay at Level 6 with no raising or lowering. Two other players act as 'status barometers': each of them is allocated to an actor and monitors his status level. These two observers stand at a front diagonal position to the players so that they can see them clearly and, as they watch the scene, each raises his hand if his player is rising above 6 and lowers it if the player falls below 6.

You will find that even at the start of the exercise there is a problem in maintaining the same status as your partner: the person to speak first usually rises in status, as does the person who introduces a new subject, or even a new word into the conversation, so the scene is a constant adjustment between a rise and a hasty lowering as the players struggle to remain static at 6. The scene usually collapses after a while as there can be no progression without change. Vocabulary and ideas are limited, there is a great deal of repetition, body sets and gestures are copied, yet the scene is familiar and has a sort of flaccid comfort about it.

We realise that this sort of mutual reassurance and shared stroking has a purpose and is often used among colleagues, for short periods, possibly as 'time out' from some stress in their working or domestic environment. As actors we can learn from it that adaptations of status are the essence of our energy and pleasure in our work. At the same time we should notice and avoid the danger of muddled priorities: in acting, the situation of the scene must be more important to the actor than the 'daily life' situation of relationships within the group. (I find that this is a common mistake and one that distorts and weakens focused energy. It is a matter of being intelligently courageous and constantly aware of the job of acting. I have frequently observed the error in auditions where the actor allows the pressure of wanting to succeed to get in the way of the character's objective.)

RAISING AND LOWERING STATUS

This game and the following games can be played without reference to playing-card numbers. They are best played in pairs; once played, A and B can reverse the Raising and Lowering.

Space, time and numbers: Any space; allow 3 minutes per pair; more than four.

1   A raises herself and lowers B; B lowers himself and raises A.
2   A raises herself and lowers B; B raises himself and lowers A.
3   A lowers herself and raises B; B lowers himself and raises A.
4   A lowers herself and raises B; B raises himself and lowers A.

Brief examples of this sequence could be:

1   A: I feel wonderful today; you look dreadful.
    B: Yes, I know; I'm a complete wreck; I wish I could look as beautiful as you always do.

2   A: I feel wonderful today; you look dreadful.
    B: You won't feel so wonderful in a minute: you're sacked for inefficiency and making rude remarks. I'm in charge now and that makes me feel wonderful.

3   A: I feel really awful today and I know I look a wreck, but you look as beautiful as always.
    B: Oh no, you look marvellous, the picture of health; I'm the one who's a wreck – I'm a complete failure.

4   A: I feel really awful today and I know I look a wreck, but you look as beautiful as always.
    B: Yes, I take care always to look my best; you certainly look dreadful, don't you think you should try to improve yourself?

Here is an example from *The Cherry Orchard*, showing how this status analysis can be useful for a scene:

> GAYEV: (*Lowers Yasha*) And you, go away. (*Lowers him further*) You smell of chickens.
> YASHA: (*Lowers Gayev*) You haven't altered much, have you, Leonid Andreyevitch?
> GAYEV: (*Lowers Yasha*) What did you say? (*Lowers him further; speaks to Varya*) What did he say?
> VARYA: (*Lowers Yasha*) Your mother's waiting to see you. (*Lowers Yasha and his mother*) She's in the servants' quarters. (*Lowers Yasha as a son*) She's been here since yesterday.
> YASHA: (*Lowers his mother*) Why doesn't she leave me alone?
> VARYA: (*Lowers Yasha*) You should be ashamed of yourself.
> YASHA: (*Lowers Varya and his mother*) What's the hurry? She could have come tomorrow. (*He goes*)

STATUS SEE-SAW

This follows on from the previous exercise. It is difficult and worth practising. The most elegant use of the exercise is to make a status change in each sentence.

> **Space, time and numbers**: A clear space; a minimum of four
> players; allow 3 minutes per pair; two other players act as 'con-
> trollers', calling out changing status numbers.

A and B enter from opposite sides, each with a controller. The rule
of the game is that the player cannot speak until the controller has said
his status number. A begins at 10, B at 2. So A's controller says '10';
and then A says his first line. They then change (A going down, B going
up) at each line until a complete reversal has happened.

The conflict should be about who has control of the space, so the
best line to begin it is with A (at 10) saying something like, 'What are
you doing in here?', and A should probably be ordered out of the space
at the end. It is important that players respect each other in this exercise. Personal comments, such as 'You've got a silly face', should be
avoided – the focus is on ownership of the space. Note that, at the
mutual '6' of the see-saw, both players are level and are friendly and
co-operative. This stage needs to be clearly marked before the big
change of power.

Here is a sample scene:

[A's controller says '10']
A: (*Playing 10 and entering to the centre of the space*) What are you
   doing in here?
[B's controller says '2']
B: (*Playing 2; shrinking at the extreme edge of the space*) Oh, I'm sorry
   . . . I didn't know . . . I thought . . .
[A's controller says '9', and so on]
A: (*Lowers to 9, with a slight relaxation*) You know that people like
   you are not allowed in here.
B: (*Rises slightly to 3; a little more confident*) But I thought that as
   it's snowing outside I might wait here, just for a few minutes
   . . .
A: (*Lowers to 8; becoming a bit nicer*) Yes, but even so, you must
   understand that if I allow one of you in here then everyone will
   want to come in.
B: (*Rising to 4; moving into the space*) But you can see how cold I am;
   I won't take up much room.

A: (*Lowers to 7, allowing B into the space*) Well, it is a large space and as it's only you, I suppose it'll be all right, just this once.

B: (*Rises to 5*) Thanks; it's nice to be warm again.

A: (*At 6, nearly level with B*) Are you sure you're OK?

B: (*At 6, rising to level with A*) Yes, I'm fine.

A: (*Lowering to 5*) Oh good. Can I get you anything?

B: (*At 7*) Your coat would be nice.

A: (*At 4, giving B her coat*) Of course. I hope it's big enough for you . . . I'm sorry it's not very clean . . .

B: (*At 8*) It's filthy. Do you really expect me to wear this?

A: (*At 3*) Er, no. I'm awfully sorry. I'm afraid that all my clothes are torn and dirty.

B: (*At 9*) I can see that. Leave the coat here – on the floor – and take yourself outside.

A: (*At 2*) Yes, of course . . . at once . . . er . . . there is a bit of a blizzard out there . . .

B: (*At 10*) The snow will clean you. Get out.

A leaves humbly.

If this exercise doesn't work it is because one of you is blocking the necessary changes. Sometimes an actor will not want to lose high status and sometimes one will not take the responsibility of rising to a position of total power. This is an example of playing that is blocking the line or story of a scene. If the insecure actor refuses to play the status transaction of the scene, because he finds that raising and lowering to be a threat to his own self-image, then that scene is being played incorrectly and needs to return to the Given Circumstances of the storyline.

Many actors find it hard to reach the extremely low status of the '2' at the start of the game; this is because they are muddled about the difference between their daily life self-confidence and that of the imagined situation. When playing '2', if you begin your first sentence (replying to the '10's aggressive 'what are you doing in here?') with a 'Well . . .', it means that you are protecting yourself with the ghost of an excuse. It is more fun to play the complete submission of the '2', knowing that the game is going to change in a minute. The excuse 'Mr Brown sent me in here' is also a diversion from the Given Circumstances of the see-saw. If you use that line – and it is surprising how many people do! – you are distorting the storyline by borrowing status from the absent Mr Brown in order to defeat your scene partner.

The see-saw is a rather crude example of a basic dramatic story: the powerful person gets put down while the powerless one rises to take his place. This can be expressed tragically or in comic terms but in both cases it must be played wholeheartedly or it will not be satisfying.

You probably noticed how in Staying at Level 6 the energy of the short scene could not be sustained; actors need to be eager to change status to get their Aim and to provide strong clear Obstacles for their partners in a scene, so that energy can be generated and sustained by the overcoming of those Obstacles.

Energy is like water. With no Obstacle it will flow along smoothly and evenly; it will be pretty but boring. To create changing rhythms, breaking waves, waterfalls, etc. there must be Obstacles in the way of its flow towards its Aim. Similarly, the actor welcomes Obstacles, especially in the form of partners with conflicting Aims, because the overcoming of these gives him energy. He never compromises his own drive to get his Aim and delights in providing strong Obstacles for his partners to overcome, as in any game.

MASTER OF THE SPACE

Focus: Exploring rapid shifts in power. This is an advanced master and servant game and should only be attempted by people who have played the earlier status games correctly.

Space, time and numbers: Needs a large space. This group activity can be a powerful experience, so should not be attempted with a new or inexperienced group. Allow plenty of time, with no interruptions. The teacher must maintain a firm control throughout, indicating who enters and when. With a large group it is best for the teacher to pull players out after a while so that they don't get tired and so that they have a chance to watch.

The Given Circumstance of this testing game is that the latest player to enter the space is master of the space and of everyone in it.

It is a 'snowball' exercise which starts with one player and gradually draws in all the others.

At the start one player enters the empty space which he then feels is his own to move or relax in. But then another player enters (indicated silently by the teacher). At the moment that the next player enters, the status of both players immediately changes: the newcomer is the master of the space and of the first player in it. This means that the first player must at once become the obedient servant of the new master and this immediate complete change-over of control happens throughout the game, as each new player enters.

> The game has great power and there will be moments of real tension and belief within the group as well as times when people can't sustain their concentration. Prepare the group for the demands of the exercise and ban the various commands that are not useful: masters should not demand to be entertained, to be told jokes, sung or danced to, etc., because those activities trivialise the game and break the atmosphere. Equally, people must not be told to do press-ups or any other exhausting physical exercise. No props, real or imaginary, must be used and any commands which have unpleasant or embarrassing implications should either be stopped by the leader or a new master should be brought in to change the activity.

The most noticeable change is that, as a new player enters, all the players already in the space lose power and wait to be told what to do, where to go, etc. All their concentration is on the master of the moment and they are ready to betray each other if necessary.

There are many ways of being a powerful master; shouting and bullying are not the only ones. A calm voice and detached manner can be intimidating as well as commands such as 'Get into a straight line', which can be hard for the group to get right. The master can of course change his 'rules' at any time . . . fairness does not come into this game. 'Kind' masters are also very effective.

There are many technical difficulties in the game: one is the speed of this handing-over of power, both on the part of the latest master and on the part of the group of 'servants', who must change their allegiance at once from the old master to the new one. The chief problem of the game is that people have a healthy resistance to being bullied! This is good in real life but the Circumstances of this game are different. Here we are behaving as if our Aim were to be as good a servant as possible, ready and willing to obey every wish and command of the master. This is a big test of the willing suspension of disbelief.

It is only a game so actors should be able to suspend their resistance and enter the world of the game with full belief, at least most of the time. Some giggling will happen, partly through nervousness, but this should be controlled as far as possible. Other resistances such as sulkiness, over-subservience, questioning commands, obeying while showing resistance should be corrected; one of the main lessons of the game is that the audience can see how every inner attitude is clearly visible through the body. If you are feeling it, we will see it.

PECKING ORDER

Focus: To illustrate the changing of an individual's status according to their place in the pecking order of their social group. It gives practice in quick thinking, responding immediately to abrupt change, and to economy and accuracy of movement. Another name for the game could be Passing the Buck, as it consists of handing the blame for a disaster down to your inferior.

Space, time and numbers: This taxing, noisy and energetic game needs a large space, plenty of time and careful preparation. Between six and 12 players at a time. The first time it is played it is useful to practise the sequence, to get it right before beginning the game.

Players, stand in a straight line: A has the highest status, B the next, C the next, etc. Player A provides the pace of the game and so must be experienced and quick in invention.

The rule is that when your superior (the player on your right in the line) taps you on the shoulder (lightly, not violently) you turn to him, kneel down and respond to his commands in a servile fashion. You must stay in that position until your superior turns away from you.

For example, if you were playing C you face the front, not joining in the game until B (on your right) taps you on the shoulder. You then turn to B and kneel down in front of him, and listen and respond humbly to his demands. You stay there until B turns away from you; this will only happen when A taps B on the shoulder again.

You can see that the rhythm of the game depends entirely on Player A's constant recalling of Player B, so that the 'message' can spread down the line of players. The minute B does turn away from you (Player C), you jump up and tap your inferior (D, on your left) on the shoulder. D immediately turns to you and kneels down; you then pass on the message or commands given to you by B, your superior. You must keep D in conversation until you yourself are tapped on the shoulder by B, and then you turn back to her and kneel down etc., as before.

So the exercise gradually spreads down the line of players until it reaches the most inferior person at the end of the line. The flow of the game depends on the quick invention of A, who must claim B's attention for a very short time at frequent intervals, so that the exercise can spread down the line. The most common mistake is for players to either turn away from their superior before he has turned away from them; or for players to forget to turn immediately to 'pass the buck' onto their inferior.

It is best to have an extreme and rather unrealistic 'crisis' from A as an improvised story for this game. Here is an example:

A: (*A taps B on the shoulder, B turns to face her and kneels down*) My coronation begins in 5 minutes. What have you done with my crown? (*A turns away from B, so B immediately jumps up and turns to C, and taps her on the shoulder. C turns to face B and kneels down*)

B: What have you done with the Queen's crown? I thought you were in charge of it?

C: Oh, my God, I'm terribly sorry, I'm sure I had it yesterday . . .

B: You idiot! Find it at once. The coronation begins in 5 minutes. You must . . . (*At this moment A taps B on the shoulder, so B turns to A and kneels down. At the same moment C jumps up, taps D on the shoulder, D kneels to him, and the following conversations happen at the same time*)

A: Haven't you got it yet? I'll have your head cut off if my crown is not here in 2 minutes.

B: Yes, your majesty. Of course, your majesty; your crown will be here in 30 seconds.

A: See that it is. (*A turns away, so that B is now free to turn to player C*)

MEANWHILE:

C: The crown is missing. It's all your fault, find it at once or I'll put you in prison.

D: Of course, of course I'll find it. I'm terribly sorry, it wasn't really my fault . . .

(*Once A has turned away from B, B is able to turn again to C, leaving D free to jump up and pass the blame to E . . .*)

The game gets very noisy as the number of conversations increases. This is why the tap on the shoulder is necessary for getting the attention of your inferior. All players, except A, are constantly kneeling down and jumping up again, and they should all be careful to turn to their left or right with a good smart movement according to whom they are speaking to. The last person in the line ends up by taking all the blame! You can use a military setting for the game, with players saluting and standing to attention, instead of kneeling, for a good sharp rhythm to the game.

Pecking Order Smiling is good fun too. The game is the same except that all players must be smiling throughout; the rhythm changes to a slower and more flexible pace – a religious or educational setting is effective.

THE CHALK CIRCLE GAME, WITH STATUS

Focus: To demonstrate the importance of playing one's Aim, no matter how strong the Obstacles seem to be. It is quite advanced and should be attempted only when players are familiar with the Chalk Circle game (see p. 22) and have experienced the basic exercises in status transactions.

Space, time and numbers: This enjoyable, energetic game requires a large space and plenty of time. This version of the game is best played with several couples at once.

What you need: Several pieces of strong material, such as a scarf (a different colour for each pair of players), and some chalk or masking tape.

Note: Remember to warn players to be careful not to hold the scarf anywhere near their faces, as accidents can happen in the excitement of trying to grab it.

As in the Chalk Circle game, the floor needs to be marked with circles, one for each pair that is playing, with one player (A) inside the circle and the other (B) outside. Player B holds a scarf, which represents the 'imprisoned' player's Aim, as once A grabs the scarf she can come out of the circle and B is put inside to play the game in reverse.

Stage one

Imprisoned Player A: Begin by playing the lowest possible status; Player B, outside the circle, you are playing very high status – a basic master and servant game. It will be, of course, extremely hard for a timid, obedient servant to grab the cloth but it can and will be done if, A, you play your Aim at the same time as correctly playing the strong Obstacle. This is a difficult balance, as your servant status must be truthfully maintained: it is not correct playing to be a rebellious or sulky servant; the effort should always to be as obedient as possible, and to grab the scarf only at a moment when the master is careless or over-confident. Always remember that the challenge of this game is to attempt to get the scarf while being true to the extreme limitations of the Given Circumstances. If it proves impossible after a while for you as servant to get the cloth under these Given Circumstances, don't worry and let the exercise stop.

Stage two

Your positions are reversed: this time the master is within the circle and the servant is outside with the cloth. A: This increases the Obstacle almost to breaking point for you, as your master will, of course, command you to hand over the cloth at once and you, as a servant, need to obey all orders willingly. The secret is for the servant to be rather stupid, or extremely nervous, though eager, and so apt to misunderstand orders, to lose the scarf accidentally, to be too frightened of criticism to dare to approach the master and so on.

Stage three

The game can progress to being played with several pairs in separate circles, each with a scarf of a different colour; the rule being that any master can be released only with the scarf that belongs to his own circle. The servants can then muddle up the differently coloured scarves among each other and bring the wrong one to their imprisoned master. Some masters could then collect the 'wrong' scarves, so that they can bargain with other masters in order to be released. Again, the servants must be sure to listen to and obey their masters (or any other master who gives them an order) and eventually they will probably have to hand over the correct scarf as ordered.

This game illustrates the basic structure of most Commedia dell'Arte scenarios and many classic comedies. You can develop rehearsed sequences from the game and build them into your own Commedia dell'Arte plots.

REVERSED-EXPECTATION STATUS

A basic comedic technique is that of reversed-expectation status. This is when the social status of a person is undermined by their personal status. An example in an improv would be an application for an overdraft from a penniless student to a bank manager. Ordinarily, the manager's social status would be 10 and the student's 2, but in this case the manager's personal status is 2 and the student's is 10, so the expected story of the scene will be reversed. This is satisfying to watch and to play . . . a sort of wish-fulfilment!

Another favourite comic situation is when a person of high status, perhaps disguised as being of lower rank, is treated as lowly by someone else. The audience enjoys the situation because they know the true status of the characters and they wait for the moment when the disguised King is finally revealed to the cocky low-status character who has been patronising him. Shakespeare uses this idea in *Henry V* and *Measure for Measure* with a more serious purpose, but there is still much humour in the situation.

The effect of economics on the status of an individual also needs consideration. I invented the Simple Simon exercise (in Chapter 3, p. 20) when working on Brecht, to demonstrate how 'strength of character' is affected by the possession or lack of the means to live. It is a brutal exercise in which the actors must have the courage to play the Given Circumstances without compromise.

Status which controls or is controlled by others can be given by social position: class, wealth, the ability to achieve power through work, talent and ambition, but there is another aspect of status, that of spiritual or mental capacity, which sometimes works in opposition to material/social status. It can be useful to relate the characters in a play to these two aspects of status and to see where they match and where they differ.

A practical way of showing this is a status line-up.

STATUS LINE-UP

The teacher or director chooses one end of the room as the high-status area, with low status at the opposite end. The company then lines up as their characters, first according to their material status, then according to their characters' spiritual status.

In both line-ups, each character states why they are in the position they have chosen; lively discussions occur when characters are lining themselves up. The difference between social and spiritual status can be very strongly marked: in *King Lear*, for instance, Lear has highest social status at the start of the play, until he gives his administrative powers away to his daughters, and even then he retains his feudal authority at 10 for some time (permanently for his few loyal subjects such as Kent and Cordelia). However, in the spiritual line-up, taking the start of the play as the situation to be analysed, he would be at 2. The Fool would be at 2 or 3 materially but at 10 spiritually. At the end of the play, having lost all material power, Lear achieves a 9 or 10 in spiritual growth. In this way, choosing points at the start, the middle and the end of a great play we can see how the characters progress and thus find one of the central ideas of the play.

Making this analysis into a physical exercise gives it a concreteness and applicability which discussion would not have; standing next to the people above and below you in the line-up makes you personally aware of the power you have and the power you lack in the world of the play; it may well lead you to your long-term Aim and will affect all your relationships and attitudes.

Choosing your character's status: Examples from *The Cherry Orchard*

We each have a favourite status in our real lives. I expect you know someone who is always 'low', always in difficulties, complaining about their inadequacies, so that you have to spend time 'raising' them, giving them lots of 'strokes' to make them feel better. If you are honest you will remember that sometimes you too use your friends like this, lowering yourself with them so that they will raise you. This is fine, as long as you give them a turn too. If you don't they may well give up on you! And other people you know are always presenting themselves as successful and more powerful than you are, so that can be hard to take too. In reality we are always oscillating between high and low inner status, and these shifting balances, like those in our general health and happiness, are part of our changing lives.

So you need to be careful when choosing the status of a character; it is easy to decide that Yasha in *The Cherry Orchard* is a 4 or 5 socially (as Ranevskaya's valet, formerly a peasant boy on the estate) but with Dunyasha and the other servants Yasha behaves as a 10, until the 'gentry' come in, when he suddenly descends to a 3 in relation to Ranevskaya, while cheekily responding to Gaev as an 8 or 9 would. You can work out each change of status through a scene and use it to draw a graph of your character's ups and downs; the technique has the precision you need to play logically and truthfully.

1 Make a *money* line-up for *The Cherry Orchard*: Lopakhin, as the richest person, would be the 10 here.

2 A *social-class* line-up: Lopakhin and Gaev switch line ends for this one.

3 An *education* line-up: Peter Trofimov is at the top here.

4 A *personal* line-up, where each character chooses where he or she would be, is usually a scramble at the top end of the line, with Yasha and Dunyasha being 'above themselves' in the opinion of the Gaev family.

You could also have line-ups for practical ability, charm, self-knowledge, intelligence, loyalty, selfishness or any other useful aspect.

Then each character can place the other characters in order of importance for them. Here you will need to know which point in the play you are working on; for instance, at the start her mother is the most important person for Anya, but at the end maybe Peter has taken over that position.

Objects and places are just as important as people in your character's world. The cherry orchard itself has very high value for the Gaev family, but low for Lopakhin; the 'dear and honoured bookcase' is a 10 for Gaev in Act 1 but everyone else in the room is embarrassed at this ridiculous 'over-raising' of a piece of furniture. For poor Varya the gold coins that Ranevskaya drops so carelessly in Act 2 have great value, while to Liuba they hardly matter. In the personal world inhabited by each character, of which they are the centre and the pivot, every outside object, event and person has its precise value. The way to find 'character' is to look outwards for the impact of the outside world on the changing sensibility of the imagined person, finding the clues in the text.

NOTES FOR THE TEACHER OF STATUS

The teacher has an important role in these status classes. He or she needs to give clear explanations and perhaps a demonstration of the first status playing-card games. It is good for the group to see the teacher playing a status from a playing card and maybe not giving an accurate signal at first. The corrections needed, involving the use of space, eye-contact, timing, vocal inflection, etc., in order to give an unmistakable message as to which status level you are playing, are not threatening and are fun to do; if the teacher is willing to have the first try, this will give confidence to the group.

It is best to get the first status work clear and accurate, working through these common problems, before progressing to the more complex exercises. I would suggest that all status games are worked through in advance of a class if you have not played them previously; the games need organisation and for Master of the Space and Pecking Order a strong control is necessary, so do not play these games until you are sure that you can control the group without stress. When improvising it is extremely useful to start from a status number: the Simple Simon progressive story is a good example of this.

8 Eye-gaze

Our eye-beams twisted, and did thread
Our eyes, upon one double string.

(John Donne, 'The Exstacie')

Understanding the 'speechless messages' – as Shakespeare calls them – of the eyes is important for the actor, especially for work on camera and in close-up. There are, of course, hundreds of subtle messages conveyed silently by the eyes; timing and duration can change the signal, as can the force of the action and the spatial movement of the gaze. In my work, I have given labels to some common patterns of eye-gaze and I explore these patterns in exercises with actors. Once actors have experienced the strong effects of these basic signals, then they can develop and explore the many variations in eye-gaze and begin to understand their use in acting.

Focus: To experience and experiment with different eye-gazes.

Space, time and numbers: Allow at least 30 minutes for the whole sequence and plenty of room to move. A group of six to 12 men and women, with even numbers of each sex, is ideal for this work, though the exercise can be used with fewer players or as part of the rehearsal process, to explore relationships in a scene.

THE HELD GAZE

The group moves around the room. Each player has the Aim of meeting the eyes of every other person. As you pass each other, hold the other's gaze for a moment or two. For this brief moment, the held gaze is neither threatening nor very intimate, as it could be if held for a longer time. I find that if an actor is willing to allow the held gaze to affect her strongly, she may wish to pause a little as the power of eye connection between herself and another individual changes her breathing and her feelings. At a signal from the teacher, look only at members of the opposite sex, while ignoring your own and then look only at members of your own sex while ignoring the opposite one. Not looking at people is as strong a message as looking at them

Eye-gaze is strongly connected to status: a dominant person will normally hold the gaze of subordinates, and a mutually held gaze between two people can indicate strong anger or the desire of both to be dominant, the first one to drop the gaze or to look away being the loser of this battle of wills. Conversely, the held gaze of lovers, or of parent and baby, is a beautiful melding of trust and love. There the pupils are seen to dilate and darken, whereas in a confrontational or disgusted gaze the pupils become like pinpricks. (Pupil size conveys such a strong subliminal message that a model's pupil size can be digitally enlarged for an advertisement to give the impression of rapture at the sight of a bottle of shampoo or a box of chocolates!)

THE DROPPED GAZE

Stage one

Move around the room wanting to make eye-contact with all the others in the group, but this time, as soon as you meet the eyes of another person you must drop your own gaze, so that you see the floor for a moment. The timing of this drop is important: because it is a strong signal of subordination; some actors will resist doing the immediate drop. If you hold the gaze for a moment or two before dropping, the message can be very different: it can be read as, 'I look at you and then reject you, or signal that I am ignoring you and would rather look at the carpet than at you.' If you feel a natural resistance to this submission, remember this is a demonstration of the power of an eye-gaze interaction between people. There are also strong cultural patterns connected to the meeting of eyes: in a mixed group of youth leaders some years ago, a Chinese gentleman left the room during this part of the exercise because he refused to 'submit' to the women in the group, and in a large group of black British male actors at a National Theatre Studio Workshop the lads found that the dropped gaze was so foreign to them that they just collapsed with laughter.

I find that in groups who are doing the dropped gaze the atmosphere changes from how it was during the held gaze. How do you find the atmosphere changing? Did you feel depressed or nervous? Maybe your breathing became shallower? Did your jaw clench, your shoulders stiffen or your pelvis freeze?

Stage two

Dividing held and dropped gazes between the sexes within the group (if there are equal numbers of men and women this is ideal, but the exercise can still function with uneven numbers). As you move around the room, men, hold the women's gaze and, women, drop your eyes when you meet a man's direct gaze. This is powerful stuff. (The teacher may need to encourage the men to invade the space of the women with their held gaze while the women may need to be reminded that for the brief time of the exercise they will be 'submitting' by dropping their gaze to the floor as soon as they meet the eyes of a man. Culturally, this is sometimes necessary for women in patriarchal societies or as a defensive strategy.) Next, the roles are reversed: the women can hold and the men must drop their eyes as soon as they meet a woman's eyes. The women may want to herd the men, in the same way as the men may have cornered the women in the previous scenario.

I find it is good to stop the work at this point and find out what reactions the players have had to the various eye-gazes we have played with so far. There is usually a burst of emotion and an urge to express the power of these messages, how the breathing changes, how people feel about themselves and the others in the group, with instances of how they have experienced the silent messages of eye-gaze transactions in their own lives.

THE FLICK

This is a combination of the two previous gazes. A flick is a meeting of eyes with a partner, followed immediately by a dropped gaze then a prolonged hold. It is elegantly played with a passing move between the two partners, as they cross the room in different directions, when the final hold can be sustained as long as you like. Flicks are fun and flirty: they give the signal of, 'I like the look of you, I feel a bit over-come, so I drop my gaze and then, when I raise my eyes to yours again, I just want to go on looking at you.' However, a flick followed by a rejection is unpleasant: in this, the flick is followed by a turning away.

Practise the flick in pairs, with one person being the receiver of the gaze and the other, more active player, being the giver. The giver: try both accepting your partner, maybe going forward to her and giving her a hug after the flick, and then rejecting her by turning away after the flick. (This work is related to the opening and closing of the body as a reaction to another person, which is explored in the section on Space in Chapter 20, pp. 209–11.)

THE SLIDE

Another, rather more dangerous sort of eye-gaze connection I call the slide. In a slide, the gaze is held while the eyes travel over all or part of the receiving player, finally returning to meet her eyes again. Slides can be done from the head to the heels, or from head to toes and back to the face again, or in reverse, from feet to face, or from the eyes to any part of the body and back again. So you can see that this is an intimate 'invasion' of the partner's personal space and so it needs to be approached with respect. A slide followed by a rejection is very powerful and many players after doing that will feel a need to return to their partner to give her a hug, as reassurance. A slide followed by an acceptance is a pleasant experience for both the giver and the receiver of the gaze.

Robert Redford does a brilliant slide when he meets a desirable woman; he meets her eyes, then swiftly slides before returning to her face with his initial appreciation reinforced by seeing that she is completely gorgeous! It is worth considering this aspect of technique: think about an actor whose work you admire on film and watch the use of his or her eyes; notice when this actor blinks: a blink on camera can be used to mark an emotional change, to punctuate the rhythm of a scene, maybe as a full stop when the scene ends. Steve McQueen is also an expert eye-gaze player.

It is useful to divide the group into two lines facing each other, with one person in each opposing pair being the giver and the other the receiver of the gaze. The active partner decides in advance which gaze or combination of gazes they will play, then performs that planned sequence while the receiving partner notes and then describes what he perceived.

There are also slides that aid thought. These are usually personal, in that they are not directly aimed at another person. When we want to remember something we need to provide a blank canvas, free of visual stimulus, so we usually look upwards and slightly to the right during a pause for thought while we scroll through the memory. I have heard it said that an upward glance to the left side indicates that the person is lying, but I have no proof of this.

A slide that turns into a ROLLING gaze can be used as a clear non-verbal message; it is often used when a spoken comment would be dangerous or impolite. Eye-gaze connections are a great way of uniting with other members of a group, often as a silent comment on the behaviour or words of a person in authority. A quick roll of the eyes in an upward direction, often combined with a turning-down of the mouth can express disbelief, criticism or general fed-upness.

A GLANCE is a sideways look or, as Princess Diana used it, a look upwards through the lashes, with a lowered head; this can be a 'come-hither' invitation, or an indication of shyness or guilt.

There are several interruptions to continued eye-gaze: I have already mentioned blinking in relation to film and there is also winking, one of the clearest silent signals between people, and the classic flutter of the lashes – an attempt to attract. I like to divide the closing of both eyes into two categories according to the timing of the closure: I call a quick closing a SHUT and a slower one a CLOSE. The raising of the eyelids afterwards can also be fast or slow. Shutting can indicate shock, disbelief, denial, a cutting-off of attention or a reinforcement of a strongly felt statement, such as a heartfelt apology. If a shut happens after a sliding gaze it can add powerfully to the message of rejection or disgust. Closing the eyes slowly can be a signal of love and trust; it is used by lovers – and by cats, too!

Meeting or 'catching' the eyes of another person can at times get us what we want, such as a drink at a busy bar or the bill from the waiter in a restaurant; it can change our lives with a gaze held or avoided by another person; it can provoke aggression when it is perceived as an invasion of the personal space of another person. We seem to sense when someone is looking at us, and when our own gaze is noticed in that way we have avoidance signals, such as looking away or pretending to be interested in our book, to protect us. Some ways of looking at people can be offensive and scary, some can give comfort and strength at painful moments. All this work on gaze is applicable to objects as well as to people; when acting, you need to find out what your character enjoys looking at and what he dislikes.

There are many more 'speechless messages' for you to find, to name and to play with as a vital part of the acting 'science of human behaviour'.

NOTES FOR THE TEACHER OF THE EYE-GAZE EXERCISES

Allow enough time for each aspect of eye-gaze to be practised with precision. Working with a large group it is easy for players to 'cheat' on an instruction, which changes the experience of the game for them and for their partners. When working with people of differing cultures it would be respectful to discuss their eye-gaze and personal-space rules before starting the games.

I think these exercises would be too challenging for young and inexperienced players, especially in a group of boys and girls; it is safer to use them only with adults or with a group that you know well, with a mutual trust. Even then, be careful with a shifting gaze, to keep the area where the gaze lands in its journey from the eyes of the partner to another part of their body to a comparatively safe place such as the shoulders or feet.

When you demonstrate this, you can remind players to be respectful of each other in this way, as you are exploring a most sensitive area of privacy and emotion. If players become careless in this, it is best to stop the exercise at once and allow time to discuss the mistake. Having learned the basics through these exercises, actors and directors can find the techniques most useful in rehearsal, to enliven a scene or explore a relationship.

Notice everything. Correct a little. Cherish the brethren.
(Saint Bernard of Clairvaux)

9 Confidence, poise and balance

In all my work on myself as an actor and a human body and in my work with actors I have been puzzling over ways of finding a true, natural poise which would enable the actor to do his best work at all times, in class, rehearsal and performance. Many practitioners have found answers which help a bit but may not be completely useful because the physical problem at the centre of the puzzle has not been made clear. My son, Dominic Barter, an actor, director and teacher, has been exploring this area and has allowed me to use his work, which is still in progress, as a part of this book.

If we accept that tension is energy in the wrong place, i.e. that muscles contract for no useful purpose during the action we are taking, we need to discover why this unwanted contraction happens. The body has economy of effort: it uses only the muscles it needs to use to perform an action, so what is the need of the body when it contracts those muscles? Why would a muscle contract for no useful purpose? Because the body's need is to keep upright, to be balanced.

We all had economy of effort as young children. Without it, we would not have had the ability first to raise the head, then to sit, stand, walk and run, so this work we are doing now is a return to a natural balance, not a strange new effort. Balance is a dynamic relationship, not a given, or a static state. As the earth moves, we move; balance is a moving relationship between two things; so we look at the pivot: the point of contact between the moving body and its moving support, the ground (or the chair on the ground). A pivot's chain of influence works by sending information about the point of contact through the senses in the muscles of that point to the brain or into the spinal cord and the nerve information relays to the muscles, which organise themselves to find equilibrium for the pivot (the moving point of contact).

Tension from 'stage fright' means that I am concentrating (my attention turned inwards, closed off from the world around me), rather than being open and focused, with my attention directed outwards to what is actually going on. I have lost my natural dynamic, which is the response of the individual to his external surroundings and to his internal state.

So, we define concentration/isolation as being focused on one thing only to the exclusion of others, and focus/connection as being focused on one thing within the context of everything else. With concentration's effort to exclude what is actually happening, the body is not receiving enough true, present-moment information in order to keep its pivot in natural balance. In fact, it is receiving faulty information from and about its surroundings and so cannot be sure of its balance, so it asks you to do unnecessary things (to contract muscles): this leads to tensions in places where balance-maintenance is not needed. Examples often seen in actors are clenched shoulders, a tight jaw, braced knees, a frozen face, a held stomach and chest. Because body and mind/emotions are inseparable, fear then comes from these tensions: fear is a shorthand for these bodily changes; it is physical. Panic is the perception of this fear.

So, how do we regain balance?

Balance means the exchange of weight for support. Gravity or weight and support are the same event looked at from two different angles. We call the perception of one angle (from the top downwards) 'weight' and the perception of the other angle (from the ground upwards) 'support'. However, support is not that simple: the ground or floor will give support only to the weight that is on top of it. I will get back solely what I give. If I do not allow the floor to take my weight I will not get back any support from the floor and if I am tense I am holding that amount of my weight away from the floor. If you resist you weaken. If you meet you strengthen. So if you resist the support of the floor you will not get support from it.

In my teaching, I introduce the idea of the actor's 'silent friends', the physical supports and surroundings that are always present for us. Because a joke is easy to remember, I call these Freddy Floor, Charlie Chair and Sammy Space and remind people to sustain the connection with these friends at all times, both physically and imaginatively.

Include the audience in your perception; do not resist by pretending they are not there. They are like a floor – not a 'fourth wall' but another floor – there to support you. Nothing is more powerful than accepting attention from another person. An audience gives high group-attention to the actor and this supports him much more than in normal life; if you resist this you suffer and if you accept it you get high! On stage, balance becomes even more fine-tuned when the attention of the audience is accepted: there is a mutual transference of dynamic energy. Actors and audience are being influenced by each other so you get this big change; you are all being supported while you watch and listen to the story of the scene and you can then make wiser discoveries about and within that story through identification with the characters, especially the hero.

THE WOBBLE BOARD

Dominic teaches a process of experiencing natural balance that he calls Daily Practice, but without access to his practical work I find that the most reliable way of accessing the liberation of corrected balance – when the space between joining bones expands naturally, making free movement possible, at the same time opening the attention to an increased awareness of one's inner and outer surrounding circum-stances – is to use a 'wobble board'. These are cheap and easily made; mine are made of light plywood with a handle-space so that I can carry them. I have several and use them constantly in class and rehearsal, and most actors I work with enjoy them so much that they make their own, or ask a friend or relative to make one for them. (The dimensions shown in the diagram are wide and deep enough to take a man's feet.)

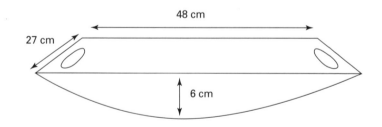

Wobble boards have many uses: as I write I am resting my feet on one, which keeps my balance fluid; I sometimes get anxious when writing and continually need to allow my chair to support my weight; stress and excitement pull my weight up into my upper chest, inhibit my breath, and tighten my jaw and facial muscles. When I return to a natural state of surrendering to the pivot-point of weight-meeting-support, and my body releases from being frozen into flexibility, thoughts and the mechanical actions of typing become easy . . . even my dyslexia improves. To watch people as they stand on a wobble board is such a rewarding experience; they look beautiful and feel themselves and are seen by others newly. I want to say, with Miranda in *The Tempest*, 'O, brave new world, that has such creatures in it!' It is noticeable that the person standing on the board can accept the full attention of his 'audience' with no anxieties; this is true of even the shyest person.

It is useful to ask what different sensations the person has when standing on the board. Is the breathing different? It usually drops down from the shallow area of the upper chest and this can be perceived in the breath support given to the voice; voices can change dramatically as the throat and jaw open. Do the feet, knees, pelvis, shoulders feel different? Observers will usually see a widening in the shoulder-girdle, both front and back, and a corresponding widening in the cheekbones, with a relaxation of the many tiny facial muscles, which make the face look younger and more beautiful. People often experience clearer hearing and sight because of the release of these muscles: the room can appear brighter and detail is noticed for the first time as the attention opens with the opening of muscles. Energy moves into the back and the spine feels warmly supported and wider.

As the person gets off the board, after spending between 30 seconds and a minute on it, the floor often feels 'soft' and friendly and they enjoy the sensuousness of walking, connected to their surroundings. The word 'soft' crops up frequently in this work: it seems to mean a connecting or merging of the individual with his surroundings, beautiful to feel and to watch, as the audience shares the experience of the actor. Usually the sensations on the board are cheery and people often find that headaches and feelings of tiredness and discomfort vanish, but occasionally, when people are very tired, the exhaustion suddenly recognised by the body can overwhelm them and then they need to sit down or cry and be looked after for a while. The board seems to provide a balance of its own for each person: an anxious person can be balanced to cheerfulness, a person resisting tiredness can be brought to recognise it, a shy person is given confidence.

The wobble board is not magic! It is important to remember that it is just a piece of plywood a couple of inches off the ground on a flexible pivot and that the changes it helps to make in the individual standing on it for a minute or even less come from the body's acceptance of a living balance rather than a static holding of the body. On the board, the body naturally adapts to the shifting wobble by exchanging weight with support and people have the delightful experience of returning to the living balance of their childhood, leaving the frozen state of trying not to fall over/fearing to fail that they associate with performance and being judged. The 'magical' effects come from the natural alignment of the body and the new connection of the individual with his environment.

You will be (here 'broad' means free):

> Whole as the marble, founded as the rock,
> As broad and general as the casing air.
>
> (*Macbeth*, Act 3, Sc. 4)

WILLIAM JAMES

The American psychologist and philosopher William James (1842–1910) wrote about habitual tension, or, as he put it, 'the effect on the over-contracted person's spiritual life'.[1]

> For, by the sensations that so incessantly pour in from the over-tense, excited body, the over-tense and excited habit of mind is kept up; and the sultry, threatening, exhausting, thunderous inner atmosphere never quite clears away. If you never wholly give yourself up to the chair you sit in, but always keep your leg and body muscles half-contracted for a rise; if you breathe eighteen or nineteen, instead of sixteen times a minute and never quite breathe out at that – what mental mood *can* you be in but one of inner panting and expectancy, and how can the future and its worries possibly forsake your mind? On the other hand, how can they gain admission to your mind if your brow be unruffled, your respiration calm and complete and your muscles all relaxed?[2]

What a good description that is of the struggling actor's state, when he is 'searching for feelings inside himself' rather than focusing his attention on the situation of the moment. James found 'a law of very deep and wide-spread importance in the conduct of our lives', which was 'that strong feeling about one's self tends to arrest the free association of one's objective ideas and motor processes'. He explained that feelings of self-doubt, anxiety, inner pressure to 'get it right' and even a 'great or sudden pleasure' may 'paralyse the flow of thought'. He advised the forming of a new habit, 'when once a decision is reached and execution is the order of the day, dismiss absolutely all care and responsibility about the outcome. UNCLAMP, in a word, your intellectual and practical machinery and let it run free and the service it will do you will be twice as good . . . Prepare yourself in the subject so well, that it shall always be on tap and then . . . trust your spontaneity and fling away all further care.'

THE FALSE SMILE

Katya Benjamin, who teaches Movement at RADA, offers this very helpful description of what happens to our bodies when we attempt to hide uncertainties behind the 'please approve of me' smile:

> The false smile is made with the mouth, not with the eyes; it is an unconscious plea to be liked and it happens when you are not convinced by what you are doing or saying. This is a halfway state and a defence at times of uncertainty. The false smile closes resonating spaces in the mouth and nose and tightens the jaw. It blocks the larynx and contracts the diaphragm, so that you want to push and shout your lines because you know that neither your voice's sound nor sense is receivable. The false smile also pulls the top of your head down so that you lose the resonating spaces in your head; the pulled weight of the top of the skull onto the lower areas presses progressively downwards from the jaw to the neck and voice box to the chest and downwards through the body, ending with the feet being stuck to the floor.
>
> This pressure is because in that state you are not able to receive the person who is speaking to you and are isolated in your inability to connect with them or your surroundings. The false smile means that you are pushing *at*, rather than connecting *with*, your scene

partners. The answer is to focus on receiving the other person, rather than pushing or shouting unfocused sound at them.

Take a moment to allow your collarbone to widen – I like to imagine wings extending laterally from the balls of my shoulders – and to relax and soften your pelvis: when you do this you can breathe naturally and effortlessly, which gives you great confidence and easiness; you can forget the false smile, because you don't need it. The approval that you want comes from inside you and, really, that inner peace of mind can only come from you, yourself; if we look for it from others we will never be satisfied.

Imagine a string of stretchy elastic between you and your scene partner, which fills the intervening space with your understanding of each other; even in a scene where characters misunderstand or have opposing aims, your energy must go into striving for clarity of purpose and comprehension.[3]

Running a scene with the 'no smiling' rule is very helpful (see p. 166). So often, actors don't even know when their false smile is happening, it is such a habit, and they are relieved to be rid of it and able to feel sincerely and to connect freely in the situation.

I think the false smile is also connected to the problem of shouting – confusing volume with meaning, as a student described it to me recently – and to that little habitual 'sorry' which creeps in when the person in the 'actor's state' makes what he interprets as a mistake.

Part Three The rehearsal process

The rehearsal process can be compared to the making of a jigsaw: after the first look at the picture on the box (the whole play), we break it up into small pieces, each of which has its own place and must be joined to all the pieces around it. As rehearsals progress to the performance, each of these separate pieces must be joined together seamlessly to form the correct picture.

The first series of techniques in this Part offer ways of exploring the play text and dramatic structure of a story. The second series provide practical approaches to the playing of a character, followed by suggestions for the actor's homework, how to put on a play and notes for the director.

I am using Act 1 of Anton Chekhov's *The Cherry Orchard* – his last and arguably greatest play – as the text for Part Three. In this play, Chekhov provides a believable background for each character, so the actor can build up his life outside the scene in order to bring that life on stage. Each character has their own unique voice, their own response to the events and people around them and their own special value to the themes and storyline of the play. Motives, Obstacles and Strategies are crystal-clear to the actors and the audience, although so many characters do not understand themselves; this human muddle, in which we can see our own aspirations, ambitions and mistakes, connects, teaches and makes us laugh and cry with the characters in the same way as Shakespeare does. As actors we have to inhabit the life of the character without commenting on it; working with Chekhov texts gives vital practice in playing with uncompromising fidelity and connection.

The version I use was translated by Peter Gill, a brilliant playwright and director; it is friendly to the speaker while being true to the setting of Russia in 1904.[1]

10 Meeting the play

THE FIVE 'WH' QUESTIONS

A useful way to start work is to use the five 'Wh' questions to collect the information we need from the text and also to research and imagine any gaps that there might be in the web of the Given Circumstances. (An actor I worked with recently called this being a 'text detective'.)

What happens in the play? What is the story? What does each character want and what does s/he do to get it? (What does s/he *do*, not what does s/he 'feel' or 'think'? 'Character is action,' said Aristotle.)

Where is the play taking place? Where is each scene happening? A scene played outdoors has a very different feel to one indoors; being at home is different to being in a strange house: each place we are in dictates our behaviour to some degree. We often need to do some research to find the geographical world of the play.

When is the play happening? When does each scene take place? 4pm is not 4am; everything changes for people according to what time of day or night it is and in response to the changing seasons. What is the political and social time of the play?

Who are the people in the play? Especially, who is your character? The answers to this question, as with every Wh question, lie in the text. (See the 'invisible characters' diagram, p. 118.)

Why does this imagined person behave as s/he does? What motives impel the story? Also, why did the playwright create the play?

This fascinating work takes up a great deal of rehearsal and preparation time and involves research into the world of the play, the social conditions of the When and Where, the financial, moral, family, domestic, religious, political and psychological backgrounds of all the roles.

You can never know too much about the background of the play and the life of your part, but you do not need to drag your researches around with you like heavy luggage during the scene. Think of your own life: you have lived through every minute of that number of years and all those formative experiences; you carry the genes and the inheritance of personality from your ancestors. They are part of you; you bring your past into the room with you with no effort of thought on your part although you cannot exist without it; all your attention is on your present situation.

And there is one other 'Wh' question, but it is different: **how** does all this happen? The How of acting can only be answered in action with the other people in a scene. Using the different spelling of 'How' as a reminder, we could say that for this aspect of acting we remove the W, which is the first letter of Work, from the question: no work here, just connection. Remember, you cannot prepare to feel, therefore you cannot prepare your reactions to others, because the only thing you can be sure of is that they will be different every time they happen.

You cannot prepare exactly **how** you will behave even though you know a great deal about the What, Why, Where, When and Who of the scene. The essence of good acting is that you stay in the moment and allow yourself to be changed by what happens in the scene.

Life is one unexpected thing after another. If you wish to bring true living onto the stage, then you must allow your character the freedom to be surprised. From a strong personal centre, experienced in the awareness of the body, the actor can extend his imagination into the experience of an imagined Other. It is the same empathy, coming from an inner security, we look for in life.

George Eliot sums this up in this passage from *Middlemarch*: she is describing the feelings of Dorothea in her marriage to the elderly scholar Mr Casaubon:

> It had been easier for her to imagine how she would devote herself to Mr Casaubon, and become wise and strong in his strength and wisdom, than to conceive with that distinctness which is no longer

reflection but feeling – an idea wrought back to the directness of sense, like the solidity of objects – that he had an equivalent centre of self, whence the lights and shadows must always fall with a certain difference.

(Chapter 21).

'That distinctness which is no longer reflection but feeling' is our aim in acting. Eliot takes care to define 'feeling' as a physical reality; it must be 'wrought back to the directness of sense, like the solidity of objects' as we recognise and accept the 'equivalent centre of self' of the character we are playing.

THE SECRET OF THE PLAY

To define your thoughts about the play imagine that you are answering the question 'What is the play about?', asked by an intelligent 10-year-old. Use one sentence if possible. For *The Cherry Orchard*, the sentence might be 'The play is about a family who let their home be destroyed because they all want other things more than saving it.' Do you agree? What would you say? You could start with one answer and see if another arises during your rehearsal period.

George Bernard Shaw tells us that we must try to find the *secret* of the play, which is an excellent aim for directors and actors. Sometimes it is not easy to define at first; the best way is to get a starting-point and be ready to change it as the play reveals itself.

FRENCH SCENES, EVENTS AND UNITS

A play script is like a large cake; it needs to be divided into bits in order to be digested. The playwright has divided it into acts and scenes; actors and the director need to divide it further, in order to clarify the dramatic structure, story and characters, and to devise a coherent rehearsal process.

French scenes

Classic French play texts mark a division at every entrance and exit of any character in a scene. Each such section is headed by the names of the characters remaining on the stage. Numbered French scenes make it easier to organise rehearsals so that actors are called only when needed.

In the first act of *The Cherry Orchard* I find three French scenes close together at the beginning:

Scene 1 is the empty stage
Scene 2 Dunyasha's entrance
Scene 3 Lopakhin and Dunyasha

Then:

4 Epihodov, Dunyasha, Lopakhin
5 Epihodov, Lopakhin
6 Epihodov, Lopakhin, Dunyasha
7 Lopakhin, Dunyasha
8 The empty room
9 Firs crossing
10 Ranevskaya, Anya, Gaev, Pischik, Varya, Lopakhin, Dunyasha, Charlotte, servants.

And so on.

As you can see, some French scenes are very short and there is a choice at the beginning whether you give the empty room a scene number and whether you bring Lopakhin and Dunyasha on at the same moment. I am following Stanislavski's original production of the play in my list as it seems right to give time for the place to establish itself. He filled our French scene 8 with the noises of the family's arrival off-stage, building up to the general entrance.

Events

Having done the formal French scene divisions, we now divide the text into events, giving each one a title, so that we can see the physical and psychological actions that occur in each act clearly. An Event is a main section of the action. You could divide Act 1 of *The Cherry Orchard* into:

1 Waiting for the mistress to come home
2 Coming home
3 The home must be sold

or you could take rather smaller divisions if you felt that was helpful. What you are looking for is a clear, simple through-line of action so that you know the main drive of each event sequence.

Units

Units are smaller divisions of action, like paragraphs in a book. Their purpose is to mark changes of subject, rhythm and feeling within a scene. It is most useful for the group of actors to use units divided by changes of subject, because then they are dealing with the rhythmic changes of the scene and making those decisions together. The focus is to discover the dramatic narrative structure of the scene and this is not hard to do. As a result, the actors' energies are directed to the whole scene, rather than just to the character they are playing, and this puts them in charge, as a group, of the storyline and of their part in it. (Stanislavski used the word 'task' for the purposeful action of a character within a unit.)

A new unit is often indicated by a pitch or rhythm change, that is, we signal a change of subject as we talk by marking it with a different pitch (the highs and lows of the vocal line), sometimes with a change of volume and always with a change of tempo. These are such universal signals that to ignore them and to change a subject without such vocal changes will often get a laugh from an audience and so is a technique of comedic delivery – an effective one, but do not use it too often or it will quickly lose its power.

Units can also change with a change of focus: that is, the action and rhythm change when a new person is addressed. Changes of action, such as moves, will naturally coincide with unit changes. A unit change also indicates a new strategy in the attempt to achieve the Aim of the scene.

The secret of exciting immediate playing is to keep your attention totally in the unit of the moment, not anticipating the coming change. Do not use one unit to prepare for the next one; play it for itself alone and in performance the next change will come upon you as a surprise – as it would to the character you play – with a renewal of energy. When units are lifted off the page and integrated into acting we find that they solve the problem of staying in the moment; the unit works as a secure 'firewall' for the immediate problem-solving strategy, cordoning off that specific action so that the actor can focus only on that unique exchange of energy with his scene partner, free of the baggage of the past and with no anticipation of the future. This means that the character is enabled to 'play to win', as he would in real life, even when the actor knows that the scene will end in failure or disappointment.

In order to establish this good practice right from the start of work on a play I ask my actors to unit each scene that they are in; they can do this at home while I, as the director, unit the whole play. At the next rehearsal we compare our choices of unit and come to a company agreement on when these divisions are, so that we share a common understanding of the dramatic structure of each scene. (This is in order to save time; decisions are made by the actors in the scene, with the director. In the first scene of any play the director may have to ask for a few more unit changes, because the playwright is introducing new characters, relationships and situations which the audience needs to hear and retain in order to understand the story.)[2]

In later rehearsals and performances, these divisions will join into the changing rhythms of the narrative action. There is nearly always a new unit when there is a new French scene, because the arrival or departure of a person changes things. Units just as pencil marks on a page are useless: the changes need to be in the actors' bodies, impulses for breath, speech and action. (See Breath, Chapter 14, p. 154.)

An example from *The Cherry Orchard*

I will start the numbering from the beginning of the play. When marking a script always use a pencil, so that you can make changes; I mark unit divisions with a little '/'. Here I've numbered them as well.

Unit 1 LOPAKHIN: Thank God the train's in. What time is it?

DUNYASHA: Nearly two o'clock. *Blows out a candle.* Look it's already light.

LOPAKHIN: That train must be two hours late.

/Unit 2 I feel such a fool. I came here specially to meet them and I fell asleep in the chair; damned stupid thing to do. Why didn't you wake me?

DUNYASHA: I thought you'd gone with the others.

/(Unit 3 *listens*: There they are.

LOPAKHIN: No they're not. They won't be here yet. There's the luggage and everything.)

/Unit 4 I wonder if she's changed at all . . . wonderful woman. She was always very good to me . . . I always felt at ease with her. I remember when I was about fifteen, my father . . . he had a shop in the village then, beat me for something and made my nose bleed. We'd come up here for some reason, I don't know why, and he was drunk.

/Unit 5 Liuba Andreyevna, she was only a girl herself, brought me here, to the nursery it was then, and washed my face for me. 'Never mind, little peasant', she said, 'it'll be better before your wedding day.'

/Unit 6 *pause* Little peasant . . . quite right. Here I am in my waistcoat and leather boots but I'm still a peasant, like a pig loose in the drawing room. I may have money, I may have lots of money but I'm still a peasant, you can't hide that.

/Unit 6a I've been reading this book. Couldn't make head or tail of it. Fell asleep over it.

/Unit 7 DUNYASHA: The dogs haven't slept all night. They know, you see.

LOPAKHIN: What's the matter with you, Dunyasha?

DUNYASHA: I feel faint. My hands are shaking.

LOPAKHIN: That's because you think you're a lady. You're too sensitive that's the trouble. Why don't you dress properly and wear your hair properly? You should remember your place.

/Unit 8 *Enter Epihodov with a bunch of flowers. As he enters he drops the flowers. He picks the flowers up.*

EPIHODOV: These are for the dining room. The gardener sent them. *He gives them to Dunyasha.*

LOPAKHIN: Fetch me some kvass will you?

DUNYASHA: Yes sir. *Goes out.*

/**Unit 9** EPIHODOV: Three degrees of frost and the cherry trees are covered in blossom. What a climate. *Sighs.* I don't know what to make of it, I'm sure. It's shocking, you know it is. Dear, dear, it makes no sense this weather. Completely nonsensical. I don't think much of it anyway.

/**Unit 10** I bought myself a pair of boots the day before yesterday and they squeak, so that doesn't help matters. Should I put something on them do you think?

LOPAKHIN: I don't know. Leave me alone. I'm tired.

EPIHODOV: Every day something frightful happens. I'm not complaining. I'm used to it. I think it's quite funny.

/**Unit 11** *Enter Dunyasha.*

Did those divisions make sense to you or would you have divided the scene differently? Remember that one of the purposes of the divisions is to facilitate learning; another is to honour the narrative information in a speech, to advance the story, which is why more units are usually necessary in the first scene of a play. The audience must hear and understand every word but there are some words and sentences that they need not only to hear but to remember, so that they can follow the story.

Unit 1 concerns the arrival of the train, maybe triggered by the distant sound of the whistle which has brought Lopakhin and Dunyasha into the nursery from different doors.

Unit 2 is about Lopakhin's feelings about himself and his failure to meet the train as he had planned.

Unit 3 I have put in brackets because it is a short interruption to the main flow of dialogue, heightening the anticipation felt by the characters and the audience. This I call a bracket unit.

Unit 4 introduces Ranevskaya without giving her name; we just hear that there is a 'wonderful woman' on that train. You could make the story of the drunken father a 'follow-on' unit (see below), but I like to let it run.

Unit 5. This choice is solely because of the name 'Liuba Andreyevna'; it is the first time we hear the name of a character in the play.

Unit 6. Chekhov requires a pause here and this is always a signal from the playwright that a change of rhythm is necessary.

Unit 6a. A little 'follow-on', or bracket unit, it connects with Lopakhin's sense of himself as an uneducated peasant, but there is a slight shift of subject there.

Unit 7. Both Lopakhin and Dunyasha have moved upwards from 'their place'; he through his money and she because of her idea of herself as a 'lady'.

Unit 8. Units change with a new French scene.

Unit 9. There is another change of rhythm as Dunyasha leaves.

Unit 10. Although there is a change of subject here, from the weather to the state of Epihodov's new boots, it might be fun to play as an unbroken continuation in tone, ignoring the usual vocal change of subject, as evidence of Epihodov's grasshopper thinking.

Unit 11. Dunyasha returns with Lopakhin's drink and Epihodov leaves.

Follow-on and bracket units

Sometimes within a unit you can detect a noticeable directional change that doesn't seem to quite warrant a new unit; here you can use a 'follow-on' unit. A 'follow-on' is like a curve in the road: it is a change from the previous unit but only a slight change of direction. Some actors will want a new unit and some think it unnecessary; calling it a 'follow-on' is an immediate solution until the full value can be realised in the action of the scene. Unit 6a above is a good example. Bracket units are also helpful: they are like a lengthened subordinate clause and should be phrased in the same way, taken with less volume, faster speed and less inflective variation than the main units surrounding them. See unit 3 above.

The change of subject and focus usually dictates a change of movement, either a travelling move or a gesture or shift of position.

Try this exercise with another scene; it is not difficult and it is good when everyone does it together, because then you are all digging into the play and making those changes belong to you. Company discussions based so closely on the text are helpful; general discussions which take up rehearsal time are not always so useful.

The text is the map. It is not the journey. The journey is your direct experience of the life of your character in the Given Circumstances of the play. But before any travelling into the unknown you must study that map for every detail of information you need. All the answers are in the text. The secret is to know what questions to ask of it and not to give up until it yields its answers to you.

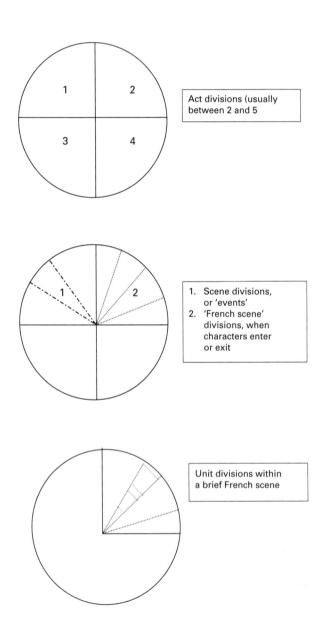

Act divisions (usually between 2 and 5

1. Scene divisions, or 'events'
2. 'French scene' divisions, when characters enter or exit

Unit divisions within a brief French scene

A SIMPLE AND CONFIDENT START TO A SCENE

Focus: To find a practical route into the playing of a scene.

At times it can be difficult or scary to begin putting a scene into action. You want to avoid the deadening process of wandering around holding the script and reading your lines; I find that this makes true lively action impossible, as the actor's focus is entirely in the actor's state of 'I want to play this scene' rather than in the creative state of interaction between the characters.

The following process works well; it can be used as the very first step in rehearsal, or you can wait to use it after you have spent some time on the text, so you can start with number 1, 2 or 3 on the list below.

(If you start with number 3, make time to go through numbers 1 and 2 later on.)

1 For any play you do, it is worth going carefully through the scene in your own words, to make sure that you understand the full sense; one sentence at a time works well. The Pointing and Receiving exercises are especially useful here, as you will be working with one or more scene partners.
2 Unit the scene, checking your decisions with your partners.
3 Make a list of the physical actions demanded by the playwright.

At the start of *The Cherry Orchard* these are:

a. Dunyasha enters, carrying a candle.
b. Lopakhin, with a book in his hand, comes in from another door.
c. Dunyasha blows out the candle.
d. She listens, thinking she has heard the arrival.
e. She feels faint and her hands are shaking.
f. Epihodov enters with a bunch of flowers.
g. He drops them and picks them up again.
h. He gives them to Dunyasha.
i. Dunyasha goes out.
j. Epihodov sighs.

k. Dunyasha comes in with a glass of kvass (a sort of beer made with pears).

l. Epihodov stumbles against a chair as he starts to go out, knocking the chair over.

m. He goes out.

(*Note*: Make sure that the locations are clear. Think where the imagined stairs down to the entrance of the house on one side and the internal rooms on the other side are. Decide which side Dunyasha comes from – if she comes from the stairwell, then Lopakhin would come from an inner room (or maybe it's the other way round, as Lopakhin is a visitor). Epihodov, coming up from the garden, would enter from the stairwell.)

This approach to actioning the scene is fun and puts you in charge of the visible storyline, giving physical confidence and a sense of truthful communication and makes you want to use the text, so that you are not frightened of speaking the lines.

4 With your scene partners you then learn and play the physical actions silently; you are free to look at and react to others, to feel a sense of the imagined place and to allow spontaneous impulses to happen.

5 After this you can sit down together and go through the text, finding the details of the story and the central lines of the dialogue. You are now going to improvise your way through the scene, just sitting down and talking to each other as the characters, using your own words. Notice what imagery your character uses in the text and incorporate that into your improvised speaking. Remember that we use images when there is no other way of expressing our meaning, so an image often represents an important feeling that needs to be expressed.

6 When you are all ready after the improvised scene, it is time to get up and go back to your list of actions, but this time you can add your improvised lines, so the scene now has the firm structure of the required actions plus the freedom of your spontaneous dialogue.

7 By now, I hope you will be feeling a bit frustrated with using your own words for the scene and you will want to rediscover Chekhov's text, so you can start to learn your lines together, using the snowball units system (p. 132) or perhaps first trying the Ghost exercise (p. 45), while sitting down with your scene partners.

Only when you can go through the whole scene with perfect accuracy of text should you get up again and once more join text and action.

And there is your scene! Lively, truthful, accurate and fun to play.

WITHIN THE UNIT

Focus: To examine the dramatic structure of each unit.

In scene groups or pairs, look at each line or sentence within a unit to examine its dramatic purpose. The first step is, of course, to find where each unit begins, taking the definition of a unit as a point where the subject or focus of the dialogue changes (see the earlier example from *The Cherry Orchard*, p. 101–2).

Lines of dramatic dialogue can be seen as having different purposes:

Narrative lines are lines or sentences giving information on the background or present situation of the characters and their story. Exposition is necessary at the start of any story and we can see how Chekhov handles this in the opening scenes of *The Cherry Orchard*. Names and family relationships need to be clearly placed; although they are familiar to the characters, they are new to the audience. Some lines advance the story, such as those lines that impel action. Other lines recapitulate or reinforce important information in the storyline.

Personal lines are lines or sentences that reveal a character's emotions, reactions, hidden agenda or 'subtext', and the changing relationships between people. Lopakhin's long speech at the beginning of *The Cherry Orchard* is full of personal lines, interwoven with points of information such as the fact that he now has lots of money.

Theme lines: In many plays the central themes, often presented as the values of the characters, are made clear in dialogue and action. In *The Cherry Orchard*, Firs, for example, seems to represent the old values of loyalty to the family, the house and the orchard, although, as he says, the 'proper recipe' is 'gone, forgotten, no one can remember it'. Firs is talking about a recipe for dried cherries but the theme is about lost certainties, as opposed to Lopakhin's drive for new energy to 'change country life completely' when newcomers will 'cultivate their land and your cherry orchard will have to make way for rich, prosperous lives'.

Key lines: A useful exercise is to find out which lines or sentences fit into each category (narrative, personal or thematic) and then to find just one sentence within each unit that sums up that unit; this will usually be a narrative line which advances the story. When you have listed these essential lines, you can learn them and play them as a sequence, before going back and restoring the many lines you had to miss out. In this way, you can find what is most important in the scene, which will then release the pressure of emphasis and undue stressing on most lines, giving ease and elegance to your phrasing. It makes acting and speaking more natural, more available to the audience and is especially useful in comedy. The exercise is useful for line learning, as it will give you a series of stepping-stones or fixed points to guide you through the story of the scene. It can also be used for a swift run-through of the play, when only the key lines are spoken. An example from the first scene could be the very first line of the play, 'Thank God the train's in!'

11 Bringing the text to life

THE FIRST READ-THROUGHS

Focus: To avoid stress and 'auditioning' from the actors and to see the play as a whole.

The first read-through

A useful device is for the director (or the cast, if there is no director) to change the casting by reversing the male and female roles, so that the men are played by women and vice versa. Another trick is simply to change the casting so that players are reading a different character from the one that they will be playing. For times when casting is not certain, more than one read-through with changing casting is useful; it enables the director to see new possibilities in the group and to get past the first impressions produced by a player who is a good sight-reader and another person who may be dyslexic or nervous when reading aloud. In subsequent read-throughs the Pointing exercise (p. 110) is invaluable as it makes all relationships clear. The Receiving exercise (p. 127) is also helpful as it gives players a chance to listen to each other and provides, as does the Pointing, a firm basis for learning lines.

If an actor is willing to slow down and quieten down, then real, creative work can begin.

Second read-through

This technique can be used for rehearsed readings of a play. It is useful for actors to know when they are in or out of a scene. For this reading, arrange two circles of chairs, one inner circle for those characters in the scene and an outer circle for the off-stage players. Characters come in and out of the central circle of chairs for the start and end of their scenes. The exercise clarifies the composition of each scene and brings useful physical actions into the reading. In the scene, you need to make eye-contact with each other, and those in the off-stage circle need to watch the current scene, rather than read your own next scene. Ask yourself which is more important, the person or the page?

THE POINTING EXERCISE

In this exercise, which can also be used for an early read-through of the script, the work must be slow and, above all, accurate. It utilises the basic instinct that we all have, to 'point out' (literally) what we are talking about, so as to clarify our message for our listener. Specificity equals storytelling; generalisation gives rise to 'acting custard', which covers the dramatic structure with unfocused waves of forced emotion.

Like the Ghost exercise, this exercise aims to free you from the old habit of reading aloud, when your eye races ahead of your voice to prepare the next part of your speech. When you lose your connection with the present moment you lose your way. So many actors keep 50 per cent of their attention on 'the next thing' (which, like tomorrow, never comes); they also often have 25 per cent of their mind on what they have just done – Was it good or bad? What did it sound like? – leaving only 25 per cent for the present moment. No wonder so much acting is unconvincing and boring!

Acting should be like sport, where every ounce of the player's energy is being used in the action of the NOW.

Your first public meeting with your character and the other people in the world of the play is important: it sets the tone of your future relationships in the same way as the arrival of a new person affects a family. I like to think that the characters in a play search for the actor to embody them, rather than that the actor 'tries to find the character', who, after all, does not even exist except in the imagined world of the play. All the actor has to do is to be open, ready and swept clean of fear and ego for the character to move in and take action.

So it is vital that this first experience of the text being shared aloud by the company should allow *time* for the roots of the character to go down and for the lateral web of interpersonal relationships to grow. There is always the choice between planting seeds of creativity that can grow organically, or just shoving in plastic flowers at the first reading, which might look instantly impressive but will lack possibilities of growth or change.

When we slow the reading down we give time for our active imaginations to work: the 'internal film' of imaginative images arises spontaneously as we speak, so that the muscular activity of speaking the word or phrase is the same thing as the bright, clear image in the mind, as it is in life when we speak to convey our internal world to others.

If we do a conventional first read-through there is no time for this to happen: the imaginative work and the building of relationships through correct focusing (knowing who you are talking to, and who and what you are talking about), eye-contact and active involvement in the scene, listening to each other and being changed by your partners – all these essentials have to be dealt with after that reading.

The Pointing exercise is simple but not easy and it takes time to understand that it is not a miming game or a mechanical arm-waving process but an opportunity to allow the play to penetrate deep into your imagination, arousing strong, concrete emotions and discoveries about the world you are entering together for the first time.

The director must therefore have practised the exercise herself in advance to familiarise herself with its demands and difficulties and be prepared to correct actors who try to push forwards and forget to make eye-contact with their partners, or who cop out of the exercise by just rushing through it. Some exercises are like casseroles: you can adapt them and even change the ingredients without spoiling the dish. But some are like soufflés: these must be done strictly according to the recipe or they just won't work. The Pointing and Ghost exercises are just such.

You will notice that this exercise brings physical action into the work at the first contact with the text. We start in the way we mean to go on. Once players have learned the discipline and uses of Pointing, then they can go on to join it to the Ghost exercise; the two exercises combined make a wonderful beginning to text work and truthful acting. They also help a lot in the learning of lines, as the learning process has begun creatively, with direct experience and lively visual images. However, if you use the Pointing exercise only as a line-learning device it won't work for you.

Looking at the first scene of *The Cherry Orchard*, I will illustrate the Pointing exercise up to the end of Lopakhin's first long speech. First we have to discover what people and places we need to point at:

Places

'Here', the room where the action takes place: use the table or centre of the room you are in. For 'abroad', point to a far corner of the room which will stand also for Paris later on.

You also need:

- a place in the room which represents the station and the train; that could be over by the window of the rehearsal room
- a place to represent the village and in it a place to represent the shop where Lopakhin's father worked; the village could be by the door and a chair there could stand for the shop
- the room where Lopakhin has just fallen asleep
- the drawing room.

Objects

Although the exercise is not really about props, sometimes an actor finds it useful to have some. For this scene it would help to have a book and some money for Lopakhin to connect with when he talks of them. You can point to some bags for the luggage.

People

- The most important person for Lopakhin is Ranevskaya so it might be useful to point to her even when he says 'they', though that 'they' should also include Anya, Charlotte, Yasha.
- It is best if the people who have come from Paris on the train (Ranevskaya, Anya, Charlotte and Yasha) sit together for Act 1,

with another group of those who went to meet them at the station (Gaev, Pischik, Varya) and the rest who have stayed at the house (Lopakhin, Dunyasha, Firs, Epihodov, the servants).

- God – He can be above. This is a world where God is very much a part of life, so the exercise begins to establish the invisible world of belief as well as the concrete world of the house and family.
- Lopakhin's father is one of the dead people who affect the living in this play; the director or stage manager can stand in for him.
- Someone or something to be the pig!
- Dunyasha will need some dogs.
- In most scenes, of course, you ('I', 'me') and the person you are speaking to ('you') get most of the pointings.

You will see that the exercise means that you must point at characters who are not actually in the scene with you – dead people, etc. You may need to make labels for those characters, which players not in the scene will hold, so that the speaking actor can point to them (Lopakhin's father, for example).

Ambiguous questions such as 'Who is using patchouli?' (later in Act 1) actually have a precise focus: with that question Gaev is attacking Lopakhin for using cheap scent. The word 'one', as in 'If one looks at things from a certain point of view', means either 'I' or 'you', depending on the context. The precision of this demand – that the speaker knows exactly what his meaning is – is one of the great benefits of this exercise.

Once you have sorted this out you can begin. Remember that the exercise works only if you *slow down* and *look* at *each pointing*.

The rule is that you never speak when you are looking at the page; your eyes must be free to look at the others, so you will have to pause frequently to look down between phrases to find your next word-cluster, which you will speak while looking at your partner. This is why the Ghost exercise (p. 45) is such a good combination with Pointing, because in that exercise you are fed each line and need no contact at all with the script.

Speak *only* when you have eye-contact with a partner. You get a gold star each time you lose your place, because that proves that you have not anticipated the next thought. And *stay* with your partner's eyes until he has received (acknowledged) your sentence before you continue to the next thought. This requirement is even tougher than the previous one. The speaker is always anxious to press on, as he can see that he has several lines to deliver before his partner replies. It takes unselfish courage to allow for the few seconds that your partner needs to absorb the implications of what you have just said to her, and to respond to this, and for you, in turn, to take in and be changed by her response, only then going on to your next sentence.

I will illustrate the Points in the first scene of *The Cherry Orchard* in bold.

> LOPAKHIN: Thank **God** the **train**'s in. What time is it?
>
> DUNYASHA: Nearly two o'clock. **Look, it**'s already light.
>
> LOPAKHIN: That **train** must be nearly two hours late. **I** feel such a fool. **I** came **here** especially to go and meet **them** and then **I** fell asleep in the **chair**. Damn stupid thing to do. Why didn't **you** wake me?
>
> DUNYASHA: **I** thought **you**'d gone with the **others**. There **they** are.
>
> LOPAKHIN: No **they**'re not. **They** won't be **here** yet. There's the **luggage** and everything. **I** wonder what **she**'ll be like after five years **abroad**. **I** wonder if **she**'s changed at all. **Wonderful woman. She** was always very good to **me**. **I** always felt at ease with **her**. **I** remember when **I** was about fifteen, **my** / **father, he** had a **shop** in the **village** then, beat **me** for some reason and made **my** / **nose** bleed. **We**'d come up **here** for some reason, **I** don't know why, and **he** was drunk. **Liuba Andreyevna, she** was only a girl **herself**, brought **me** in **here**, the nursery **it** was then, and washed **my** / **face** for **me**. Never mind, little **peasant, she** said, **it**'ll be better before **your** wedding day. Little **peasant**, quite right. **Here** / **I** am, in **my** / **waistcoat** and **leather boots** but **I**'m still a **peasant** . . . like a **pig** loose in the **drawing room**. **I** may have **money, I** may have plenty of **money** but **I**'m still a **peasant, you** can't hide that. **I**'ve been reading this **book**. Couldn't make head or tail of **it**. Fell asleep over **it**.

I have marked the double Pointings with a '/' between words, as in: **my** (point to yourself) / **father** (point to Father), because it is so important to be precise over each focus. You can see how S.L.O.W.L.Y. you must work to do all this correctly. If you were learning a dance routine or a new song, you would not worry about working slowly at first, constantly stopping in order to change (see Bound Flow in Chapter 19, p. 200), going back over difficult bits until you understand what is needed, but realising without panic that you will have to practise a lot before being able to work up to speed. It is only in reading aloud and acting that people lose this wisdom and expect themselves to somehow achieve a performance level with no preliminary work.

There is the danger of becoming quite good at doing this – being an expert bluffer – this will not satisfy you and your talent will rust in its place. Talent does not stay still; it either improves with practice or it fades away.

NOTES FOR THE TEACHER OF THE POINTING EXERCISE

The Pointing exercise can be hard to teach; with some school students it can be too much of a challenge, as they find it embarrassing to point and look at each other. In this case I just demonstrate it and enjoy their response of understanding and connection with the speech. A speech I find useful as a demonstration is part of Friar Lawrence's last long speech in the last scene of *Romeo and Juliet*. Most people know the story of the play roughly and the speech recapitulates it.

Allow time to 'cast' the people mentioned in the speech and to find corners of the room, or points to use as the places mentioned. Usually one person is the focus of the speaker's words, but if the focus changes, be sure that the speaker then turns to talk to this new listener. Most people starting the Pointing exercise will 'cheat' by looking down to find the next few lines, rather than focusing on the person they should be pointing and looking at. They can feel awkward about taking the time necessary to play correctly, and need reassurance and encouragement. They may also avoid a clear Pointing gesture. The teacher needs to be firm about this: do not let the speaker get away with fudging the exercise. Be sure that the speaker allows time for the listener to react to what is said, before he goes on to the next few words.

The Pointing exercise is so valuable when it is used correctly; it can be the breakthrough to real truthful acting, often for the first time. If you are teaching it for the first time, I suggest that you practise with a friend, asking them to help you keep to the rules of focus and patience.

INVISIBLE CHARACTERS

Not all the characters that we need to know about in *The Cherry Orchard* are alive; the influence of the long-dead and those people who have died within the memory of the living characters is important and we need to find out who they are. Also, living people are talked of who do not appear.

Here is a list of the dead who are mentioned in Act 1:

- Grisha, Ranevskaya's little son who was drowned in the river here six years ago
- Ranevsky, Ranevskaya's husband who 'died of champagne', also six years ago
- The Gaev grandfather
- The Gaev parents, the mother being especially present in the orchard
- For Firs, the Gaev father and grandfather are very present
- Lopakhin's father (and generations of serfs)
- The Gaev nanny
- Anastasia, probably an old servant of Gaev's

And the absent living people are:

- The lover, who has treated Ranevskaya so badly, to whom she returns at the end of the play. He is a threat to the happiness of many of the characters, as the estate money has been spent on him.
- Dashenka, Pischik's daughter
- The gardener who gives the flowers to Epihodov
- The people in Paris and on the journey home
- Fiodor Kosoyedov, Dunyasha's father

- Petrushka, a Gaev servant who has left the estate and is now working for the police
- The peasant woman on the train who commented on Peter Trofimov's shabby appearance
- The summer visitors who are buying houses in the country
- Yasha's mother, waiting to see him in the kitchen
- The rich Gaev aunt in Yaroslavl
- Gaev's friends at the district court
- The servants: Yefim, Polya, Yevstigny and Karp
- The beggars and travellers who come to the house for food

The diagram shows the characters and places mentioned in Act 1 of *The Cherry Orchard.* The characters we see on stage are in capital letters; the dead characters are linked to the living by a dotted line and the live characters and places that are mentioned but not seen are marked by a wavy line. The central circle contains the world of the play seen on stage in Act 1; the outer circle represents the surrounding area, and the people and places outside the circle are the wider outside world, beyond Russia, including some deceased characters. It is useful in Act 1 to understand the journeys and arrivals of Ranevskaya and her entourage; this links with the departure of the family at the end of the play, when the cherry orchard is destroyed.

CHARACTERS IN A CIRCLE: THE THREE STATEMENTS EXERCISE

Focus: A useful exercise that sorts out the social and family relationships between the characters, gives a starting point for exploring each character's personal aims, and establishes for the actors the importance of eye-contact and a direct approach to one's partners right from the start of work.

An exercise for the whole cast. I use it at the beginning of rehearsals and I find that actors often wish to play it again later on in the process. Actors: sit around in a circle with one of you in the centre. The central actor addresses each of the others in turn. He then comes out of the

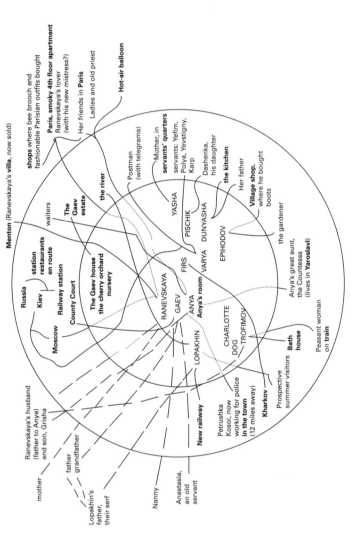

Invisible characters in
The Cherry Orchard, Act 1

centre and another person moves into the centre to do the same, until everyone has had a turn. The exercise consists of three statements that each 'pair' (the central person and the actor he is addressing) says to each other, while looking at each other.

First statement: The full name of your character.
Second statement: You and your partner's social relationship to each other.
Third statement: A personal Aim relating to the person you are speaking to; this is expressed as a request for a simple feasible physical action that can be responded to at the moment of asking. The request can be granted or refused by your partner; if it is granted in the exercise it could still possibly be refused in the scene. (You will notice a link with the Christmas Day exercise on p. 26.)

Example: We'll imagine that the actor playing Anya is in the middle of the circle and that the first person she turns to look at is Ranevskaya.

First statement

ANYA: I am Anya Ranevskaya.
RANEVSKAYA: I am Liuba Andreyevna Ranevskaya.

Second statement

ANYA: I am your daughter.
RANEVSKAYA: I am your mother.
(Be careful with this statement; it must be only the social/family relationship, not an emotional comment on it.)

Third statement

ANYA: At this moment I want you to put your arms round me and say, 'My dearest daughter, I will never leave you.'
RANEVSKAYA: At this moment I want you to put your arms round me and say, 'Darling, beautiful Mum, I forgive you for everything; you are completely free and I'll love you no matter what you choose to do.'

Note that the third statement must begin with 'At this moment, I want you to . . .' followed by an active verb.

This is just a starting point for your personal Aim, which must always be directed specifically to one other person, so that, as well as your long-term objective and the main Aim that carries you through a scene, you know exactly how you would wish each other character to behave towards you. The fact that other people do not always behave as we would wish them to does not stop us from wanting them to do so and trying to influence them to give us what only they can give.

Some actors find the directness and power of this exercise difficult; they try to compromise on the third statement, or do not address it straight to their partner. It is most important that they make strong, simple statements with eye-contact; then each time they meet each other in a scene this connection will be present and of ever-increasing interest to them.

To continue with the exercise, Anya, sitting in the centre of the circle of characters, then turns to Gaev:

First statement
ANYA: I am Anya Ranevskaya.
GAEV: I am Leonid Andreyev Gaev.

Second statement
ANYA: I am your niece.
GAEV: I am your uncle.

Third statement
ANYA: At this moment I want you hold my hand and say, 'You have nothing to worry about; I promise I will save our home.
GAEV: At this moment I want you to look at me with trust and say, 'Uncle, you're so clever; I know you will save the cherry orchard for us.'

In the third statement we need to know which point in the play we are talking about – here it is Act 1. You may well find that personal aims change during the course of the action; the only Aim that remains constant is the long-term Aim, as it is the through-line of the play. (However, in some plays even the second statement changes: for instance, in Ibsen's *Ghosts*, Regina would state that she is Oswald's servant in Act 1; his fiancée in Act 2 and his half-sister in Act 3.)

Anya then addresses Epihodov, a character she has very little contact with in the play, but, all the same, they have a social relationship and opinions about each other.

First statement

ANYA: I am Anya Ranevskaya.

EPIHODOV: I am Epihodov.

Second statement

ANYA: I am the daughter and niece of your employers.

EPIHODOV: I am the clerk of your family estate.

Third statement

ANYA: At this moment I want you to say, 'Dunyasha, please marry me tomorrow', then I want you to leave the room.

EPIHODOV: At this moment I want you to say, 'Dunyasha, marry that wonderful intelligent man Epihodov', and give me a congratulatory kiss.

And so on, Anya speaking to everyone in the circle, until it is someone else's turn in the centre.

Remember to think of what your third statement might be before starting a scene in rehearsals; the simple physical request gives an active clarity of purpose and innate energy right from the start.

THE GHOST EXERCISE, FOR A SCENE

Focus: To begin work on a scene without preparation, to experience it freshly, as a speaker and listener.

Description: This exercise is used in Chapter 6 (p. 45) with primary source material, from transcripts of real people talking. When using the technique with a scene, each actor in the scene needs another player who isn't in that scene to be his 'ghost'. The player sits facing into the scene, his 'ghost' behind him, facing away, holding the script and whispering the player's lines in his ear.

The players are now fully supported by their ghost helpers and are free to watch and listen to the other characters in the scene, not knowing when it will be their turn to speak, what they will say or what others will say to them. They can react spontaneously and truthfully in their first acquaintance with the scene; the necessary slowness of the exercise also helps because it gives time for a full receiving of what is said and heard.

Having had this initial experience of the scene, the player feels the beginning of certainty about his function within the group of characters; because he has been liberated from the stress of making decisions too early and from the pressure of interpretation, he is able to continue to respond to the Given Circumstances of his character moment by moment, taking the story where it needs to go.

VISUALISATION

When your character mentions absent people, past events or distant places, you must allow yourself time to create them in your imagination. In your real life you will have met the people, lived through the past events and seen the distant places so, when you talk about them, sense memories arise vividly in your mind and you recreate them effortlessly. When you play a character, you have not had any of these direct experiences, so you need to spend some time in creating them. This is called 'visualisation' or the 'internal film' and there are exercises in its practice in Chapter 5 (Betty Plum, p. 32, and He Stood There, p. 36).

The technique is one for the rehearsal period only; in performance, either the mental pictures will arise spontaneously as you speak or you will find that you are not consciously aware of them; they have already been established to provide a basis of truth for you to rely on. But if you are having difficulty in a scene, if you lose belief or concentration suddenly, then you can find it again through the use of your 'internal film'.

To understand the visualisation idea as a tool for acting, imagine that you are on a film set, creating a background for one brief shot, let's say a shot of a character moving through a corridor on the way to open the door. Although the corridor shot lasts only for a few seconds and will not be remembered or even noticed in any detail by the audience, still a great deal of thought and work goes into its design, construction, lighting and furnishing; all this careful work takes time. The audience may not remember that shot when they have left the cinema, but at the moment of seeing it in the film that is all that they see. That shot, brief though it is, is their experience in that moment. If the work had not been done satisfactorily they would have noticed and have lost belief in the situation of the scene. So it is with our preparatory work.

Do the work and then forget it is the secret: do not go on stage unprepared and do not prepare during a performance. Do the work at the correct time, in early rehearsal, and then be ready for the changing moment, with that security within. Anthony Hopkins says that 'if you have prepared well for your job, that's when inspiration comes. When you feel secure that the foundation is there, that's when you can take off.'

The technique of visualisation is especially useful for moments when a character is remembering.

An example is Anya's recollections of her time in Paris, as she tells them to Varya. The specificity of visualisation will protect you from wandering off into a vague middle-distance gaze as you 'relive' that past event and feel again all those emotions. Actors enjoy doing this and feel very sensitive as they do it. They have a special 'I am reliving this experience' tone to their voices, which is seldom heard in real life. The real truth of human behaviour, which must always be the deciding factor for actors, is that in recounting a past event, however traumatic that event might have been, the speaker's attention is focused onto the listener, not onto himself. The task is to impart, not to relive. In order to tell the experience clearly your efforts are focused on controlling your emotion.

So our exercise now is to establish Anya's memory; when she plays the scene in the future she will have that to rest on and will be able to play 'I want Varya to understand what I have been through', which is the correct Aim for that part of the scene.

> ANYA: Paris was cold. It was snowing when we arrived and Mama was living in the most awful place right up on the fifth floor, and my French is awful. She had visitors when I arrived. Some French ladies and an old priest with a book. The room was full of cigarette smoke. You can't imagine how untidy and poky it was. I suddenly felt sorry for her and I took her head in my hands and couldn't let her go. She was so loving and she cried all the time.

You will have started with the Pointing exercise (p. 110), so you will already have good strong images for this speech, plus the contact with Varya. After all, she is the reason that Anya is saying all this. Now you need to ask specific questions of the speech to find out more.

- How long had you been in the train? (The journey from Russia in those days took almost a week.) Did you hope and expect that someone would be at the station to meet you? Did you imagine that your mother, who you have not see for five years (she left home when you were 12, just after your father and little brother died) might be on the platform to greet you?
- Tell me about the journey to your mum's flat; did you and Charlotte take a taxi? (Anya would not have seen an apartment before; she is used to a big house, so Ranevskaya's lodgings would have been quite a shock, especially as so much of the estate money had been sent to her.)
- What was it like when you opened the door and saw that room? Had you imagined the meeting differently? Who exactly had you imagined?
- Suddenly, when you see your mother again, she becomes the sad child and you have to 'mother' her. How do you feel about her now?
- Tell me about the staircase up to the fifth floor . . . what did it smell like, look like; did you take your luggage up there or did you leave it in the hall?

You see how much you need to know! You cannot know too much about those past events. Once you have established it, rest on it. Do not play the memory; play the telling of it, focused on Varya, your listener. This is where emotion memory can be a useful tool.

EMOTION MEMORY

Emotion memory is used simply to help you to connect with the experience of the character. It is not there to replace the experience of the character with the actor's own personal experience. This is where people get muddled and start to distort the play to fit their own feelings. They say 'My character would not say that', because they themselves would not say that.

Let us suppose that the actor playing Anya cannot connect fully with those experiences in that speech: it might help her to think of a time in her life when she looked forward to meeting a long-absent friend and found that her hopes were disappointed and then found that the meeting was very different from what she had expected, yet touching and important for the future relationship. The brief touch of her personal emotion memory has helped the actor to trust the truth of her imagination and to take action impelled by the Magic 'If'.

After recalling that experience and perhaps hearing that other people have had similar experiences, Anya can try the speech again, having made a personal connection between her own life and the life of her character. Having thus engaged her imagination and awakened her genuine emotions, she can transfer them, with whatever adjustments are necessary, to the world of the play. So, if you are playing Ranevskaya when she breaks down on seeing Trofimov for the first time since Grisha's death, you might need to think for a moment about a time of grief in your own life to understand the power of Ranevskaya's emotion. But, having done that personal memory once, you leave it and play the character, not yourself. You do not have to relive the death of your kitten each time you play the death of Grisha! The death of Grisha has all the power you need. We do not need to squeeze our hearts or to assault our private memories in order to experience emotion in acting: imagination aroused by specific physical actions does the job without fail.

IMPROVISING OFF-STAGE SCENES

Improvising off-stage scenes solves many problems. It provides the 'line of the day', as Stanislavski called it: the continuum of experience for the characters between the scenes of the play, so that they know where they are coming from and what happened between scenes. If you have problems with a scene, improvising the last time you met your partner or some central off-stage moment will often solve it for you.

The secret here is to transfer immediately from the improv to the scene, making a seamless join. If you stop between the two, you often lose the benefit of the improv. Rehearsing *The Cherry Orchard* I have found that improvising episodes such as the death of Grisha – we had Trofimov bring the 'body' (a heavy coat) into the nursery as he told the family how the little boy had drowned – and going from that tragic experience straight into the scene in Act 1 when Trofimov returns to that room for the first time, bringing the shock and sorrow back into the minds of everyone present, makes the scene itself as powerful for the actors as it would have been for the characters.

I remember doing this when the actor playing Ranevskaya had a big 'block' because she tried to prepare to burst into tears. Of course she could not do this and she 'lost' at least two pages of the previous scene as she left the present moment to prepare to squeeze out some emotion when Trofimov entered. She therefore left the play almost completely, leaving the 'state of the character' for the 'state of the actor'. We had to make it possible for her to experience Ranevskaya's state so fully that she had no time to 'prepare to feel', and this improv did that for her, and for the others in the scene. And this is the demand: that the experience of the actors should matter as much to them as it does to the characters, at each moment of the scene.

It is better for the group to have these direct experiences together, than for them to sit and discuss it for hours or to decide in isolation from each other what their off-stage transactions have been.

LEARNING LINES

Impatience is the main Obstacle in learning; we need to remember the process of dyeing a piece of white cloth: it is dipped into the bowl of blue dye once, then left to dry into a pale wash of colour; then dipped and dried again and again until the true deep colour permeates the material.

How can the learning of lines be an enjoyable part of the creative rehearsal process rather than a painful chore and problem for the actor?

I ask my actors to learn their lines ONLY in rehearsal, not to study them at home. I know that this is unusual but the result is very valuable, to the actors and to the production of any play. Surprisingly, this method takes less time than the conventional one, where rehearsals are so often a stressful period – actors are so busy trying to remember their lines that no real work can be done on a scene. Here, using the Receiving exercise, much valuable foundation work is done while the line learning is happening: meaning, phrasing, breathing and the cueing of the scene can be explored so that they become an integral part of the actor's process as he creates the character. Meanwhile, he is constantly developing an emotional connection with his lines and his partners in the scene.

A good process makes for a good result. You cannot create a good meal from a messy kitchen and stale ingredients: begin the way you mean to go on, with sincerity, imagination and precision.

Many actors are good at speaking their lines, but few are good at receiving, and it is the responsive reception of a heard line or action that is the mark of the true artist. During the Ghost and Pointing exercises, you will have seen some good receiving, largely because of the slow, broken rhythms of the exercises, which give time for a response from speaker to listener and back again. From this we have learned that Slow Time is essential for healthy learning (see Laban on Time, Chapter 21, p. 221).

In the following exercise, the listening partner is functioning simply as a Receiver, not as her character, who may well, in the scene, have a reaction to the speaker's line that is more than a simple reception of it. However, it will make clear the necessity for a specific, clear response, as happens in real life between people. We react physically to everything that happens: to events, to the words and actions of others, to our internal thoughts and feelings – and these changes in breathing, tension, posture and movement are read by those watching.

The Receiving process is a circular one: that is, the first response to a line or action is itself received by the initiator, changing him, which changes the first receiver and so on, in an uninterrupted circle of impetus/response.

THE RECEIVING EXERCISE

Focus: Accurate listening and responding to scene partners.

A quiet talking exercise, usually played in pairs. Holding the script of the scene, sit facing another player. The exercise consists of taking the sentences in a speech one by one and allowing time at the end of each sentence or phrase for your listening partner to repeat that sentence back, paraphrasing at times so that the repetition does not become mechanical. Once each spoken phrase has been thoroughly received by the listener, then the speaker can continue, or the listener respond with his own line, to be 'received', or reflected back to him, as before. This Receiving is, I believe, the most important gift that actors can give each other; it can be used outside rehearsals as practice in truthful communication and also helps in learning lines and discovering character relationships.

> The simplicity of the exercise makes it quite radical and advanced for beginner actors. In fact, any technique that demands patience, listening and full attention on the action of the moment needs very careful teaching and constant monitoring as it progresses.

As an example I will use a scene between Anya and Varya in Act 1 of *The Cherry Orchard*. Anya's first speech is divided up sentence by sentence, to allow Varya time for her response. After each response, the speaker's line is repeated, this time with more truthful energy, fuelled by her experience of being acknowledged and understood.

ANYA: Has he asked you yet, Varya?
VARYA: (*Improvised response*) Has he asked me yet? What do you think? No, he hasn't.
ANYA: Has he asked you yet? But why not?
VARYA: (*Improvised*) You want to know why not?
ANYA: But why not? Why don't you talk to him?
VARYA: (*Improvised*) Why don't I talk to him? What could I say?
ANYA: Why don't you talk to him? You know he loves you.
VARYA: (*Improvised*) Do I know he loves me? Does he love me?
ANYA: You know he loves you. Why don't you?
VARYA: (*Improvised*) Why don't I? You mean, why don't I talk to him?

We now continue with Varya's speech and Anya's improvised responses:

VARYA: I don't think we'll ever get married now.
ANYA: (*Improvised*) You don't think you'll ever marry Lopakhin now?

VARYA: I don't think we'll ever get married now. I don't think he's got time for me.

ANYA: (*Improvised*) You don't think he's got any time for you?

VARYA: I don't think he's got time for me. He's got too many other things to think of.

ANYA: (*Improvised*) You feel that he's got too many other things to think of, besides you?

VARYA: He's got too many other things to think of. He's too busy.

ANYA: (*Improvised*) He's always too busy?

VARYA: He's too busy. He hardly notices me.

ANYA: (*Improvised*) You feel that he hardly notices you?

VARYA: He hardly notices me. I honestly wish he wouldn't come here any more.

ANYA: (*Improvised*) And you're wishing he wouldn't come here any more.

VARYA: I honestly wish he wouldn't come here any more.

What is happening here is a simple exchange of information, with a receiving from the listener full of empathy and connection; the spoken word changes the hearer. It is so easy to lose this connection when rehearsing a play, because of the necessary repetition of lines. At this stage of the rehearsal process, the response is only this empathic one; later on, the exercise can be extended to take in the character's response to what is said, which might well be antagonistic or unsympathetic to the speaker, in a situation where there are opposing aims or unwished-for strategies being used.[1]

THE SILENT RECEIVING EXERCISE

The Receiving exercise can be played silently, either while a scene is being enacted, or as a seated exercise just focusing on the demands of the technique. The process is simple and must, of course, be played honestly. The best help you can give each other is mutual respect.

You can play this in pairs or in a group of characters in a scene. The first speaker says her line, one sentence at a time, as in the spoken version of Receiving. The receiver of these words then gives a small nod of 'Yes, I did receive that; it reached me; I understood it and let it change me in some internal way.' Or, the receiver might find that the speaker's words did not fully reach her – maybe they only just got as far as her edges but they did not fully penetrate her understanding. In that case the receiver gives a shake of her head, as if to say 'No, I didn't quite hear that; it didn't reach me.' So then the speaker says the words again, to see if this time, with more focus and a clearer intention to connect, the lines do reach the listener.

Of course, this is not about getting louder or pushing words at your listener! You already know that that never works: your listener will retreat from any outer force. What you have the chance of doing now is to find that real elastic connection of meaning between you and the other person and you will probably realise that you were not allowing time for that to happen with complete truth before this experience. And for the listener: you realise that you were not really listening to your partner before this; yes, you heard the noise of someone speaking but you did not give yourself enough time and attention to the meaning; now you understand how necessary real listening is and how helpful it is to receive the impulse that triggers your next words and actions.

Note: For the listener who is giving the 'Yes' nod and the 'No' head shake, remember that this is an exercise not a rehearsal, so even at the times when your character would be responding positively or negatively to the offer of the speaker, in this exercise you are working as an actor, helping your partner, not as your character.

SPOKEN RESPONSES

As in the Receiving exercise, sit facing your scene partner (at later stages of rehearsal you could try this during the action of the scene). If you are the speaker, give some necessary gaps or pauses in your lines, as you did in the Receiving exercise. The listener, in character, then has a chance to speak his responses to what he is hearing. These are the unspoken thoughts and feelings that his character experiences as he listens.

The benefit of Spoken Responses is to define these reactions – which will, of course, vary to some extent each time the scene is played – and to allow the silent changes to be felt and expressed in the body, as happens all the time in life. The mistaken idea that listening actors should stay frozen, so as not to pull focus or distract from whoever is speaking – especially in Shakespeare and classical plays – makes for unreal playing and kills the life of the scene. As an audience we tend to look at the listener while hearing the speaker.

Note: When I first invented this rehearsal exercise I called it Spoken Thoughts. Then, I found that the listening actor often kept on talking for far too long, digressing from the immediate situation and impeding the action of the scene. So I changed the title to Spoken Responses and asked the listening actor to keep her reaction brief and to the point at each moment allowed to her by the actor speaking his lines from the text.

The following example uses unit 7 from Act 1 of *The Cherry Orchard* (see p. 101). It gives an idea of what Dunyasha's and Lopakhin's thoughts might be while they wait for Ranevskaya and the family to arrive from the station. The lines from the script are in bold. When playing this exercise, both characters might be speaking their thoughts at the same time as each other; however, it is important to allow time for the scripted sentences to be spoken and heard clearly, because what is spoken (as well as what is seen) triggers reactions.

DUNYASHA: It's so boring listening to you going on about being a peasant. I'm a very different sort of person, I'm sensitive and special . . . I have an amazing awareness of animals too . . . **The dogs haven't slept all night. They know, you see.**

LOPAKHIN: You silly girl, what on earth is that about? 'The dogs know . . .!' Grow up! **What's the matter with you, Dunyasha?**

DUNYASHA: You don't understand me . . . Look how sensitive and lady-like I am . . . I feel faint. I want you to notice me . . . **My hands are shaking** . . . Look at my hands, they're so white and elegant . . .

LOPAKHIN: **That's because you think you're a lady** you silly little servant girl . . .

(DUNYASHA: Yes, I am a lady, I am . . . I'm just like Anya, I'm not just a servant . . .)

LOPAKHIN: **You're too sensitive, that's the trouble. Why don't you dress properly and wear your hair properly?** I can't bear people who don't keep to their proper place; just look at yourself, wearing those unsuitable clothes and your hair should be combed back in a bun or under a scarf. **You should**

remember your place. Oh, damn, should I be remembering my place too? Now here's that idiot Epihodov, that's the last straw . . .

DUNYASHA: My place? You're a fine one to talk! Pig in the drawing room, that's what you are, bossing me around just 'cos you've got money. You'll never understand how real ladies feel. Oh, here's Epihodov, now you'll see a really clever man . . . One of my admirers . . .

SNOWBALL UNITS

Focus: To use an active, practical way of learning lines while building character and relationships.

Lines are learned in unit chunks, which conditions the choice of unit divisions, in that they need to be of a useful length to learn: if we use the analogy of the text being a cake, divided by the playwright into acts, then by us into French scenes, then units, we need 'bite-sized' pieces to learn, not crumbs.

Learning *with* heart, not *by* heart

Your motive as an actor is important when using this technique of learning lines: if you are merely trying to get the lines into your head you would probably be happier using your usual method of learning by rote, on your own, with little reference to the other lines and people in the scene. Having done this mechanical learning, you will then have to inject life and responses to others into your acting at a later stage. To benefit from the active co-operative learning, your actor's Aim is to enjoy communicating with and listening to your scene partner; you are willing to start with a truthful connection which will then grow in strength and power, keeping spontaneity with the security of knowing that the words and thoughts of the character are firmly built into your memory.

Using French scene and unit divisions, sit together as a cast, speaking quietly, maintaining eye-contact as much as possible. Learning in 'snowball units' means that first you learn unit 1 together, then, when that is secure, you continue, to learn unit 2. Once unit 2 is secure, go back to unit 1 again, which you may well find you have temporarily forgotten. Reinforce unit 1 and join it with unit 2 (the snowball gets bigger as it is rolled along) and so on to unit 3, then back to units 1, 2 and 3 and so on until the scene is learned. This is a most efficient way of learning. It may seem to take up too much time, but actually it saves a great amount of time and stress. Even when rehearsals are several days apart, you will find that you can remember a scene effortlessly and, most importantly, that the scene belongs to you; you will enjoy it together and continue to develop it each time you play it over.

Learning your lines in this way gives you the essential skill of being in the 'firewalled' moment right from the start of your work; it forms a correct habit of playing which will not let you down and will sustain you throughout rehearsals and performance. There is a natural rhythm of breathing that goes together with the learning of lines: as we observe in human behaviour, a new breath will come with a new thought or impulse. However, when acting we need to be aware of using correct breathing rhythms and bringing them under our conscious control, otherwise intrusive habits, like unnecessary gaps between sentences or in the middle of them, will creep in and interfere with the natural rhythms that the character would have in the situation of the scene. The only way to avoid this problem, which makes so many performances boring and untrue, is to be aware of the danger right from the start of work. So, some conscious thought about when new breaths want to come within a unit and how a breath can usefully be sustained to flow through the exchange of words is really helpful and fun to play around with. (See Breath, Chapter 14, p. 154.)

> All things are ready, if our minds be so.
>
> (*Henry V*, Act 3, Sc. 4)

12 The actor's work on
a character

THE WRITING EXERCISE

Focus: To find the depth and variety of a character's experience at a specific moment in the scene.

Space, time and numbers: A quiet exercise in pairs, needing at least 30 minutes; all pairs work at the same time for the first 10 minutes, then each pair needs time to read back what they have written while the rest of the group listens to them.

What you need: Each player needs several sheets of paper and a pencil or pen.

Some work on a role is 'horizontal' in nature, some is 'vertical'. Horizontal work looks at the narrative line of the play, the character's through-line of action, the drive and shape of a scene. Vertical work focuses on a short moment of the play or on the depth of a character, looking at her hidden inner self, her memories, private thoughts, beliefs and world-view; this is what the Writing exercise achieves.

For the exercise each player needs to be with a partner who plays opposite him in a particular scene. They choose an exchange of lines, keeping the lines as short as possible. They sit opposite each other, with paper and pen, in a place where they can write comfortably. It is best not to speak the chosen lines before the exercise begins.

Here are sample exchanges from Act 1 of *The Cherry Orchard*:

DUNYASHA: We've been waiting and waiting for you.
ANYA: I haven't slept properly for four nights. I'm frozen.

or

DUNYASHA: Yasha, I hardly recognised you. Going abroad has changed you.
YASHA: Has it? Hmm.

Each writes the line they are going to say at the top of the page. When everyone is ready with their line, their attention, paper and pen, so that the room is quiet, each pair of players speaks their lines to each other quietly, looking at each other. They then immediately start to write down what they are thinking. The secret of the exercise is not to stop writing; the pen must keep moving non-stop because players are accessing the creative unconscious through the conscious, through this physical action of writing.

Before the exercise begins I like to reinforce this idea of the writing being continuous. When players get stuck, because they almost certainly will after around 2 minutes of writing, I ask them to just repeat the last word they wrote until they break through the little block and find that they have much more that they want to say. So you might write, 'I don't know what to say say say say say', until you find that you DO know.

I usually let the writing run for 8 to 10 minutes, which is a very long time; then I say, 'Finish the thought or sentence that you are writing now', and I wait until all the players have stopped writing. When I ask them how long the writing lasted they usually say '4 or 5 minutes' – about half the time they actually had. This is because they were functioning in 'real time' or 'creative time', which is different from 'clock- time'. Plays happen in 'real time', which is the eternal moment of 'now'. The changed sense of time is a signal of creative endeavour; there is a point in the rehearsal process when scenes which previously felt endless suddenly become swift and easy to play and to watch.

The disappearing moment of the experience is the firmest reality.

The next part of the exercise has to be carefully monitored by the teacher/director; some important in-depth work has been done and it must be treated with respect. I tell the players that if they have written anything that they do not wish to read aloud to the group, then they should just miss that part out. Choosing one pair, I check with them which lines they have chosen. I explain to the rest of the group what characters the two actors are playing and roughly which part of the play their lines come in. This is to avoid the speaking of the actual lines, which must not be said until the very end of each pair's reading of their thoughts.

The actor with the first line reads her thoughts, followed immediately and with no discussion by the second person's written thoughts, then, again immediately with no interruptions, each of them speaks their line to the other. And you will find that this time the actors keep looking at each other as they speak and for as long as they can afterwards; they cannot tear themselves away from that true communication, they wish to hold onto the scene and their partner's eyes for as long as they can. Suddenly acting has become easy and inevitable, not a problem to be solved but a reality to be experienced together.

To hear what another person really felt about us is extraordinary. Here we have that unusual experience but safely within the world of the play. It is good to ask, after the exercise, what the actors found in the writing and speaking. Often people say that they realised for the first time how much the situation mattered to the character, and how surprising aspects of that person arose during the exercise. They find that any fixed concepts they held about 'what my character is like' were limiting; they became open to the character and allowed the situation of the scene to change them, which is the essence of acting.

The test of true creativity is when we surprise ourselves. In this exercise we have taken Stanislavski's advice: 'In work one must always start from oneself, from one's own natural quality and then continue according to the laws of creativity. Art begins when there is no role, when there is only the 'I' in the given circumstances of the play.'[2]

Here are some examples of the writing exercise done by young actors at RADA who were rehearsing *The Cherry Orchard*: Penny

Needler played Dunyasha and Indira Varma, Anya. I have not edited their writing, so there are some repeated words where the actor got stuck for a moment. The exchange of lines from Act 1 that they used was:

DUNYASHA: Epihodov proposed to me just after Easter.
ANYA: That's all you ever talk about.

Dunyasha's written thoughts

What do you mean, that's all I ever talk about? At least be excited. You're supposed to be my friend, soul mate, confidante; this is not the reaction I want. Aren't I important to you? I thought you'd be impressed, in awe, I don't know. I've been waiting so long to see you. I've missed you terribly; I've been awake all night waiting for you, you in particular, my darling angel. I can see you're exhausted but I want to stay up all night on your return, talking to you about MY romance. About Epihodov. I've missed talking to you; I've missed sharing things with you. I've no one else to talk to. At least you should understand that I love you very much. I know maybe it's because you're exhausted after your adventure. I'm so over-joyed to have you home. You've come back to me at last, at last at last at last. I wanted to share my excitement with you. I've been wanting to explode with this whole episode. I need your advice. What shall I do? Be happy for me. I love you, I love you. Show me you've missed me. I know you would be interested normally, but everything is too much for you now. You like Epihodov, you know you do.

Anya's written thoughts

What about me? Of course he proposed, he always proposes, nothing ever changes. Mama's back and it's awful . . . no one seems to realise just how bad everything is . . . I . . . I . . . I . . . I should be looked after. Why am I the one who takes the brunt of everyone's pain? I feel pain but I have no one to talk to at all, not even Dunyasha. But I am sure she loves me, maybe she's just overwhelmed. It's so good to be back, especially with Mama. I can't believe we've been all the way to Paris and back and I wish I hadn't seen Mama in such a humiliating state. Why does she pretend even when she knows I've seen the truth? Oh, it's such a relief to see Dunyasha's lovely face. Familiar and alive and full of love. I wish she'd marry Epihodov; Oh, I love her so much but I wish I could tell her about what's happened. Everyone's pretending nothing's gone on. Paris is out of mind but . . . but . . . but . . . Mama's so flighty and she looks so unhappy but everyone else's joy makes up for it. I suppose their happiness will soothe her for a bit. Dunyasha isn't listening to anything I say. But I know she's pleased to see me. I do love her and she cares for me in her own way but I need to talk to someone, I need someone to look after me; my head is going to burst. I don't know if I can take this pressure but everyone's uplifting, their excitement is wonderful.

There is always so much more in your mind than you can write down; this exercise is an encouraging experience for actors as they find out how much they understand about the character, how they can link up the rhythm of an imagined character's thoughts, vocabulary and belief system and how clear those repeated, uncompromising aims are, driving through the scene as the character tries every possible strategy to get what she wants.

THREE ASPECTS OF CHARACTER

Each of us has three aspects of the Self. When playing an imagined character, it is useful to examine these aspects both within ourselves and in the character we play. In some ways we may find similarities between us and the character invented by the playwright and, of course, in other ways there will be marked differences between the two.

These three aspects of a person are:

1 Material
2 Social
3 Spiritual

1   The **material** aspect includes the physical appearance, age, clothing and financial state of a person and also her feelings about how she looks; her health; the appearance she wishes to present; her love of wealth; fear of poverty; how she feels about her home; her vanity or modesty; and her self-respect.

2   The **social** aspect includes the relationships a person has with others and with himself: his desire to please, to be noticed and admired; his sociability; ambition; envy; the objects of his love; his pursuit of fame; his honour; his feelings of shame, guilt, pride, or achievement; his happiness, contentment, satisfaction or dissatisfaction with himself as a social being within his circle of family and friends, at work, and in the wider world.

3   The **spiritual** aspect includes a person's intellectual, moral, political and religious aspirations; how conscientious he is; his sense of superiority or inferiority in his mental or moral thinking and behaviour. These abstract, spiritual values are often the most powerful motives for action in a person; these are the values that can lead someone to choose death for the sake of their beliefs, or to abandon important parts of their material or social contentment.

The world picture of an individual is an important clue to their inner life and outer behaviour. If you feel that the world is a dangerous, treacherous place, so that you need to be suspicious or wary of the people you live with, or that you can only find safety within your own small family circle, which you need to protect against a hostile world, then this will lead you to defensive and at times aggressive thoughts and actions. If, however, you see the world as a place of trust, beauty and love, filled with people who are basically good (though they may at times behave in ways that you don't like) then you, or the character you are playing, will have a more open and friendly relationship with your surroundings. You/your character may indeed be seen as too trusting, too ready to believe a liar and too easy to cheat, just as the person with the opposite world picture may lose his happiness through his overriding distrust of others. Most of us have a more balanced view of our world, though it may at times change quite radically in reaction to events in our lives.

A crisis of loss of trust in another or a happier discovery that one's love and work are valued and rewarded can change our world picture from sunshine to darkness, or vice versa. It is helpful to find those moments of change in a play and to be aware of them within ourselves. (We can connect this work with the open and closed responses to space in Chapter 20, pp. 209–11.)

In order to free yourself from worrying about the personality, rather than the true, fully rounded character of the part you are playing, look for your character's ruling idea and for what his world picture is. Hamlet's world is full of disease and pain, darkness and death; he describes it in detail in Act 2, Sc. 2 ('the earth . . . appeareth nothing to me but a foul and pestilent congregation of vapours . . .'), whereas before his father's death his world was secure and sunlit. And in *The Cherry Orchard*, Firs' world is the house and orchard, representing the past, which must be preserved, while Lopakhin's view of the same house and orchard is that they are 'no use' and must be destroyed to make room for the future.

I remember a fairy story in which a wicked magician stole the Prince's eyes. The Prince had to find his own eyes in a pile of other eyes; when he chose one pair he saw nothing but foxes; with another pair he could see nothing but hawks, so he knew that he had found first the eyes of a fox, then those of a hawk. The actor needs to 'put on the eyes' of a character so as to see the world through these new 'spectacles', so that the energy of his acting is correctly directed outwards.

It is also useful to consider:

1 Who a character thinks he is.
2 Who he really is.
3 How people see him – the character is viewed differently by each person who encounters him.

To discover these aspects from the text make three lists:

1 What the character says about himself.
2 What clues are given as to who he really is. These are often gleaned by contrasting the actions of the character with what he says.
3 What other characters say about him.

The four F-words: Forget the feelings. Focus on the Facts.
  Your focus on the facts will engender the spontaneous feelings of the character at each moment of the changing situation, every time you play the scene.

SUGGESTIONS FOR THE ACTOR'S HOMEWORK ON A ROLE

To act, you must make the thing written your own. You must steal the words, steal the thought, and convey the stolen treasure with great art.

(Ellen Terry)[2]

1 Read the whole play through thoroughly, at least twice (and read it through again the night before you first perform it, as if it were completely new to you).
2 Write out the storyline of the play and then that of your character.
3 Find the answers to the five 'Wh' questions (see p. 95).
4 What central themes do you find in the play?
5 What recurrent imagery do you find?[3]
6 What imagery does your character use? We use images when we can find no other way of expressing what we mean. They are a useful clue to how we see the world and our place in it.
7 Why is your character essential to the story?
8 What actions does s/he take to change the course of the narrative?
9 What function does s/he play in the central themes?
10 Write out your 'back story'.
11 Write out what you say about yourself and what other characters say about you. What do you think is true and what false?
12 Looking at the actions of your character:

   a. List the central universal values/needs (those which we all share) expressed by his/her actions. (The following are taken from a list drawn up by Marshall B. Rosenberg, founder of the NVC (Nonviolent Communication) movement.[4]) These are the triggers or impulses that create action and the character's aims.

At any one time there is an urgent Present Need to be met:

- Physical needs: for food, air, shelter, protection, sexual expression
- Interdependence: for acceptance, love, respect, trust
- Autonomy (freedom to choose one's own goals, dreams and values and to make plans for fulfilling them)
- Celebration of life and dreams
- Mourning the loss of life and dreams
- Integrity, being true to one's values
- Play
- Spiritual values, such as beauty, order, peace, harmony

b. List the Obstacles that occur in your story that make the achievement of your aims difficult. List also the people and events in the story that assist your aims.

c. List the strategies (both successful and unsuccessful) used by your character to overcome the Obstacles and achieve his/her aims.

As we all share these central human needs and values, it is through the strategies a person employs to meet those needs that we recognise what we call 'character'. Some strategies are efficient, in that they succeed in meeting the Present Need; some succeed only in the short term, or succeed in meeting one Present Need while not satisfying another; and some strategies fail completely and at once, to tragic or comic effect.

So, play the situation and you get the character for free![5]

13 Draw a chart or a diagram of the relationships surrounding your character. Who is most important to you? Who do you want to get rid of?

14 Draw a map of your journeys before, after and during the period of the play. What happens to you after the time of the play?

15 Write out what you do between the scenes in which you appear.

16 Draw the character. (Use free drawing (p. 5) rather than trying for a portrait.)

17 Draw the other characters in the play from the point of view of your character.

18 If your character were living now, what would s/he be wearing/ doing/working at/enjoying/avoiding, etc.?

19 Write or draw a recent dream your character has had.

20 See if you can find a picture of your character.

21 Have you ever played the game where you describe someone in terms of music, animals, paintings, etc.? Taking the very first image that presents itself, answer these and other questions about your character: what animal does s/he remind you of? What bird? Insect? Music? Artistic object? Building? Landscape? Weather? Colour? Domestic object? Texture? Metal? Jewellery? Historical period? Natural sound? And so on. You can do this with a partner who asks the questions or you can write it out.

22 **When your character speaks he could be silent; when he is silent he could speak.** Find the moments when your character decides not to speak or when his speech is prevented; also take responsibility for his choice to speak when he could choose to be silent.

23 What other questions or useful ideas do you have for getting into the skin of an imagined character in an imagined situation? Share them with your group.

INTELLIGENCE   IMAGINATION   INDIVIDUALITY   INDUSTRY

Part Four Tips and techniques

Technique enables the imagination to flower.

The dictionary definitions of 'technique' and 'technician' include: 'a useful art or language of a particular art'; 'one skilled in a practical art'. I like this passage from *The Mirror of the Sea*, where Joseph Conrad writes about technique. In this context he writes about the skill of yacht building, but what he says can be applied to all art:

> The skill of technique is more than honesty; it is something wider, embracing honesty and grace and rule in an elevated and clear sentiment, not altogether utilitarian, which may be called the honour of labour. It is made up of accumulated tradition, kept alive by individual pride, rendered exact by professional opinion and, like the higher arts, it is spurred on and sustained by discriminating praise. This is why the attainment of proficiency, the pushing of your skill with attention to the most delicate shades of excellence, is a matter of vital concern. Efficiency of a practically flawless kind may be reached naturally in the struggle for bread. But there is something beyond – a higher point, a subtle and unmistakable touch of love and pride beyond mere skill; almost an inspiration which gives to all work that finish which is almost art – which IS art.
>
> (Chapter 7).

13 Unstrung pearls

TUNNELS

In almost every creative process there will be a period of some darkness or dip of confidence, a lack of enjoyment or clarity of purpose. I call these times 'tunnels' because it is important to recognise and name them, so as to survive and manage them. If the tunnel is prolonged and deep, it can be felt as a black hole, from which there is no rescue, but if one recognises it as a tunnel, with light at each end and as a part of the moving journey, one can cope with it with more grace.

Tunnels can occur during the rehearsal process. When this dip in energy and focus occurs, it is useful to recognise and discuss this openly, without blame. Sometimes exhausted actors need time off – it is worth a director cancelling a rehearsal to give this respite. Sometimes the group will be feeling frustrated or anxious because they need more uninterrupted run-throughs of the play to give them confidence. The important thing is not to get into blame or guilt; the tidal nature of energy with its natural ebbs and flows needs to be recognised and accepted. When energy is at a low ebb it means that the work will continue, perhaps more quietly but with the focus on precision and detail; when the tide of energy is high, a strongly risk-taking run-through is a great experience.

EMOTION

Looking at hands

To avoid the painful and inefficient approach of preparing or trying to feel an emotion, it is useful to find simple physical ways of opening up to a truthful emotion. For sadness, I find that just looking down at one's hands is very effective, especially when one is sitting. Notice when and why people look down at their hands in real life; it seems that it is often a moment when words fail them or when inner emotion floods to the surface.

Crying

Brecht says that in real life people attempt not to cry, whereas in acting they try to cry. The actor's struggle to squeeze out real tears is not connected to the grief of the character in the scene; mostly in life one struggles to repress tears or sobs in order to speak; if your character is speaking during these sorrowful moments, then that is her action; her focus is on the communication of her story to the listener in spite of her tears.

A simple physical action that works well for me is just to put a hand up to wipe away an imagined tear from my eye; this immediately brings the truth of grief to me. If you remember a time when you or a friend were telling a story while repressing tears, or if you watch an interview on TV when this is happening, you will observe that grief controlled is so much more moving than grief indulged. Also, with big Shakespearean speeches the actor needs to balance the truth of emotion with the necessities of clear speaking, the demands of the verse and the richness of the language.

Laughing

Prolonged or uncontrollable laughter can be difficult to access truthfully. I think the clue is the same as for weeping: attempt to control your laughter and it will bubble up spontaneously – if the situation of the scene demands this control it is even more fun to play.

Kissing

To have to kiss a scene partner can be embarrassing and awkward for inexperienced actors. I like to delay a kiss in the rehearsal process until the players have come to know each other a bit, then I put aside some time with them alone and gently approach the physical contact between them. It is useful to begin with both players sitting on the floor and to start with a touch on the hand and from there to ask the player who is accepting the caress what further touch she might enjoy. Does she like to be supported, to lean against her partner? If so, is it pleasant for both players if he strokes her hair, or her cheek, or kisses her neck very gently? Once these enjoyable strokes have been accepted, trust is established. The actual kisses at this point must be 'butterfly kisses', very soft, dry, quick, frequent and close together. The closer, longer kisses and embraces can then come later in the process, when they seem more natural and inevitable to the players. You may well find that these more delicate and enjoyable kisses and embraces work better in performance than conventional clinches and tongue-tangling – for myself as an audience I often find these boring and sometimes embarrassing to watch.

Surprise and shock

Surprise and shock are tricky to play, because of course the actor knows what's coming and must guard against anticipation. I once saw an actor picking up the phone to answer an unexpected call before it rang! A sensible strategy just before a surprise is to turn your head slightly away from the speaker or event that is going to shock your character, so that at the moment of hearing or seeing the unexpected event, you can turn sharply towards it.

Stillness is also natural while a person takes in new information. To mark this, the actor can use movement just before the shock. In life, a big shock takes time to be absorbed; the greater the shock, the longer the time of denial or inability to accept it; in stage time this period has to be shortened but it should still be understood and clearly played. In the Laban chapter on Time you will find an exercise on 'Stops' which gives you practice in the truthful playing of shock and those strongly dramatic moments of change in the life of a character (p. 225).

Blips

It seems inevitable that at times any actor will lose belief in what he is doing. These unexpected and scary moments can be called blips. Sometimes a blip will happen when one has just played a line or a moment rather well; the actor takes over from the character for a few seconds, to congratulate himself on his cleverness, or, conversely, a blip can occur when the actor is berating himself for fluffing a line, missing a cue or not coping well with a cougher in the audience. The sensation can be, 'What on earth am I doing, pretending to be someone I'm not with all these people looking at me?' Blips come, I think, from nervous tension; most people experience them in social contexts when they are uncertain of acceptance or approval from their peers; often there seems to be no direct explanation for them.

In acting, the way out of a blip is not to panic, it is most unlikely that anyone will have noticed. The blip may feel as if it is happening for ages, but in real time it will be a matter of a few seconds only. Bring yourself back into the scene with a simple physical action. Don't try to think yourself into the character because that often increases the power of the 'out of it' sensation. An unobtrusive action, such as focusing on how your hand feels against your thigh, pressing it gently against your leg and thinking only of that pleasant sensation, will take you out of the muddle in your thinking and back to where you actually are in the scene.

My favourite solution is to allow the floor (or the chair if I am sitting) to take my weight; I feel supported and safe again, knowing that the more of my weight I surrender to the floor, the more support I will receive from it. This also reconnects me with my breathing, which is probably rather shallow and stressed in the upper chest in my brief moment of panic and loss of connection with my partners. (See Chapter 9, p. 87.)

Gaps or pauses

There is a crucial difference between a gap and a pause in acting. In a pause the thought and action continue and develop; in a gap the engine stalls and the actor's state as opposed to the creative state takes over. If an actor is gapping constantly it is worth finding out what the problem is: it may be uncertainty about lines, acute self-consciousness or a general lack of foundation in the life of the character and the through-line of action.

The free jaw

A loose lower jaw, which naturally drops down as it opens, is essential for clear speech. Many people hold a lot of tension in the jaw and mistake a forced grimace of the lips for free relaxation. A good trick is to gently pull your earlobes down, pinching them between your thumbs and the knuckle of your index fingers; this can feel quite pleasant and often gives a sense of opening in the throat as the hinge of the jaw relaxes with the pull of the earlobes. Practise this as much as possible, so that you begin to notice a tightly held jaw and acquire the freedom to let it go. We need to keep our lips closed most of the time, as an open mouth is considered unsightly, but the teeth should not be clamped together in a bite unless we are actually eating, and the jaw can remain loosely dropped while the lips are gently closed.

Filling

Sometimes in playing a role, there can be moments that feel rather starved and empty. These are usually because the actor doesn't fully understand what is happening in the scene. If this happens to you, maybe you need to return to the five 'Wh' questions (p. 95). Alternatively, if there is time, try using the Writing exercise (p. 134) or focusing strongly on your scene partner; imagine, perhaps, that you are going to paint that person. What colours would you use? How do the shadows fall? What does the background look like and what is the precise position of that person from moment to moment? Stanislavski's advice is to look for the expression in your partner's eyes and try to change it. Other people are endlessly fascinating and mysterious; can we ever know what someone else is feeling or thinking? Surrender to this passionate curiosity and every moment of your playing will be full to overflowing with life and truthful action.

The Little Plus

The Little Plus means that combination of extra imposed voice and action that the actor resorts to with the intention of being interesting or effective. You can see it used in daily life too, when a person wishes to impress or get attention – we have probably all used it ourselves at times – but it actually doesn't work because the listeners can tell at once that it comes from a false energy. Little Plus can inform a whole performance, a scene or just a line or reaction, and it is worth considering why the Plus is thought necessary – it could be that the actor does not fully understand the line or motive, because she has lost faith in the scene or in her own playing, or because the part she is playing is close to herself and she feels that she has to demonstrate that she is really acting to avoid being criticised as 'just being herself'. There is a big sense of relief once the Plus is dropped and true energy is released.

When your acting voice is louder than your normal speaking voice, you won't be able to express yourself clearly or respond to others; so many actors confuse vocal volume with meaning! There is a story that actors in former times would advise inexperienced actors to cover their uncertainties with extra loudness: 'When in doubt, shout.' You need to be aware of this danger and avoid it at all times.

The Little Minus can also be a problem. This comes from the mistaken idea that mumbling and lack of vocal and physical expression are more real than lively, natural action. Just notice real life and see how clear and strong people are in their motives and strategies; observe in yourself and others how vital it is to get what you want when you want it – now! Both the Little Plus and the Little Minus are related to Showing, Trying and Simply Doing (p. 12).

Comedy, farce and clowning

The secret with farce and clowning is to never try to be funny. The ridiculous situation takes care of the comedy. It is a very good lesson in taking action to solve the present problem. In comedic situations it is the problem and the strategies, often hopelessly inefficient, employed to solve that problem, such as putting a bicycle into a paper bag, that are the joke. The serious efforts of the character, the respect paid by the actor to his activities, must be the priority. As the celebrated eighteenth-century English actor David Garrick is reputed to have said, 'Any fool can play tragedy, but comedy, sir, is a damned serious business.'

14 Breath

Action starts with the breath; the knowledge and control of breathing is the centre of the actor's technique. When you have your breathing under control then you can express fully whatever you wish to convey with your voice and body, and when you choose to alter the rhythm of your breathing your emotions, thoughts and mood will change.

Controlled breath is the fuel and the engine; no amount of talent and imagination will make up for the lack of it. Apart from technical voice work, which is not the province of this book, there are some useful exercises that you can practise to improve your breathing when working on a role.

A rule to remember is:

A sentence = a thought
A thought = a breath
Therefore: A sentence = a breath

You should aim for one breath for one sentence, as long as the sentence and your lungs can combine the two. Thinking and breathing work together. In real life you always have enough breath for what you want to say, and when your Aim and your technique are strong enough, you will have the same capacity in your acting. Any physical activity changes the breath and the breathing pattern changes the psychological state.

PHRASING

The control and conscious choice of where the new breath comes is called phrasing: this is the grouping of words on the breath so that the sense and feeling are conveyed simply and elegantly. The physical decisions you make in rehearsal are crucial here; if you do not decide where to breathe then you will fade and gasp in the middle of a line; you will be like a car that suddenly runs out of petrol in the middle of a race. You need to find the breathing rhythm of each speech because that will be both your inner truth and your means of conveying it. The secret is to learn a breathing pattern at the same time as you learn your lines. Then you will have a firm foundation which will be there for you when you need it but which can be changed effortlessly in the flow of action in a scene. In a good play the text will provide you with these changing tempi – this is especially so in Shakespeare – so your job is to find and use the rhythms of the playwright, as you would do if you were a singer.

PACE V. SPEED

Phrasing looks after the speeches you have, pace is the interaction of thought and breathing between players in a scene. Pace is the pulse of the scene, therefore it depends on the closest interaction between the actors and on good use of their unit changes. Pace is not speed, though the words are often used interchangeably. Speed usually means rush and gabble in acting, so it is not a useful word for us. Pace, on the other hand, is like the hand-over in a relay race: the moving player in the race approaches the waiting player and hands on the baton; the waiting player is focused on his approaching partner so that he can grab the baton at the precise moment, in order that the race can continue fluidly with no clumsiness or waste of time. The baton in this analogy is the breath – the bodily action of emotion.

PICKING UP CUES

Almost the most important conscious choice of where to breathe is your cue-breath: the rule here is that you breathe for your next line on the word or action of your partner that impels that next line (probably his single stress word [see Chapter 16, pp. 179–80]). So you need to look closely at your cues to find out which word acts as the trigger or impulse for your character. This helps the learning of lines: if you really hear what your partner says, then your next line will become inevitable. This cue-breath happens in real, unrehearsed life – just be aware of your breathing when you are talking to someone: as you have the thought in silent response or a spoken answer, so the breath will gather at that instant.

The word 'inspiration', with its double meaning of the arrival of an idea and the intake of breath, is a great help here; for the actor, the two meanings of that word – its intangible and its physical application – are one thing, one experience felt through the body. Sometimes in life you have a strong impulse to speak while someone else is speaking: your inspiration (both senses of the word) happens to you, but you cannot always interrupt the speaker. This common experience probably happens to your character: do let it happen; don't let your breathing and feeling be soggy just because you do not have any lines in that part of the scene.

When listening, your breathing changes carry your thoughts across clearly and silently; breathing cannot lie. Just watch people listening in real life and notice how their breathing rhythms inform you of what they are thinking . . . you can almost hear those 'silent lines'. Use the Spoken Responses exercise (p. 130) to define your character's silent lines; they are another way of understanding your through-line of action in the scene.

BREATHING WITH UNIT CHANGES

For the brief time of a unit it is useful to share the breathing rhythm. A shared rhythm happens naturally when people are in agreement, as an opposing rhythm will often be evident when people have conflicting aims. Each person in the scene breathes in at the same moment at the start of a new unit. Sharing a rhythm with one or more people can be stimulating and rewarding – think of singing together, laughing or even crying together, the satisfaction of speaking in unison or any mutual action which gives us assurance that another person exactly reflects our feelings. At times, an opposing Aim can also be expressed in a shared rhythm – in a row it is easy to join your enemy's volume level so that you are both shouting, or to whine and moan at each other when you are feeling hard-done-by.

15 Playing the scene

THE SPACE

Upstage/downstage

The back of the stage area is called upstage and the front, nearest the audience, is downstage. These names come from the time when stages were raked, on a slight slope, from back to front. To upstage a scene partner means to position oneself above or further back from them so that they have to turn away from the audience in order to face you. This behaviour is considered selfish and unprofessional if you are doing it in order to focus all the attention on yourself. Some actors also upstage themselves unconsciously by turning away from the audience and may need to be reminded to allow themselves to be visible.

Alternatively, many actors are too aware of the audience; they may stand with their head turned, looking at their scene partner but the body below the head will be firmly facing out front. This is uncomfortable and unreal to play and to watch; the convention of the 'fourth wall' or 'fish-tank' play is that the audience is looking in at a private world where the characters are living their lives unobserved. The actor needs to establish a delicate balance between the truth of this private life and the need of the audience to hear, see and enjoy the action of the play. The play has its own truth; it is not the reality of daily life.

Bus queues

A bus queue is a straight line of actors. Any number of three or more people can easily form a straight line without realising how boring and unnatural this looks. The mistake comes from an unawareness of the depth of the playing space; often, the actors are only aware of the width of the space (see 'invisible walls' below). Every actor needs to look out for a bus queue and to take responsibility for breaking up the straight line, unobtrusively opening up the space by varying the distance between his partners as well as dropping up- or downstage to break the line into a more naturally uneven grouping. Thinking in diagonals is the answer.

Easing

If you are good at easing you will be the director's favourite actor! Easing simply means being aware of where you are in the stage pattern, avoiding straight lines, being ready to move out of the way of others, so they they can be seen and can move easily, and shifting weight very lightly to move the shadow of your face off the face of your scene partner (very important for camera work). You may find that using the step position (see below in 'Movement') gives you the possibility of easy, fluid adaptation and a friendly relationship with the stage space. I think actors are often uncertain of how much they are supposed to move without being directed; in my experience as a director, the actor who is inventive, willing to take action and initiate is a treasure.

Invisible walls

In any playing space, including those of class and rehearsal, there seem to be invisible walls, places within the space that are not explored, where the action of the scene or exercise does not penetrate. Most often these invisible walls keep action stuck within a narrow corridor running horizontally across the middle of the space, ignoring the dimension of depth and safely away from both the audience and the upstage area. Invisible walls show the fears and self-imposed limitations of the players; if one or two people stay in the centre for safety then it is likely that others will join them, but if one or two players decide to break free, to use diagonals, curves and deep spatial relationships – up and down in the space rather than just right to left – then the scene will come alive and there will be a sense of freedom and playfulness.

I find that it is useful to explain about invisible walls and even to draw the edges of them on the floor with chalk, then to challenge the actors to go past those non-existent boundaries. The placing of furniture also helps to free players from that 'trapped corridor' feeling. An exercise in 'balancing the space' is useful; the group move around the space attempting to keep an even balance between all players, so that A will move into a gap in the moving group, but, as he does, B will also be moving to fill that space, so A, B and C will need to be aware of other gaps in the group that need to be filled. The Laban exercises on Space will be helpful here (pp. 207–20).

Meeting the space

The playing space is a vital character in the scene. The actor responds to the space, is influenced by it and has a strong personal connection with it. The actor needs to ask these questions:

Does the space belong to your character?
Are you familiar and comfortable in it or is it strange to you?
Do you need to explore or change it?
How do you feel upon entering the space?
Why are you coming in? (An entrance is an arrival and you need to know where you have come from.)
Who is in the space already?
Who is the most important person for you?
How do you feel when a new person comes in or when someone leaves?
Why and how do you leave the space? Where are you going?
What has happened between your entrances? Where have you been and what have you been doing?

MOVEMENT

The step position

Researching acting methods of the past, I discovered that actors in the nineteenth century would stand with their feet in a step position, that is, with one foot slightly in advance of the other. Nowadays we do a lot of work with the feet in parallel, which is useful for stable balance while working on breathing, but not always helpful in a scene. The step position allows for a fluid and easy transference of weight for moving in any direction, while the parallel position means that, in order to move off, one has to take a moment to transfer the evenly balanced weight onto one foot so as to free the other to make a first step, so generally one is not so flexible in response or action as in the step position.

'Full' and 'empty' legs

Many people stand habitually with their weight unevenly distributed between one leg and the other; this can be called having one leg 'emptier' than the other. A habit is by definition unconscious so it is helpful to point out this tendency towards uneven balance to the actor so as to give him the chance of consciously choosing how he stands. Imbalanced load-bearing in the legs can distort the pelvis and thus the whole torso, where it affects the breathing; the imbalance can then be seen in the shoulders, in a tight jaw, neck and tongue and generally in a pattern of held muscles and tension; this distortion limits action and is uncomfortable for the audience to watch. (See Chapter 9, p. 87.)

The 'Richard III question' is frequently raised when I recommend equal balance for the actor. The answer is that any physical imbalance required for a character (such as a limp or a raised shoulder) needs to be carefully planned so that the central skeletal structure that holds the breathing and vocal mechanism can function freely, undisturbed by any distortion of the shoulder-girdle or knee joint. Richard III is a long and tiring role; if you are lucky enough to play it, you need to be in good condition with plenty of breath support and vocal power.

Turning

Actors often forget the logic of a natural turn; it is satisfying to see a completed turn rather than all the time seeing a half turn, which is then reversed. So, if A does a half turn away from B, following his right shoulder round, he then has a choice as he turns back to her again, either to reverse his first half turn by following his left shoulder round and back to face her, or to complete his turn by following his right shoulder round once again.

Mirroring your scene partner

Be aware of copying the gesture or position of your scene partner. If A has his arms folded, then B should keep her arms free; if B is leaning her head on her hand, then A should not mirror her gesture, unless this is necessary for a comedic effect or the action of the scene.

Asides

Asides are private moments between the actor and the audience. They are inaudible to other characters in the scene. An aside is taken in the same way as a bracket or subordinate clause, that is, it should run smoothly on from the scene-action, with just the marked change of focus – usually running faster, less inflected, at lower pitch and volume than the main clause or action of the scene – as the character 'puts his head through the picture-frame of the scene' to comment privately to the audience. The important thing is for the other characters in the scene to occupy themselves in some way so that they do not look at the speaker of the aside. If one character looks at another, the audience perceives that they can hear what is being said, but the point of an aside is that it can be heard only by the audience. Eye-contact in an aside should be directly to one or more members of the audience. If there are several asides, the eye-contact needs to be shared so that many members of the audience receive the direct contact.

Buttoning the scene

This means establishing an ending or full stop to a scene; it can also be used to complete an exit or for the neat conclusion of an audition speech. A button is a physical and vocal action, a rhythmic logical gathering of energy like a closing chord in music. Buttons are connected to the elegant playing of comedy; they are immensely satisfying to an audience – without a button there is a feeling of disappointment and incompletion. Shakespeare usually closes a scene with a rhyming couplet, forming a neat 'button' to the text. Tidy buttoning in comedy is useful at the conclusion of a unit or at the end of a line where it will get a laugh from the audience. Buttons are often physical actions – I find Rowan Atkinson's 'Mr Bean' can be an excellent example of tidy rhythmic actions.

COMMON MISTAKES

Koala bears

'Koala bears' is when actors, usually women, cling to each other, like a koala bear hugs a tree trunk. Players do this when they need support and comfort, and once they are in this hug they often find it very difficult to release each other and free themselves. Sometimes women start stroking each other's hair and can't stop; this seems to be comfort grooming. If this starts in rehearsal it needs to be controlled before the performance. The answer is to find individual support from the floor and to understand that the job is to look after yourself; you are not responsible for your scene partner.

Pumping hands

'Pumping hands' is like koala bears with less physical connection between the two players. It happens when actors clutch at each other's hands and cannot let go; the tension in the four hands seems to make for an up-and-down pumping or wringing action. The answer is the same as for koala bears; each actor needs to be the first to release the clutched hands.

Drowning together

'Drowning together' is the result of pumping and being a koala bear. The mistake is to lean on your scene partner physically, emotionally and vocally; the result is that energy fades and the life of the scene quickly dies. The answer is to play your own role and allow your partner to play his.

Hairpins

Old-fashioned hairpins are shaped like a horseshoe or a staple. A hairpinning actor collapses her chest and pokes her head forward, usually pumping her arms from the elbows or shoulder. The impulse is to make contact with her partner but it comes from an insecure centre. Breathing is shallow, voice constricted and with a whining minor key. The solution is to regain support from the floor and keep the power within yourself, not spill it out all over other people.

Relying on surface talent

We all have three or four acting skills that work successfully for us and when at all lost we return to those comforts. However, repeated tricks are soon seen through and become boring to the actor and the audience. The job is to enjoy widening and deepening the range of your expressive action.

WHAT GOOD ACTING FEELS LIKE

It is hard for an actor to know when he has played well. Maybe you have had the unsettling experience of feeling that you had at last done a really good performance or rehearsal only to be told by the director that your playing was a disappointment; or, when you feel that you have not done well, to be told 'Well done! That was excellent.' Stanislavski gave helpful advice here: saying that if you come off-stage remembering what your scene partners did, how they looked and spoke, then you will have played well, because your attention has been directed outwards (as the character's attention would be) and you have been in the 'creative state' rather than the uncomfortable 'actor's state'. Stanislavski said that the actor playing well is 'fascinated by the sensations of the moment'. What a wonderful phrase that is! It combines clear focus with physical and sensory awareness of every fully inhabited second of playing.

LATER RUN-THROUGHS: SOME IDEAS FOR THE DIRECTOR

As many runs as you can manage, using essential props and marking costume changes, even in other spaces, are helpful. As director, I give my actors an Aim for each run: a run can be for clear storytelling; for accuracy of unit changes of thought and focus; for relationships; for clear grouping; clear speaking; neat exits; focus on the central themes of the play, etc. (It would be interesting, for example, to focus on the themes of disease or hearing/spying in *Hamlet*.)

Rough runs

If you have time, it is very helpful to do some rough runs of the whole play at later stages of rehearsal. Their function is to refresh and rediscover the play by playing it through without the usual moves and habits of speech and action. I suggest using possibly one or two of the list below if the cast is getting stale and would enjoy a change.

1   Find two or more of the main themes of the play and put up big labels with the theme word clearly written on different walls of the room. For instance, you might use the themes of truth and lies in *Hamlet*, so that whenever a character is lying he goes to the end of the room where LIE is and when he is telling the truth or speaking about truth, he will rush off to the opposite TRUTH end of the room. For *The Cherry Orchard* you could use the themes of money versus love, and of course you can use more than two themes at a time.

2   'Whose side are you on?' This is a very useful rough run, as it clarifies relationships and deepens true emotion. In this run, whenever a character is mentioned who is not actually present in the scene, that character comes into the scene, in an appropriate active relationship with the speaker. So, when Ranevskaya talks of Paris, thinking of her absent lover there, an actor playing this 'invisible character' will come in and maybe kneel by her side, or embrace her gently, not speaking and not interfering with the dialogue; then possibly Gaev or Anya might want to detach him from Ranevskaya so that her attention can be given wholly to family

and home. In Chapter 11 I mention a rehearsal where we reacted to the scene of Trofimov bringing in the news of Grisha's death by drowning; a rough run of Act 1 of *The Cherry Orchard*, using people to enact Grisha, the Gaev parents, etc., is very valuable in building a direct past experience of the characters.

3 A no-smiling run is extremely useful, especially for comedy; it is always important to break through the charm barrier which actors, often unintentionally, hide behind in their need for approval.

4 A public/private run is helpful too; one end of the room is the public area and the opposite is for private moments.

5 Just before the dress rehearsal, it is good to release actors from their preoccupations with performance; a simple way to do this is to have a quiet and intense word run sitting round a table or in a comfortable group, coming in and out of the circle as you did in early read-throughs of the play. This also helps to correct paraphrasing habits.

6 An extension of this quiet run is the 'Nothing Run'. For this you need plenty of time, preferably a whole evening, because the run will take considerably longer than usual; also, a comfortable, warm room with mats or carpet on the floor and dim lighting, not overhead neon. The company will need to have eaten first, to have some water with them and to be able to go out to use the bathroom, when they are not in a scene. It is helpful to have a prompter by the light. The only rule is that people must stay awake! The centre mats or carpet are the playing space; everyone is grouped around this, sitting on the floor and coming in onto the mats for their scene. The run is played lying or sitting down, so there is really nothing to impede communication. With a responsible and professional group of players, a Nothing Run can be a magical experience, opening up new possibilities of meaning and connection between characters. The usual reaction afterwards is 'Can we always play it like this?'

7 Bad Acting. This short warm-up before the performance helps to release nervous tension. Choose a group scene, hopefully involving all of the actors and a moment in the play that will survive this rather rough handling, then encourage the cast to act it out as badly as they can, using huge over-the-top gestures and voices, especially in their reactions to others. You may find that there is a hidden fear of overacting which subdues clear expression and energy, so this is a good opportunity to dispel that needless anxiety.

Part Five An introduction to playing Shakespeare

16 Shakespeare's language

[Shakespeare wrote] for a theatre in which no visual illusion, as we interpret the term, was possible. His resource – all others beside it negligible – was the spoken word. No question of the wonders he works with this . . . The playwright devises, the actors interpret, and the rights of the audience are to a language of words and movement which they can currently understand. Where all concerned are in familiar touch, no difficulty should arise. But in three hundred years even the theatre has seen changes. Shakespeare stands at one end of a road that has many turnings, and we at the other. He offers and asks for one thing; we are ready enough to offer and like another. How far will the new thing supplement the old, how far does it nullify it – that, roughly, is what one has to discover.

(Harley Granville-Barker)[1]

Shakespeare was primarily an actor writing for other actors in his company, in a hard-working theatre that had few rehearsals, and no director to help or hinder the performances of his plays. So he wrote clear, unequivocal 'directions' so that scenes would be played in the way that he wished, helping actors to speak the lines through the musicality and imagery of his verse and prose, supporting them in leading and minor roles, by giving a clear dynamic to each speech, scene and act in the same way that a composer creates an opera with appropriate lyric passages, climaxes and dramatic tensions.

We have an almost unbroken line of connection from the originators of these parts, the actors for whom they were written, to ourselves; I like to think of all those forgotten players who came before us, finding their own solutions to the technical and emotional demands of Shakespeare's plays, as we do the form and content of his language: the form is the structure of the verse which contains and shapes the content as a bottle contains wine; the wine is more important than the bottle, but we need both.

To play Shakespeare well and truthfully is not easy, but it is possible with application; we do not expect a friend with a pleasant singing voice to be able to play the Countess in Mozart's *Marriage of Figaro* without years of study plus a great deal of talent and we do not claim for ourselves that because we enjoy dancing at a party we can dance the ballet of *Swan Lake* without training for years, but we do seem to expect ourselves to be able to 'do Shakespeare' just like that, relying on our 'feelings' to get us through. The actor working on Shakespeare needs technique, knowledge and practice in order to reach the uncompromising simplicity and power of the plays. The following basic exercises take the form of Shakespeare's verse as a beginning. The plays are dramatic poems as well as dramatic action.[2]

THE BLANK VERSE BEAT

Shakespeare's plays are mostly written in iambic pentameters, which have 5 strong beats in a (usually) 10-syllable verse-line; we call this beat the blank verse rhythm. The verse is 'blank' because it does not rhyme, though the term 'blank verse' is also used to cover iambic pentameter lines with rhyming line endings. The blank verse beat is a basic rhythm of English speech: it consists of 5 weak beats and 5 strong beats in a skipping rhythm, with a weak beat beginning the line:

and ONE and TWO and THREE and FOUR and FIVE

Try saying this, counting and beating out the rhythm by clapping your hands or tapping the floor, lightly on the weak 'ands' and strongly on the words in capitals. Then, find the rhythm in the following sentences:

I'd like you all to do this exercise.
I hope that it is not too difficult.
I am quite sure you'll do it very well,
and find it easy to speak Shakespeare's verse.

This basic rhythm is like a heartbeat supporting the life of a line, or a drum beat under the melody in music; the firm base gives strength and security to the verse-line, allowing it to be regular or syncopated. The beat must not be emphasised when speaking, but it cannot be ignored. We are concentrating on it briefly at the start of our work, but as soon as possible it must be absorbed so that it can be 'forgotten' in performance. Irregularities in this 'heartbeat' give the actor valuable clues as to the inner state of a character at each moment of the scene. By choosing correctly where to breathe and following the Flow, Space, Time and Force (see Part Six, below) of the language, we can be true to Shakespeare's idea of the play.

If we try to say our birthdays in the blank verse beat, we will come across some of the natural variations used by Shakespeare:

'My BIRTHday IS the FOURteenth DAY of JUNE.'
'JuLY the TWENty-FIRST is MY birthday.'
'My BIRTHday IS the SIXTH day OF SepTEMber.'

Strong and weak endings

Now, what happened in that last sentence of 11 syllables? You can't change the sentence to 'My birthday is the sixth day of Septem' because that doesn't make sense, so you need to add an extra weak beat to the end of the line, to get the whole word in. This weak beat is called a 'feminine' or 'weak' ending, I regret to say. Sometimes Shakespeare uses a weak ending just to make the line fit, as we have done here, but at other times the rhythmic change is there to help the actor. That famous line in *Hamlet* does not have the regular firm beat of

The question is to be or not to be

but a more open, uncertain shape, continued in the subsequent lines, ending on a weak beat:

To be, or not to be, that is the question:
whether 'tis nobler in the mind to suffer
the slings and arrows of outrageous fortune,

or to take arms against a sea of troubles
and by opposing end them. To die – to sleep
(Act 3, Sc. 1)

The 'open' endings of the first four lines convey the flexible, wavering rhythm of Hamlet's uncertainty, ending with the closing thump of the fifth line's strong sentence. Here we can also see that a sentence can end and a new one begin in the middle of a line, giving a more broken rhythm and an abrupt change of direction that differs from the regularity of a sentence ending on the strong beat at the end of a strong line.

Because a new sentence demands a new breath, pitch and rhythm to mark the change of subject, you will need a tiny pause within the lines in which a new thought begins halfway through. For example, you need a new breath before the phrase 'To die – to sleep'.

Shared lines

An iambic pentameter can be shared among two or more speakers:

PEASEBLOSSOM: Ready!
COBWEB: And I!
MOTH: And I!
MUSTARDSEED: And I!
ALL FOUR: Where shall we go?
(*A Midsummer Night's Dream*, Act 3, Sc. 1)

This is quite a tightly packed line, in that there are a lot of syllables to fit into the pentameter, but that gives it great energy and charm. The way it is printed on the page gives the clue to the fact that it is a shared verse-line.

HAMLET: Hold you the watch tonight?
BARNARDO AND MARCELLUS: We do, my lord.
HAMLET: Arm'd, say you?
BARNARDO AND MARCELLUS: Arm'd, my lord.
HAMLET: From top to toe?
BARNARDO AND MARCELLUS: My lord, from head to foot.
(*Hamlet*, Act 1, Sc. 2)

This sharing of the pentameter gives urgency to the scene; it is essential that each actor has his breath ready to come in instantly, to keep the beat going. Here I would suggest that Hamlet keeps one breath going throughout his three short lines, and Marcellus also, so that they almost overlap each other in the questions and answers. We can be sure that Shakespeare did not want any pauses in a shared line sequence! Remember that Shakespeare chose his 'rule' in order to have fun with it, stretching it, generally playing with it. We, in turn, must be in charge of the rule, so that we are not trapped by the metrical stresses when they don't assist the sense of the line.

Added syllables

In the passage above from *Hamlet* you will have noticed the apostrophe in the word 'arm'd'; this is to indicate that the word is pronounced as one syllable; when it is printed in full as 'armed' the actor should pronounce it with two syllables – 'armED', in order to provide the necessary number of syllables for a pentameter line. This is simply a device to help the verse rhythm, so of course it is not necessary in prose speeches.

Here are two examples of the extra syllable used for the verse beat. In the first, the inflected 'è' adds the necessary beat.

> HAMLET: Rest, rest, perturbèd spirit . . .
> The time is out of joint. O cursèd spite,
> that ever I was born to set it right.
> (*Hamlet*, Act 1, Sc. 5)

Note that not all editions of the plays will use the apostrophe or the accent.

Words ending with 'ion' must have been pronounced differently from our 'shn' single syllable in Shakespeare's day, because the rhythm of a verse-line indicates that two syllables are necessary:

> HELENA: Have you conspir'd, have you with these contriv'd
> to bait me with this foul derision? . . .
> So we grew together,
> like to a double cherry: seeming parted,
> but yet a union in partition.
> (*A Midsummer Night's Dream*, Act 3, Sc. 2)

173

But of course we do not pronounce those two syllables of the 'ion' ending nowadays, as it sounds wrong to an audience and too 'precious' for the actor to be convincing; you need to recognise this small problem and find a way to honour the beat while keeping a natural inflection.

For some lines you will need to syncopate or to contract a word or two, in order to fit the beat; I call these 'tightly packed' lines; sometimes you will notice several apostrophes scattered about:

> POLONIUS: Beware
> of entrance to a quarrel, but being in,
> bear't that th'opposed may beware of thee.
> *(Hamlet*, Act 1, Sc. 3)

In that last line, you must think the contracted words 'it' and 'the' but allow them to slide into the word before or after them, so that the listener can hear the full sense of the complete word in the contraction; it is no more than the contractions we use in our ordinary speech: 'I'll' for 'I will'; 'That's' for 'that is', etc., but it looks a bit intimidating on the page until you get used to it.

Rhyming couplets

A rhyming couplet is often used to mark the end of a scene, like a strong chord in music; Shakespeare's theatre had no scene or lighting changes, so each scene needed a definite conclusion within the text, which could signal to actors waiting off-stage that their turn was coming:

> Till then sit still, my soul. Foul deeds will rise,
> though all the earth o'erwhelm them, to men's eyes.
> *(Hamlet*, Act 1, Sc. 2)

The end-of-scene rhyming couplets nearly always have strong endings, as they serve the function of a full stop or the end of a chapter in a story.

PUNCTUATION AND PHRASING

A skilfully edited edition of Shakespeare can be a great help to an actor, but we must always remember that the text has been punctuated to suit the needs of the reader, rather than the player. We have to provide our own speaker's punctuation, which for the actor is entirely centred on the breath. There is always a temptation to hit heavily on the first strong syllable of the pentameter; this must be avoided to get the continuity of thought through to the end of the sentence. Another common trap is stopping for a breath at the end of each verse-line; it is hard to avoid this because of the look of the lines on the page, so I now write out my Shakespeare scripts as unpunctuated text (see below) to help actors to discover the verse or prose rhythms themselves and to make their phrasing decisions according to the sense of each sentence. Even when printing the verse in lines I avoid capitals at the start of each verse-line, saving them for the beginning of a new sentence, so that actors can see where the new thought and breath must happen. (For more help, look at Chapter 14 on Breath.)

Punctuation marks for the actor indicate new thoughts (which mean new breaths), changes of pace, pitch and volume for subordinate clauses and all the practical vocal adaptations of rhythm that convey the sense and emotional drive of a speech. The actress Dame Edith Evans tells us to 'ignore the commas', which is excellent advice. I like to use only full stops, question marks, a few exclamation marks and lots of brackets in re-punctuating Shakespeare for the actor; phrasing is not just an academic exercise for us, but a way to grasp the deepest content of a speech, transferring the black marks on the white page into clear, heartfelt verbal communication.

The Unpunctuated Text exercise

In this first exercise, you must discover if the following unpunctuated passage is in blank verse or in prose. If you think it is in verse, then put a bar-mark . . ./ . . . at the end of each verse-line. If the passage is in verse, it will begin at the start of an iambic pentameter. Extra and contracted syllables are not indicated. Do not be too proud to beat out the blank verse rhythm on your fingers: 5 weak and 5 strong beats, with an occasional extra weak beat at the end of a line. I will comment on each passage afterwards, so that you can do the exercise and then see how you succeeded.

> HELENA: O spite O hell I see you all are bent to set against me for your merriment if you were civil and knew courtesy you would not do me thus much injury can you not hate me as I know you do but you must join in souls to mock me too if you were men as men you are in show you would not use a gentle lady so to vow and swear and superpraise my parts when I am sure you hate me with your hearts.
>
> (*A Midsummer Night's Dream*, Act 3, Sc. 2)

This passage is not too difficult as the verse beat is so regular. Did you notice the rhyming couplets all through the speech, which made it easier to find the line endings? Where did you put your punctuation marks? Remember that you are only to use full stops, brackets and question or exclamation marks, maybe a dash, but no commas. The reason for this is that commas do not always indicate a new breath or a marked change of pitch and rhythm; it is clearer for your breathing and rhythm decisions to put subordinate phrases and clauses in brackets if you want to take a new breath for them or to indicate that extra, less-important thought that is tucked into the main sentence. When you punctuate, the decisions are your own, just as the editor of whichever edition of Shakespeare you are using made their own decisions. You are not taking an exam, but making a creative, interpretative choice for yourself. Those of us with smaller ribcages and less breath capacity may need to find more occasions to breathe than those with larger frames.

The idea is to make your choices consciously as you study and learn your lines; then that technique will be there for you in the exciting process of performance; it will support you through all the changes that come naturally during a scene. To find the breathing patterns of your character is to access his deepest inner truth; it is the Method of Physical Action at its most basic and powerful level. As you take the character's breathing into yourself, then you will feel with him and need to say the words of your speech as the only possible expression of your Aim at that moment of the scene. You will also have the security of knowing that you are paying attention to Shakespeare's directions to you as an actor.

Here is Helena's speech, with, first, the line endings in the script, then my choices of punctuation for acting.

O spite O hell I see you all are bent / to set against me for your merriment / if you were civil and knew courtesy / you would not do me thus much injury / can you not hate me as I know you do / but you must join in souls to mock me too / if you were men as men you are in show / you would not use a gentle lady so / to vow and swear and superpraise my parts / when I am sure you hate me with your hearts /

O spite! O hell! I see you all are bent to set against me for your merriment. If you were civil and knew courtesy you would not do me thus much injury. Can you not hate me (as I know you do) but you must join in souls to mock me too? If you were men (as men you are in show) you would not use a gentle lady so: to vow and swear and superpraise my parts when I am sure you hate me with your hearts.

This punctuation gives me a through-line of thought and rhythm, which conveys Helena's indignation without destroying the verse form. I have given myself four full stops here (including the question mark), so that I can take four separate breaths (after the first two exclamations). The sentence endings come at the line endings here, which makes them all strong in emphasis. In practice, however, I might well try to go from 'I see you all are bent' to 'join in souls to mock me too' all on one long breath, as Helena is so angry and has such a strong Aim here. Also, there is more of the speech to come and it is a long scene, so it would be good to let rip, as, for the first time in her life, poor Helena expresses her rage.

You could make a different choice at the start of the speech: 'O spite O hell!' Or even: 'O spite O hell I see you all are bent to set against me for your merriment.' However, I think that the two strong exclamations at the beginning are better taken separately; when Shakespeare uses an 'O' it does need to be marked quite strongly; these are at the start of a long speech and give Helena the necessary energy to carry through her list of accusations. The brackets around 'as I know you do' and 'as men you are in show' indicate subordinate clauses; they are less important than the rest of the sentence and give variety in the pitch, volume and rhythm.

Do you see what the exercise has given you? It has put your choices clearly in front of you, so that you are in conscious control of your work, not just belting it out, gasping for breath when you run out of puff, or squeezing 'feeling' out of yourself like a sponge that will then dry out in the rest of this long and tiring scene. Remember that Helena's experience in this scene would probably be one of attempting to control her rage and pain in order to tell her former friends what she thinks of them.

When one tries to control a powerful emotion, the effect, both internally and for the listeners, is of a living, heartfelt energy; the emotion is recognised as natural and experienced as truthful. When the volcano of feelings does then erupt for short bursts it has an exciting quality of danger. Try the two parts of the exercise again with a more difficult speech from *Hamlet*:

> CLAUDIUS: no place indeed should murder sanctuarize revenge should have no bounds but good Laertes will you do this keep close within your chamber Hamlet return'd shall know you are come home we'll put on those shall praise your excellence and set a double varnish on the fame the Frenchman gave you bring you in fine together and wager o'er your heads he being remiss most generous and free from all contriving will not peruse the foils so that with ease or with a little shuffling you may choose a sword unbated and in a pass of practice requite him for your father.
>
> (*Hamlet*, Act 4, Sc. 7)

In the section below, you will see this speech as it is seen in your script, but I hope to persuade you that the printing of the verse speeches as prose is more useful to the actor. The verse beat is so powerful that it can look after itself, once the actor understands it. When a sentence takes up two or more lines of verse you need to run the sense of the line onwards with the breath, over the line endings. (In sentences running over six to eight lines you will need, of course, to find suitable points during the sentence to 'top up' with new breath as unobtrusively as possible.) You really do have to concentrate on not letting that line ending and the white gap on the right-hand side of the page stop you. Try writing out your speeches in sentences, as prose, without the verse form, and learn them like that, with your breathing.

Another important aspect of handling poetic speech is the avoidance of a 'poetry voice' or a 'Shakespearean delivery'. The marks of this are a 'floating' or 'singing' tone in the vowel sounds, which are 'held' longer than usual and given a false musical note which is not natural to the pitch of the vowel. Each vowel sound in English has its own individual pitch and these should be left to sound naturally, not 'lifted' or prolonged for extra effect.

Single stress

You should also consider single stress. That is, as Stanislavski put it, the 'subject noun' – the 'one word without which the sentence could not happen'. Your one main word will most probably be a noun at or towards the end of the sentence (the sentence, not the line). See the examples from the beginning of Act 3, Sc. 1 of *Hamlet*:

CLAUDIUS:　　And can you by no drift of conference
　　　　　　　get from him why he puts on this confusion,
　　　　　　　grating so harshly all his days of quiet
　　　　　　　with turbulent and dangerous **lunacy**?
ROSENCRANTZ:　He does confess he feels himself distracted,
　　　　　　　but from what cause a will by no means **speak**.
GUILDENSTERN:　Nor do we find him forward to be sounded,
　　　　　　　but with a crafty madness keeps aloof
　　　　　　　when we would bring him on to some confession
　　　　　　　of his **true state**.
GERTRUDE:　　　　　　　　　　Did he receive you **well**?
ROSENCRANTZ:　Most like a **gentleman**.
GUILDENSTERN:　But with much **forcing** of his disposition.
ROSENCRANTZ:　Niggard of question, but of our demands
　　　　　　　most free in his reply.
GERTRUDE:　　　　　　　　　　Did you assay him
　　　　　　　to any **pastime**?
ROSENCRANTZ:　Madam, it so fell out that certain **players**
　　　　　　　we o'erraught on the way. Of these we told him,
　　　　　　　and there did seem in him a kind of joy
　　　　　　　to hear of it. They are about the court,
　　　　　　　and, as I think, they have already order
　　　　　　　this night to play before him.

According to Toporkov (89), Stanislavski suggested that the way to play single stress was to take the vocal pressure off the other words in the sentence. Be aware that if you use the Pointing exercise with Shakespeare (p. 110), you may unconsciously retain those unnatural stresses on names and pronouns. Descriptive words and phrases should not be 'coloured', made 'special' or have their poetic qualities thrust at the audience; the reason for an actor doing this is usually to show how sensitive or clever he is, but it only distracts from the story of the scene.

Breathing

When you are listening to your partner in the scene you take your first breath at the moment of the word or action that impels your next line; if your partner has chosen his single-stress word well, then your intake of breath may often coincide with his key word, though if his key word is at the end of the sentence, you may need to breathe two or three words before it. There are also times in his speech or action when your character would like to answer; you can find these precisely by using the Spoken Responses exercise (p. 130). Even though your character does not actually say anything during a partner's speech, you can still take a breath as a silent response to what is happening; this is most helpful to the speaker if he has a long speech which you are listening to: it provides the Obstacle or the reinforcement which he needs to impel his next lines.

Here is Claudius' speech (Act 4, Sc. 7) printed in verse-lines, but unpunctuated:

> no place indeed should murder sanctuarize
> revenge should have no bounds but good Laertes
> will you do this keep close within your chamber
> Hamlet return'd shall know you are come home
> we'll put on those shall praise your excellence
> and set a double varnish on the fame
> the Frenchman gave you bring you in fine together
> and wager o'er your heads he being remiss
> most generous and free from all contriving
> will not peruse the foils so that with ease
> or with a little shuffling you may choose

a sword unbated and in a pass of practice
requite him for your father

Now with my choices of punctuation for phrasing:

No place (indeed) should murder sanctuarize.
Revenge should have no bounds. But (good Laertes)
will you do this: keep close within your chamber?
Hamlet (return'd) shall know you are come home.
We'll put on those shall praise your excellence
and set a double varnish on the fame
the Frenchman gave you. Bring you (in fine) together
and wager o'er your heads. He (being remiss
(most generous and free from all contriving))
will not peruse the foils – so that (with ease
(or with a little shuffling)) you may choose
a sword unbated and (in a pass of practice)
requite him for your father.

When you have a short subordinate clause, or a short phrase that is less important than the main sentence, you do not need a new breath for it: just let the clause ride on your main breath, drop the volume and pitch slightly and allow the clause to run a bit faster than the main sentence, so that it is fully audible but clearly of less importance than your main message. The last sentence in this speech is quite lengthy: two half-lines and four complete lines, containing those two fairly long brackets, so that you might need a top-up breath after 'foils'.

Have a look at another speech from *Hamlet*:

I heard thee speak me a speech once but it was never acted or if it was not above once for the play I remember pleased not the million 'twas caviare to the general but it was as I received it and others whose judgements in such matters cried in the top of mine an excellent play well digested in the scenes set down with as much modesty as cunning I remember one said there were no sallets in the lines to make the matter savoury nor no matter in the phrase that might indict the author of affection but called it an honest method as wholesome as sweet and by very much more handsome than fine

(Act 2, Sc. 2)

Did you find the iambic pentameters in that speech? Don't worry
. . . there aren't any. The speech is prose, so all you have to do is to
punctuate it for sense:

> I heard thee speak me a speech once but it was never acted – or (if
> it was) not above once (for the play (I remember) pleased not the
> million ('twas caviare to the general)) but it was (as I received it
> (and others whose judgements in such matters cried in the top of
> mine)) an excellent play: well digested in the scenes; set down with
> as much modesty as cunning. I remember one said there were no
> sallets in the lines to make the matter savoury (nor no matter in
> the phrase that might indict the author of affection) but called it
> an honest method: as wholesome as sweet and by very much more
> handsome than fine.

Two long, complicated sentences there, needing a lot of breath
control to keep the through-line of sense clear. A useful exercise for
seeing the through-line of thought is to practise the speech leaving
out the subordinate clauses and the brackets at least once in rehearsal:
'I heard thee speak me a speech once but it was never acted or not
above once but it was an excellent play . . .'

Another helpful tip is to omit all adjectives and/or imagery in a long
speech, so as to clarify it, just as an exercise; when you return to the
adjectives and imagery, which are often contained in a subordinate
phrase or clause, you rediscover them with new delight. In both exper-
iments you can add each deleted phrase, adjective or image cluster one
by one, incorporating them into the main thrust of the speech and so
understanding their necessity.

Short rhyming lines

Here is the last unpunctuated text passage to look at:

> ROBIN: through the forest have I gone but Athenian found I
> none on whose eyes I might approve this flower's force in
> stirring love night and silence who is here weeds of Athens he
> doth wear this is he my master said despised the Athenian maid
> and here the maiden sleeping sound on the dank and dirty

ground pretty soul she durst not lie near this lack-love this kill-courtesy

> (*A Midsummer Night's Dream*, Act 2, Sc. 2)

This speech is neither in prose nor in the blank verse beat; this is quite a different verse rhythm, with short rhyming lines with the beat of ONE and TWO and THREE and FOUR. Shakespeare uses it in *A Midsummer Night's Dream* and *Macbeth* for magic spells.

> Through the forest have I gone
> but Athenian found I none
> on whose eyes I might approve
> this flower's force in stirring love.
> Night and silence! Who is here?
> Weeds of Athens he doth wear:
> this is he my master said
> despiséd the Athenian maid;
> and here the maiden sleeping sound
> on the dank and dirty ground.
> Pretty soul, she durst not lie
> near this lack-love, this kill-courtesy.

17 Handling Shakespeare's language

THE POINTING EXERCISE

Though the Pointing exercise has already been explained in Chapter 11 (p. 110), I think it is useful to show its application to a Shakespeare speech. The technique is simple: the actor points to and looks at the person or place that he is talking about.

> **Focus**: The aim of this exercise is to allow time for the actor to make the speech specific and personal; it can be used in the early stages of rehearsal or study and can also be used more swiftly and freely once the scene has been learned.

For this speech from *Hamlet* the actor speaking will first need to pick a listener to represent the audience listening to this soliloquy. Then he needs to choose which other actors in the group will represent the other figures mentioned in the speech: the players, sinners (you can choose some sinners but I think 'they' means Claudius in this case, so you could point at him), Murder (personified), Hamlet's father and the Devil (Heaven's voice).

> HAMLET: Hum – **I** have heard
> that **guilty creatures** (sinners (Claudius)) sitting at a
> **play** (indicate players)
> have, by the very cunning of the **scene** (players),
> been struck so to the **soul** (sinners' (Claudius') souls)
> that presently

they (the sinners (Claudius)) have proclaimed **their**
(the sinners' (Claudius')) malefactions.
For **murder** (personalise Murder), though **it** (Murder)
have no tongue, will speak,
with most miraculous organ (Heaven's voice). I'll have
these players (indicate players)
play something like the murder of **my** / **father**
before **mine** / **uncle**. **I'll** observe **his** (Uncle's) looks;
I'll tent **him** (Uncle) to the quick. If **he** (Uncle) a do
blench,
I know **my** course. The **spirit** (Father) that **I** have seen
may be a **devil**, and the **devil** hath power
t'assume **a pleasing shape** (Father), yea, and perhaps,
out of **my** weakness and **my** melancholy,
as **he** (Devil) is very potent with such **spirits** (Father),
abuses **me** to damn **me**. **I'll** have grounds
more relative than this (the Ghost). The **play**'s the
thing
wherein **I'll** catch the conscience of the **King**.
(*Hamlet*, Act 2, Sc. 2)

This exercise should be used with the whole play or right through every scene you are working on, using the main characters as themselves, and others, or labels, for 'extras' such as the devil or Heaven's voice in the speech above. It is a great help to the actor in understanding the text and relationships, and for starting to learn lines, as it creates such strong personal connections. Never forget how important Heaven is in Shakespeare (Hell, too, very often) and how God or supernatural powers are believed to influence the lives of the characters.

PARAPHRASING

Shakespeare's language and references are not always easy for us to understand. I like to go through every scene paraphrasing the lines with the actors, putting them into our own words and making absolutely sure that everyone understands them. The director should let the actors know that this exercise will be done, so that people can have a chance to prepare their speeches; otherwise the paraphrasing can take too long. Once the actors are more experienced and confident with paraphrasing it is fun to use it in parallel with the text

Parallel paraphrasing

Focus: To analyse meaning, aims and relationships in a scene.

This exercise in pairs, which is quite messy and informal, is close to Spoken Responses (p. 130) and is a good introduction to that technique. The idea is to mix the text and your own words together, working on the technique of 'hitting the target', changing the expression in your partner's eyes with the line, and waiting for the 'yes' or 'no' from your partner to be sure that the sense of the line has got across to her, as in Silent Receiving (p. 129).

Example from *A Midsummer Night's Dream* (Act 3, Sc. 2):

OBERON: Now listen to me carefully, Puck, and concentrate this time . . . we must get it right because **thou seest these lovers seek a place to fight,** they're going to kill each other and then our magic can't help them, what can I do to save them . . .? I know!

Hie, therefore, Robin, overcast the night. Yes, we'll make it pitch dark so that they can't find each other; I must make Robin understand how dark it must be, no starlight or anything.

The starry welkin cover thou anon – at once, we have no time to waste,

with drooping fog, as black as Acheron, as black as the gates of hell, Robin, do you remember how frightening that was when I showed them to you?

And lead these testy rivals so astray as one comes not within another's way. You must separate Lysander and Demetrius who are trying to kill each other This is good but it might not be enough . . . let's have some fun with them . . .

> **Like to Lysander sometime frame thy tongue, then**
> **stir Demetrius up with bitter wrong, and some-**
> **time rail thou like Demetrius**. You heard them
> shouting and swearing at each other just now . . . so
> now you can pretend to be them yelling insults
> **and from each other look thou lead them thus,**
> **till o'er their brows death-counterfeiting sleep**
> – sleep that looks like death but isn't, now that we
> have saved them from each other
> **with leaden legs and batty wings doth creep** ...

When you are really friendly with this game, you can add the Spoken Responses of the other characters in the scene. Noisy but exciting and most valuable!

CLASSICAL REFERENCES

Shakespeare often used images from classical mythology and stories that were familiar to his audience but are unknown to us. These images and references are important to the thought and emotion of a character and therefore need to be thoroughly absorbed by the actor. For instance, in *A Midsummer Night's Dream*, Act 1, Sc. 1, Hermia, vowing her love and constancy to Lysander, refers to Dido, Queen of Carthage, who burned herself to death when her lover Aeneas left her, and to blind Cupid, the son of Venus, whose burning arrows shoot the flame of love through the eyes of lovers:

HERMIA: My good Lysander,
      I swear to thee by Cupid's strongest bow,
      by his best arrow with the golden head,
      by the simplicity of Venus' doves,
      by that which knitteth souls and prospers loves,
      and by that fire which burn'd the Carthage queen
      when the false Trojan under sail was seen,
      by all the vows which ever men have broke –
      in number more than ever women spoke –
      in that same place thou hast appointed me,
      tomorrow truly I will meet with thee.

If that image of 'the Carthage Queen' does not have much meaning for the actors playing Hermia and Lysander, even when the story has been explained, you could take a few minutes out of rehearsal time to act it through, with Hermia playing Dido and Lysander playing the false Aeneas sneaking away; they will then be able to feel that image as they speak it and make it an integral part of the scene and their relationship. You might also need to find out about Cupid and his golden arrow shot into the eyes of lovers.

THE TELEGRAM, LETTER AND IMAGERY EXERCISE

Focus: To analyse a speech in order to discover its central message.

In this exercise we call the core information the Telegram. Any additional or reinforcing information in the speech is called the Letter. The Imagery, of course, is just that: metaphors and similes and the personification of abstract nouns. This process enables you to make the essential narrative information of the speech completely clear, to understand the 'back-up' to that central story and to analyse the imagery, which gives you the clues as to the character's state of mind.

Example from *Hamlet* (Act 4, Sc. 3):

> CLAUDIUS: And England, if my love thou hold'st at aught –
> as my great power thereof may give thee sense,
> since yet thy cicatrice looks raw and red
> after the Danish sword, and thy free awe
> pays homage to us – thou mayst not coldly set
> our sovereign process, which imports at full,
> by letters congruing to that effect,
> the present death of Hamlet. Do it, England;
> for like the hectic in my blood he rages,
> and thou must cure me. Till I know 'tis done,
> howe'er my haps, my joys were ne'er begun.

I will paraphrase this speech, suggest a breathing punctuation and then divide it into Telegrams, Letters and Imagery, so that you can observe the whole process.

Paraphrase

King of England, if you rate my friendship at all – which you should feel, because of the great power I have over you, since the scars you took in the last battle where you were defeated by my Danish forces are still red and bleeding, and now you freely recognise my power over you and pay homage to me – you cannot coolly disregard my royal command, which is completely explained in my letter to you, that I wish you to put Hamlet to death at once. I want you to do this, King of England, because Hamlet is like a fever raging in my body and you must cure me. Until I know that Hamlet is dead, whatever else happens I can never feel happy.

As you can see, this is not a literal 'translation' but it conveys the sense of the speech, not leaving anything out. The actor must know precisely what all of these words mean; they must belong to him.

Phrasing and breathing

This speech is largely a series of brackets, one within another, leading up to the vital Telegram of 'the present death of Hamlet'; it is as if the King cannot at first bring himself to say those words, or feels that he has to reinforce his hold over England to make sure that the English king has no choice but to obey him.

And England (if my love thou hold'st at aught * [as my great power thereof may give thee sense since yet thy cicatrice looks raw and red after the Danish sword and thy free awe pays homage to us]) * thou mayst not coldly set our sovereign purpose * (which imports at full by letters congruing to that effect) the present death of Hamlet. Do it England (for like the hectic in my blood he rages and thou must cure me) ** Till I know 'tis done (howe'er my haps) my joys were ne'er begun.

I have put ** where I might take a major breath and * for a top-up. These choices need to be made by the actor at the same time as the words are learned, using the 'snowball units' technique (p. 132). The brackets mark subordinate clauses where I can take the speech faster and with less inflection and little stressing. You will see that the single stress comes with the Telegram: 'the present death of Hamlet'.

The letter to England is also important, because this is the one that Hamlet finds when the ship is raided by pirates on his way there. He changes the names in the letter so that Rosencrantz and Guildenstern are executed instead of himself and returns to Denmark, knowing the truth about his uncle. (Shakespeare writes 'letters' in the plural, like the word 'news', which we now use as a singular noun.) In performance it might be helpful for the King to have this letter with him.

The single stress in the second sentence is interesting; where would you put it? Maybe one could use more than one word and hit 'Do it, England' or keep it until 'cure me'. I think the heavy rhyme at the end of the final couplet, marking the end of the scene, looks after itself – I mean that the rhyme, like a repetition, makes a strong stress unnecessary. Think about your choices.

We have already found the Telegram, the vital centre of the speech: 'The present death of Hamlet. Do it, England.' The rest of the speech contains reinforcements of this message and imagery giving vivid pictures of the King's state of mind. The Letter consists of: 'and England, if my love thou hold'st at aught – as my great power thereof may give thee sense . . . and thy free awe pays homage to us – thou mayst not coldly set our sovereign process, which imports at full by letters congruing to that effect . . . Till I know 'tis done, howe'er my haps my joys were ne'er begun.'

This leaves two main images, both contained in short clauses, of wounds and illness (in fact, the dominating images throughout the play are of ulcers and disease): Claudius sees England as scarred and bleeding from his recent attack: 'since yet thy cicatrice looks raw and red after the Danish sword', and he sees Hamlet as a destroying fever in his own body, feeling that he can be cured only by Hamlet's death: 'for like the hectic in my blood he rages, and thou must cure me'.

As you work on a speech, be aware of the images used and give yourself time to visualise them; then you will understand their force within the speech. We all use images to explain ourselves in real life – we need them when there is no other way of making our meaning and feelings clear. Be aware of when you use them in daily life, when you hear them from others and what the choice of image tells you about the feelings of the speaker.

SHAKESPEARE'S DIRECTIONS TO THE ACTOR

Shakespeare, as actor and director, gives us clear instructions about how we are to play his characters. The most detailed teaching comes in Hamlet's advice to the players in Act 3, Sc. 2:

> Suit the action to the word, the word to the action, with this special observance, that you o'erstep not the modesty of nature. For anything so o'erdone is from the purpose of playing, whose end, both at the first and now, was and is to hold as 'twere the mirror up to nature; to show virtue her feature, scorn her own image, and the very age and body of the time his form and pressure.

Looking at random through *A Midsummer Night's Dream* I find that Egeus in the first scene states that he is 'full of vexation' and has come to complain about his daughter Hermia. Later, Lysander asks Hermia, 'Why is your cheek so pale?' and she replies that she feels that she will burst into tears at any minute, using an image of the roses in her cheeks being pale without the rain of her tears, which will soon drench them. Illustrations of the characters' emotions and expressions are constant in every scene – 'Aye, counterfeit sad looks, make mouths upon me when I turn my back' (Act 3, Sc. 2) – and Shakespeare also gives precise instructions as to the actions he requires: Hermia, eloping with Lysander in the midnight forest, says that she will 'rest her head' upon a bank and, when her lover attempts to lie near her, she tells him to 'lie further off yet, do not lie so near' (Act 2, Sc. 2). 'Come, Hamlet, come, and take this hand from me,' says Claudius in *Hamlet* (Act 5, Sc. 2) when he is setting up the duel with Laertes. The choosing of the foils, the duel itself and the final tragedy of multiple deaths are carefully choreographed by the playwright.

In *Hamlet*, the Ghost's actions and appearance are clearly set out each time he appears. In the 'closet scene' (Act 3, Sc. 4) between Hamlet and his mother, Hamlet tells her to 'Come, come, and sit you down, you shall not budge. You go not . . .' – clearly these repeated commands mean that Gertrude must be trying very hard to leave the room. An actor can often find out what actions he must take by observing what other characters ask or forbid him to do. So, if someone says to you, 'Dry your eyes, Do not weep', your character must be crying and if you are told, 'Rise, do not kneel', that line cannot be spoken if you are just standing there. If a command is repeated, it is obvious that it has not been obeyed the first time.

Shakespeare also helps with breathing rhythms, building them into the structure of the text and even at times giving precise instructions about a character's breathing changes – after Hamlet has left her, Claudius notices that Gertrude has 'sighs', and 'profound heaves' of breath.

A simple and confident start to Hamlet

The exercise 'A Simple and Confident Start to a Scene' gives a clear method for actors and directors to put Shakespeare's instructions into practice. See Chapter 10, p. 105, for a full explanation of the method. The following example lists the actions demanded by Shakespeare in the opening scene of *Hamlet*:

a. Barnardo and Francisco need to enter separately, as they do not at first recognise each other in the dark.
b. They challenge each other. Barnardo dismisses Francisco, as it is his turn to take over the watch.
c. As Francisco prepares to leave, he hears Horatio and Marcellus approaching.
d. Marcellus and Horatio enter together.
e. Francisco challenges them.
f. Francisco leaves.
g. Barnardo suggests that they sit down.
h. Horatio agrees and they all sit down.
i. The Ghost enters.
j. Do they rise in shock? Shakespeare does not say so, but maybe this is why he insists that they sit before the Ghost's entrance, to increase the tension and to emphasise the vision. After the Ghost's first exit, Marcellus says, 'Sit down' again, so by that time they must all be standing.

And so on.

NOTES FOR THE TEACHER OF SHAKESPEARE

For the first teaching of the blank verse rhythm, when I suggest using a birthday date for the example sentence, teachers working in schools may find that students are happier using a date other than their birthday; they could use a 'shopping list' instead, as: 'A pound of apples and a piece of cheese'; it is also good practice to ask each person to say one line in the blank verse beat to their neighbour, round the group and, if that goes well, to make pairs speak to each other in the rhythm; people often start to use rhyme at this point, just for fun.

To teach 'shared lines' I use numbers round the group, so that person A might start with:

A: And ONE and TWO . . . then B needs to continue the beat of the line with
B: and THREE and FOUR . . . and C can then finish the metre with:
C: and FIVE

Teaching the basic beat does need time and practice and it is useful to revise it until it is absorbed. Going through a play at random, students can spend time in pairs or small groups finding the beat in any speech. Unpunctuated text needs careful preparation: always start a passage at the beginning of a verse-line and choose simple examples to start with, allowing students to work in pairs to 'solve' the puzzle. You may find that you need to make a space between sentences in the passage, to help them, as the language can be hard to understand.

In order to work on the content of the speech, not solely on its verse form, you can ask students to write the speech out as prose, just punctuating it for sense, after which they can put it into verse-lines. Time spent on 'translating' for sense is the priority, of course.

Part Six Workshops in Laban movement for actors

18 The four elements

INTRODUCTION

The workshops in Part Six are designed to be used in sequence: the first four (Chapters 19–22) introduce the four basic elements of Rudolf von Laban's analysis of action, with exercises for practice and notes on the application of these rhythms to acting; the last workshop (Chapter 23) brings the four elements together and then connects them with sound and text.

The work is simple but not easy and it is important that it is absorbed in sequence, precisely, without hurry and with time for revision. The five workshops aim to provide the building blocks of Laban's vocabulary of action; as each of the four elements of Flow, Space, Time and Force are explored and understood they can be absorbed gradually, empowering the actor with the techniques of rhythmic and specific expressive action.

Actors need an accurate kinaesthetic sense – a sense of movement and muscular effort – as much as dancers or athletes do. Movement for actors means the action of voice, thought, psychology and emotion, the 'score' of a text, as well as purely physical action. The common root of the words 'motion', 'emotion' and 'motive' comes from the Latin *emovere* (to stir up, to move) indicating the intrinsic link between physical, mental and emotional experience: as the actor goes through these Laban exercises he also goes through the thoughts and emotions that each movement engenders.

The Laban analysis of movement, which is clear, practical and immediately applicable to an actor's work on character and the rhythms of text as well as to the entire rehearsal and creative process, enables the actor to develop and refine his understanding of the body, voice and mind in action. And by being able to control their movement and rhythm, actors can make conscious choices affecting the true organic emotions of scenes at all stages of rehearsal and in performance.

Rudolf von Laban (1879–1958) was born in Bratislava and studied architecture before his interest in the mechanics of physical and mental effort led him to travel in order to study the movement patterns of American Indians, Africans, the peoples of the Near East and the Chinese. Later, he became a ballet choreographer and the Director of Movement for the Berlin State Opera, but he eventually reacted against the intrigues and artificiality of that theatre world and left to set up craft centres all over Europe, where people could take courses that helped with their practical working problems, physical stresses, etc. This therapeutic and experimental work was seen as a threat by the Nazi regime and Laban had to take refuge, with some of his pupils, in England. During the war he turned his attention to industry and developed his analysis of time and motion with F. C. Lawrence, matching the individual effort patterns of each worker to tasks that suited their natural rhythms and capabilities.[1]

In later life Laban established a teaching centre for dance as an educational force and to teach Labanotation, a system for recording movement. He was for many years co-director, with Esme Church, of the Northern Theatre School in Bradford, and his pupil Jean Newlove handed on his teaching to Joan Littlewood's Theatre Workshop company. My learning of the system began with Maxwell Shaw, who had been a member of that company.

Using only the basics of Laban's system, expressed here by a brief vocabulary of action and a simple working process of exercises, it is possible to begin to achieve that physical control, and to refine the ability to observe, understand and use precisely the detail, depth and richness of human behaviour. From this reliable structure I have developed my own teaching and working method: this includes the use of Pauses, Stops, all of the exercises below, Movement Sentences, the Space, Time and Force scales and the application of Laban's Eight Effort Actions to acting and text.

THE FOUR ELEMENTS: THE MOVEMENT VOCABULARY

Laban divides movement – meaning physical, vocal and mental/emotional action – into four elements. Each of these elements of movement has two contrasting aspects to it and these provide the eight words which make up the basic vocabulary of action.

- The Flow of a movement can be either Bound or Free.
- The Space or Spatial Pathway of a movement can be either Direct or Flexible.
- The Time or Speed of a movement can be either Fast or Slow. (Laban's words for Time were 'Sudden' and 'Sustained'; they apply to both the speed and the duration of a movement. I find it useful to take the speed and the duration of a movement separately when learning the technique, so those two aspects of time are looked at in the Time workshop.)
- The Force, Weight, Intensity or Strength of a movement can be either Strong or Light.

In learning the Movement Vocabulary we work first in the extremes of each element: it is like learning to paint using at first only primary colours. The two contrasting aspects of each of the four elements are like blue and yellow: learn them and experience them thoroughly first and then you can mix your own greens. Remember, also, that we are always expressing all four elements of movement, in every action of our lives. Laban divided movement into categories solely in order to examine it; in reality it is one indivisible experience. So that when we work on one element, the other three are present at all times; it is just that they may not yet be under our conscious control.

Language reflects the outer life; movement the inner life.
(Michael Joyce, director and teacher)

---

19 Flow

FREE AND BOUND FLOW

Laban says that the element of Flow is related to precision in thought and action. Some words associated with Flow: tidal; ebb; current; stream; fluency; essence; quintessence; nature; trait; intrinsic quality; immanence; inherent; characteristic; personality; soul; heart; feeling; instinct.

The element of Flow can be either Free or Bound. Action can have either a free-flowing, streaming-onwards, almost unstoppable, unbalanced quality. Or Flow can have a bound, controlled, fully balanced quality that stays within set boundaries and provides creative structures.

Some words associated with Free Flow: yielding; soft; ductile; pliant; liberated; easy; frictionless; smooth; ready; effortless; unreserved; unimpeded; wandering; random; irrepressible; unlimited; unconditional; unconstrained; liberty; freedom; frankness; licence.

Some words associated with Bound Flow: control; balance; restraint; discipline; definition; demarcation; limitation; boundary; parenthesis; stopping; disconnection; intermittent; restriction; interruption.

Flow has a strong connection with balance: in Free Flow you play with your balance, sometimes letting yourself lose it, enjoying the feeling that the movement cannot be readily stopped, like a free-flowing river spilling over into a waterfall. In Bound Flow you enjoy complete control over your balance, you are poised, able to stop immediately and to change the course of action at any moment. Bound Flow is practical, structured, a thoughtful, considered action or an immediate response to a crisis; it is essentially a building, creative process requiring form, outline and structure.

Both Bound and Free qualities are essential for life and must be used appropriately. A bird on the ground is in Bound Flow as it hops and pecks for food; the same bird in the air will be in Free Flow to ride the wind. When you are preparing to cross a busy road you must be in Bound Flow as you look for approaching cars, then in Free Flow as you run non-stop across the road when there is a gap in the traffic. To use the inappropriate Flow would lead to a nasty accident . . .

When you are learning something you are always in Bound Flow because you need the ability to **stop in order to change** that is the definition of Bound in Laban's teaching.

If you are learning a new dance, a song, how to find the theatre, your lines, a foreign language, any new thing at all, you must be in Bound Flow until you are secure in your knowledge and can slide into Free Flow.

You will be in Bound Flow as you read this and when you are learning the exercises in the workshops; you will need to pause occasionally to consider a point of theory and to learn the practice. (Laban also described a third aspect of the element of Flow: Broken Flow, where the rhythm is jerky, arrhythmic; this is less controlled than movement in Bound Flow; the action can be spasmodic, not directed by the will and has a rather disruptive, anarchic energy. I am not offering any practice in Broken Flow, just suggesting that one is aware of it, so as to use it or correct it when necessary.)

At times, especially at brief moments of transition from one action or rhythm to another, the element of Flow can be hard to define. The changing Flow of a character is discovered through the rhythms of text and action.

THE FALLING AND SAVING IMPROVISATION

Laban explains that we can either Indulge-in or Fight-against each element of movement. Indulging-in-Flow is another way of describing Free-Flow action: abandoning yourself to the power of Free Flow to the extent of losing balance and control. When Fighting-against-Flow, which is Bound-Flow movement, your actions and balance are controlled by your will.

Focus: Experiencing contrasting Flows.

Space, time and numbers: You need a large, clear space; allow plenty of time; played in pairs. This very active exercise needs to be demonstrated and carefully supervised so as to ensure players' safety (see Notes for the teacher of the Flow workshop, pp. 205–6).

After each stage, A and B reverse roles and play that stage over again. The game uses speech and normal behavioural action. Players need to wear loose comfortable clothes, with trousers or tights, and bare feet so that they do not slip. This game is non-competitive and is played in a spirit of gentle co-operation and pleasure throughout.

Your aim is to 'convert' your partner to the aspect of Flow that you yourself are expressing, i.e. if you are the Bound-Flow player, you wish to persuade the Free-Flow person to be 'constructive' and apply some control to her movement, while if you are in Free Flow, you wish to convert your partner to a more abandoned, relaxed and enjoyably unbalanced rhythm.

Stage one

Player A: In Free Flow, begin the game by falling loosely onto the floor and rolling about gently and playfully. The joints of ankles, knees, hips, hands, wrists, elbows, shoulders and spine (especially the top of the spine: the neck and head) are all soft and bendy, playing at not taking the body's weight and not controlling balance, while always staying safe, not allowing the head or limbs to bump painfully against the floor.

Player B: In Bound Flow, attempt with patience and good humour, never using any strain or force, to get your partner to sit or stand up, or at least to apply some balance or restraint.

Player A: do not block or resist B's efforts to change you; be aware of all B's efforts and hear all that he says while remaining with the enjoyment of your active Free Flow (so making no attempt to help B); and Player B: be willing to hear and be aware of A's engagement with

Free Flow while gently suggesting and initiating an active change into the benefits of Bound Flow. Use speech: talk to your partner, with A's speech patterns in Free Flow and B's in Bound Flow.

The important thing about this approach to the game is the willingness of both players to stay in the moment of action, solving the playful problem without straining or hurrying to gain a result. It is helpful to avoid the word 'no'; try using 'yes, and . . .', rather than 'yes, but . . .' (see p. 8 for the 'Yes, and . . .' exercise).

You need to be aware of the freedom of your heads and necks during this exercise; Player A, in Free Flow, must release your head, allowing the weight of it to lead your body in its Indulging-in-Flow and your playing with loss of balance. Your face, breathing, eyes and thought-control should be relaxed through this with a heavy, rather floppy head.

Player B: You do not have to worry about being in Bound Flow; you will naturally fall into that readiness-to-change mode as you attempt to deal with your partner. It is useful to have a friend or teacher to watch out for tension, which means energy in the wrong place – rigid head, clenched teeth, held breath, tight shoulders, etc. – all of which can be safely released during this game during all its stages. Recognising when you are tense, so that you can decide to release that inhibiting clenching of muscles, is important for all your work.

Neither player can 'win' this game; it has no ending in itself and must be finished by the players themselves or by the teacher. The experience provides a useful lesson in the benefits of playing without 'end-gaining' or trying for a result, which is also the most creative approach to acting in rehearsal. Reverse the roles and play Stage one again before moving on to Stage two.

Stage two

Player A: This time you have the Aim of co-operating with your partner, insofar as you wish to sit or stand in the way that B is helping you to do. However, your head is still floppy and heavy, carrying your body down with it as it releases itself to Free Flow and the force of gravity. Your knees are also soft and your balance is still uncontrolled, so, although you might successfully manage to stand or sit up for a while, or even to walk with your partner's assistance, you slide gently back to the floor, in spite of B's help. So this is another exercise in falling and 'failing' with no winners or losers, played gently and cheer-fully, with no physical force used. (If A is heavily built and B is slight, then B must not test her strength too much; her partner will be co-operating as much as her Free Flow will allow her to. In Stage two, the danger of tightening the neck muscles and 'holding the head on' through tension is increased, because of the intention to rise and establish balance. So this is good practice in maintaining relaxed muscles even when you have an Aim, and in allowing yourself to 'fail' without struggle.)

When we relate the exercise to the practice of acting, it teaches the necessity of remaining in the moment even when you have an Aim that you wish to achieve in the near future. It also demonstrates the essence of acting the Magic 'If' (p. 28). The Free-Flow player acts as if his head is floppy and his knees are soft as cotton wool and, with the Bound-Flow partner, he is taking action to solve the playful problem. Any changing emotions and relationships come solely from the action taken to solve the playful problem. This is the trustworthy secret of the Method of Physical Action.

Reverse the roles and play Stage two again.

Stage three

The other name for this stage is 'Falling Asleep in the Snow' and it can be used also as a relaxation or very gentle warm-up or calm-down exercise. The game can be played in pairs or in a group of any size. In Stage three all players are in Free Flow throughout. You all have a strong Obstacle in that you want to lie down quietly in a situation where you are stranded in heavy snow and simply want to rest there. However, your Aim (which must always be stronger than your Obstacle) is to save your partner; you all wish 'first to save my partner's life, and only then to fall asleep in the snow myself'. The game is therefore altruistic and is not a struggle between players. Once again there are no winners or losers. A and B (or all the members of the group, if it is a group activity) just take it in turns to help each other.

The exercise must be played very slowly with no 'busyness'. The lesson is to have the confidence to allow nothing to be happening and to take action only when you feel the organic inner impulse to do so. Use the improv to listen to yourself while being aware of your partner.

You need the confidence to be 'helpless', with soft joints, as before; allow for times of inaction, while being co-operative and unselfish, and let yourself be helped; beware of the temptation to be always the helper and to be too busy to allow yourself to 'fail' and fall – that takes the power away both from your partner and yourself. The experience of the game can help you to understand more about your personal working patterns.

NOTES FOR THE TEACHER OF THE FLOW WORKSHOP

It is important for the teacher of all of the workshops to have had experience of the exercises, so find a friend to take you through the Flow sequence or at least try the gentle falling with free head and neck for yourself and notice the constant switching of Free to Bound Flow in your daily actions and in the movement of others.

I choose a partner to help me demonstrate the game at each stage, taking the part of the Free-Flow person myself; the premise of playing for the sake of play and not trying for a result can be hard for people to adapt to, but they feel a sense of liberation and laughter once they surrender to the fun of 'failing' in safety.

At the start of the first and second stages of the exercise, ask the students in pairs to find a space for themselves in the room, with a safe distance between the edges of the room and the other pairs of players; remind them to keep within that area as they play and to avoid invading the space of other pairs.

During the workshop you will need to be constantly aware of the participants' safety. As they 'fall' and 'save' each other the teacher needs to be circulating through the space, so that she can separate bodies that are rolling on the floor too close to furniture, objects or other players for safety; then it is necessary to step between them, with a quiet word of warning.

The game is an improvisation, as well as a movement exercise, so players can be encouraged to talk to each other while working together. The teacher needs to look out for Bound-Flow players who just stand still and talk to their partners, and for

Bound-Flow players who haul their floppy partners around painfully. Also for Free-Flow players who lie 'dead', or refuse to co-operate, losing the sense of play and ignoring their partners.

In the Falling Asleep in the Snow game, remind players that this is an exercise in altruism: each one wishes to save his partner but faces the strong Obstacle of his own need to fall asleep. Give plenty of time for this stage, let the group energy fade right away – after the initial stage of struggle and busyness the group will then find a natural energy and rhythm. The game is good for unwinding when people are tired at the end of a session, as long as you allow at least 20 minutes for it and can let people go away quietly afterwards.

With inexperienced players, exercises will not last very long; you may find that one or more pairs just stop and look at you, after a short playing time, expecting their signal to be picked up by you; you then have the choice as to whether to follow that signal from them and to stop the exercise, giving them time for feedback or to encourage them to continue.

After each stage that includes a change of roles for each person, from Free to Bound Flow and vice versa (this change to happen without a stop in the action), players will need time to talk about their experiences.

20 Space

Laban says that the body moves through space in a way that is either Direct or Flexible. In Direct action you take the shortest path between two points, the straight path to your Aim.

Some words associated with Direct action: straight; aim; vertical; even; linear; inflexible; aligned; outspoken; sincere; unambiguous; brittle; ordered; structured; straightforward; uncomplicated.

In Flexible action (Laban also calls this 'indirect') you take a longer, curving, circuitous route, where the Aim is approached indirectly.

Some words associated with Flexible action: convoluted; cyclical; glancing; undulating; curling; shy; sinuous; supple; wavy; rounded; easy; unbalanced; random; complex; biased; rambling; drifting; avoiding; tender; pliant; sidling; turning; plastic; elastic; melting; limp; floppy; docile.

The element of Space can be clearly seen in play texts as well as in pure or behavioural movement and character study; it can be related to thought-patterns, stage moves, the composition and delivery of a line or speech and a character's preferred method of achieving his Aim.

You will find that Direct movement is allied to Bound Flow and Flexible movement to Free Flow, but apart from that don't worry about the Flow factor for this stage of the work. You know that you will be more or less in Bound Flow for the early learning period anyway, as you consider, correct and change what you are doing.

THE SIX MAIN DIRECTIONS

Your body inhabits the space around it. Our kinaesthetic sense also tells us what physical actions are taking place inside our bodies so that we can recognise our emotional processes. The body moves through space like a fish through water, creating ripples of energy that affect everything inhabiting that space at that time.

Within your body there is also movement in Space and Flow, felt as one blocks off or moves into different areas of the body, for instance when the breathing moves down from a holding in the upper chest to the deeper, supportive area of the lower lungs and the back, and in the mental journeys of thought and continuous fluctuations of emotion.

Physical extension radiates through the body into the surrounding Space from the spinal axis, which is your centre, into the **Six Main Directions**:

High   Low   Back   Forward   Right   Left

There are also the diagonals that cross these Six Directions.

At the start of any workshop or rehearsal it is good to stretch and wake up the body: as you reach out with arms, legs and trunk, breathing into the stretch, you can use the physical exercise to relate the Six Directions to your work on a role: **High** space, above the actor, can be linked with the mental and aspirational dimensions of a character: his ideas, beliefs, thoughts and plans. **Low** space, below him, is linked to the relationship of the character to the ground and his daily life: a peasant working on the soil; an aristocrat carried over the ground in carriages or walking only on carpets in light, elegant shoes; a mechanic in heavy working boots on a concrete factory floor; a barefoot child in cool grass, etc. **Back** space, behind you, suggests the past life of the character; there has to be a great deal of research and imaginative thought to create the life of a believable human being on stage, finding the clues from the text. **Forward** space, in front of you, suggests the Aims for which the character strives and hopes, always just ahead of him. **Right-hand** space can stand for the people and circumstances of the play that assist your character to achieve his Aims. **Left-hand** space symbolises those people and events in the world of the play that create Obstacles in the way of your character's desires.

The Six Directions form the **Three Dimensions** in which we move:

Height: from high to low and vice versa
Width: from right to left and vice versa
Depth: from front to back and vice versa

Stretch into these dimensions, paying attention to the transitions from one to the next, gaining control over your spatial directions so that one movement flows seamlessly into another.

The space which the body inhabits can also be divided into **Three Extensions**:

Near	Middle	Far

These extensions can also be connected to the actor's work on a role: the **Near** extension, where the physical action is close to or even within the body, like breathing, is on a small scale, detailed, inhabiting a tiny area, like the small inner movements of feeling and thought, memory and reaction that are constantly manifesting themselves in tiny rhythmic changes. Close-ups for the camera concentrate on this Near or Inner extension. The **Middle** extension of the body is gesture, action or stride (as in walking), reaching out comfortably into the surrounding space without extending out of the easy orbit of the body. Middle extension feels that things are 'within reach', attainable or customary. **Far** extension is when the body reaches out as far as possible into the surrounding space to stretch, explore, reach, attack or risk. It is demanded by the crisis moments in a play and is linked to the extreme actions or beliefs of a character, his confidence, aggression and the peaks of his experience. When you limber and work in pure movement from now on, reach out into your Six Directions with a good Far extension, to stretch and tone the body.

OPENING AND CLOSING

Laban also describes movement which Folds Inwards (closes in) and Unfolds Outwards (opens out) to and from the body's centre. He also called these impulses 'gathering' and 'scattering'. As a generalisation, we often talk of people as 'introverts' or 'extroverts', and Folding and Unfolding are related to those psychological concepts; they are power-ful reactions to space and must be treated with care and precision.

In Gathering, Closing or Folding Inwards the action shrinks away from the surrounding space (at any extension), in defence or through insecurity, or in collecting, nurturing, holding or protecting something – another person, oneself, an idea or an object – as close as possible to one's centre. In Scattering, Opening or Unfolding Outwards the body's action opens out from the centre (at any extension) to reach towards the surrounding space in generosity, curiosity, attack or exploration.

MEETING PEOPLE OPEN AND CLOSED

Stage one

Using a partner, or, ideally, working in a group, move round the room, meeting each other. As you do so, take alternately an Opening/ Unfolding and a Closing/Folding-in impulse at the moment of meeting. Remember that the Folding-in/Closing impulse can be connected negatively to tension and isolation and positively to containment, concentration and inner stillness; while the Opening impulse can suggest attack, exploration, connection to others or invasion of wider space. With all players using the two alternatives, a Closing from one can be met with an Opening from the other, or both players can be Closing or both Opening. This stage of the exercise uses a Far extension, in that the spatial relationships of the players are more apart and formal.

Stage two

Play the exercise again with a Middle extension, with players sitting or standing fairly close to each other, as in a domestic situation and alternating their Opening or Closing impulses at the moment of eye-contact with a partner.

Stage three

Use the Near extension, when the Opening or Closing impulse is contained rather secretly within the body, felt in the breath or in small, muscular movements, using eye-contact with a partner to trigger the moment of change.

Opening and Closing can also be used with objects: try receiving a letter with an Opening of happy anticipation, then reading bad news, which Closes you in disappointment; or Opening a box with a Closing feeling of dread, then discovering a nice present inside it, which you Open out to. The actor may well find moments in a play where these impulses are necessary to the story.

When you come to learn the Eight Effort Actions, which are a combination of the elements of Space, Time and Force, you will find that they are very different in feeling and effect, depending whether you are closing or opening the body in its space.

It is really useful to look at a character in terms of this Opening and Closing; you will find that you are always doing one or the other. Try this idea with the three extensions, Near, Middle and Far, and you will see how it changes your body and your feelings. Looking at characters and the actor's process, you can see that emotionally and psychologically, people can be open or closed to new ideas and feelings.

CONSCIOUS CONTROL OF ENERGY INTO SPACE

You can experiment with connecting to or cutting off from your surrounding space by making a simple gesture such as raising your arm upwards and then to the side or front. Now, decide in your mind whether you will extend your energy into the surrounding space or whether you will cut it off at your fingertips. Then ask a friend if she can see which decision you have made; it is not what you do, it is how you do it: there is little outer difference in your gesture if you direct your energy outwards or keep it to yourself, but there is all the difference in the world as to the effect you have on yourself and the surrounding space, at any extension. You can, of course, perform a Gathering or Folding-inwards action with the energy streaming forth – cutting yourself off is not connected to what your action is but to how you do it. Here is an exercise which I use to show that the release and extension of our energy is within our control:

Stage one

Get together with a partner who is close to you in height. Put your hand, facing upwards with the palm towards the ceiling, on your partner's shoulder and ask him to put his two hands, clasped together, over your elbow joint; your arm is now loosely stretched out across the space between both of you, with your partner's hands joined and resting on the bend of your elbow.

SAFETY NOTE: This exercise is not a trial of strength; there must be no tense resistance to the firm yet gentle downward pressure of your partner's hands on your elbow joint. Your arm must always be facing upwards, palm to ceiling, so that the elbow bends naturally downwards and your partner's pressure on the joint must remain calm, with no sharp jerks which might hurt you. Now, in that position, think of keeping the flow of your energy just within the compass of your arm; that is, decide that your energy will stop at your fingertips, which are now loosely resting (not stretched out tensely) on your partner's shoulder. When you are ready, ask your partner to press slowly onto your elbow joint with his two clasped hands until your elbow naturally bends. It is most important not to resist this pressure, but to let your arm bend when it wants to.

Stage two

You will be sending your energy outwards from your fingertips right out into space; you can think of this as laser beams or as the energy of light from a star extending far out into the universe. Keep your fingers relaxed as before: you are doing this extension of power with your mind, not by tensing your muscles. When you are ready, ask your partner to press his joined hands down on your elbow, as before. He will once again be able to bend your elbow, but this time your arm will feel stronger, with the stream of energy coursing through it, so the sensation for him will be quite new and different from the first stage of the exercise. This outward flow of energy is what we call 'projection' or 'star quality'.

Now reverse the positions, so that your partner has a turn in Closing-in and Opening-out his flow of energy and find time to talk about what happened.

> Heaven does with us as we with torches do,
> Not light them for themselves; for if our virtues
> Did not go forth from us, 'twere all alike
> As if we had them not.
> > (*Measure for Measure*, Act 1, Sc. 1)

SIMULTANEOUS AND SUCCESSIVE MOVEMENT

There are two ways in which the body can Open and Close into and against the space, and these involve an element of Time as well as of Space. You can move all the body at once, as one unit, Simultaneously, as Laban says, or you can Fold and Unfold successively, moving one bit of you followed by another bit; for example, you might Fold-inwards by first curving your fingers in, then your hand, then wrist, then elbow, then arm, then shoulder and you could Unfold again, starting from either the shoulder first or the fingertips first. The Successive action would probably be related (though not exclusively) to Flexible movement and the Simultaneous, when you move a limb or the whole body together, to Direct movement.

Now exercise by going into your Six Directions, using Simultaneous and Successive actions and the Folding and Unfolding impulses, always being sure that your choices are clear. It is a good idea to ask a friend or a teacher to watch and correct you. To practise incorrectly can be worse than not to practise at all.

THE SIX EXERCISES

The Six Exercises give active experience of Laban's analysis of action, progressing from working alone to group improvisation. The exercises can be used separately for each element of action, then for any combination of Space, Time and Force. The first explanation refers to Space and the same sequence will be used for Time and Force, with additional explanations and variations where necessary.

Remember that while the emphasis seems to be exclusively on each isolated element as we work on it, all of the other three elements (Flow, Time and Force) are present in our every action and should be noticed as the work gradually combines them into a conscious unity.

All Laban exercises need time for learning and experience to be absorbed; this means that you will stay for an unnaturally long time with each rhythm, whereas in life you frequently change rhythm, occupation and focus. So, in this extended length of time in one rhythm, your action may seem limited or unfamiliar, as you play each stage of the exercise; as long as you remember the purpose of the work, you will be able to take it in your stride without worry.

THE SIX EXERCISES WITH SPACE

Exercise one: Working alone with an object

Sitting on the floor on your own, in your own space, you are going to work with a soft garment like a sweatshirt, which is your object. (You need a shirt or coat, rather than a shoe, sock, glove or scarf, because there are more things you can do with a larger object. Alternatively, you can use your bag and the objects in it.) Fold your garment, put it on, take it off, play around with it, first in Direct Space, then in Flexible Space.

Work carefully at the precision of your Space word (Direct or Flexible), finding different ways to express the quality of your movement as you play with your object. Be aware of how this specific physical 'outer' action and rhythm changes your inner mood, your attitude to what you are doing, your awareness of others in the room, all your thoughts and feelings, about yourself and others. Having already done the Laban Flow workshop you will be aware of how close Direct Space is to Bound Flow and Flexible Space to Free Flow; they are indeed closely related but they are two different elements of movement, and in this exercise you need to focus on the use of Space, allowing the Flow or quality of each action to look after itself.

Exercise two: Working alone with an object, using speech

Play with your object (garment, or bag and its contents), first Directly, then Flexibly, as in Exercise one, but this time speak your thoughts in a steady stream of consciousness as you work. Try to keep that stream of quiet words going constantly. No one is listening to you, each player is doing the same exercise by himself so it does not matter what you say. The purpose of this stage is to make you aware of the changes in vocabulary, sentence structure and mental action that occur when you change one element of your movement. When you are playing a role, these changes of rhythm and, so, of mood and sensibility, are useful aspects of the differences between the character and the actor.

Exercise three: Improvisation in pairs or in a group, played silently

First improv: In pairs or in a group, stand silently as strangers waiting for a bus, just as yourselves but having chosen to be in either Direct or Flexible mode. Whenever you make eye-contact with another player, both of you change your Space action, from Direct to Flexible or from Flexible to Direct, and continue to do this throughout the exercise.

Feel the power of this change, both in yourself and in your relationships with the other people, the space and the imagined situation. When you are working in Direct Space, you will have a Direct eye-gaze connection with partners and whatever else you may look at; Direct means a clear Aim and a straight line to get it; this is apparent in your thoughts and in the spatial pathways you use. In Flexible action the reverse applies: eye-gaze is sliding and may feel rather unfocused at first; Aims are less defined and the interest is held more by the enjoyment of the processes of movement and connection than by gaining a specific result.

Second improv: Moving around the room, covering as much ground as possible with an even pace and starting either in Direct or Flexible Space, players stop still on making eye-contact with each other and change their Space word (Direct or Flexible), before moving on to meet another player.

Exercise four: Movement alone

Now work on your own again, using pure movement, not improv and behavioural action as in the first three stages. Start moving in Direct, stretching and exercising all the parts of your body and constantly trying new ways of moving. (Refer to the Six Directions, to the diagonal lines which join them, to the Three Extensions and to the Three Dimensions; to Folding and Unfolding and to Simultaneous and Successive movement.)

Do not travel as you move as this can make the work rather messy and generalised and the working space of other players is invaded. As you move in Direct Space, notice how it makes you feel inside yourself and in relation to the space, objects and people around you. You may find the rhythm slightly restrictive, possibly aggressive at times, controlled and balanced, and, after a while, limited. Direct Space can be about angles, making sharp outlines as you shape the space around you by your movement.

Now move on to Flexible action, which you will probably find to be a release (which is why we do Direct first). You may feel a faster pace, with curving, undefined lines and an unbalanced, unplanned, carefree feeling (probably in Free Flow), which you will enjoy but which, after a while, does not seem to get anywhere in particular. You have then already discovered that if you stay with one element or one rhythm for too long, you will become bored and frustrated with it. This proves our need for constant rhythmic change so as to balance our energies. It is the same in any area of your life: you need changes of activity that bring changes of thought and feeling.

When we are acting a role we often forget this necessity, even when it is indicated by the text. We establish a constant rhythm that we call 'the character', a limited place where we feel safe, and we may be afraid to allow the character to change in response to the changes of the story. And, if we are honest, those favourite rhythms may well be our own personal ones, not those of the character; this happens when we are unsure and unready – at those times we incline to pull the character towards ourselves, rather than reaching an understanding of how another person functions. Work on the basics of Laban's system puts us in control of our choices of rhythm so that we have the ability to change constantly in a lively stream of response to the inevitable changes of life.

Be careful, also, not to get stuck in a choreographic pattern in these exercises, that is, to use a series of actions which indicate Direct or Flexible Space to you, to which you return safely without exploring other means of expressing the quality of your movement. When you play your Laban rhythm sequence again, do it using only your hands, then with your face only, then with feet, spine, breathing and so on, noting the power rhythm has to change thought and emotion.

Exercise five: Movement with a partner

Stage four is repeated in pairs with a partner. Both A and B start moving (not mirroring each other but shaping the space between them and responding to each other). They both begin in Direct, feeling that balanced energy together. Then the pair does the same using Flexible Space; the moment of change can be given by the teacher or decided by the players. Be sure that your attention is on your partner, not trapped within yourself.

Once you have tried each Space word together, play them in opposition to each other; A moves in Direct Space and B in Flexible. Still working with each other, have the feeling that you are showing your partner the benefits of your chosen Space word, so that you relate to each other as you work, in pure movement without using speech.

You could use pure sound if you wish, but no words at this stage.

Exercise six: Improvisation using speech, in pairs or in a group

Taking eye-contact between players as the signal for changing your Space word (Direct or Flexible), start moving in a natural, everyday way, talking together about some neutral subject, such as clothes or the weather.

Each player starts in either Direct or Flexible mode and is ready to change their Space word when meeting the eyes of another player as they all move and talk to each other. You will find links to status transactions and power relationships between people and need to watch out for the temptation for Direct players always to be bossy shouters and their Flexible partners to stay scatty, weak and vague. Players need to observe, respect and listen to each other for the work to be specific and varied; the radical simplicity of Laban's analysis of action demands great depth and precision from the student.

THE SPACE SCALE

As with Flow we all balance our use of Space between the extremes of Direct and Flexible action that we have been using in these exercises.

However, most people have a tendency towards either one Space word or the other as a habitual or characteristic norm. Find out where you stand by observing yourself and asking your friends, and use the possibilities of change when you play a part.

This Space Scale might help. Mark with an X where you think you are at this moment, or where you feel you are habitually; then mark where you think your character might be habitually or at a precise moment in the play. You are not allowed to be at zero, which is the exact balance between the two extremes but you could be at ¼ or ½, if you wish.

The Space Scale

DIRECT										FLEXIBLE
5	4	3	2	1	0	1	2	3	4	5

It is interesting to mark where you think you are as a general state, then to check your observation with that of other people. I find that most observers put me at around 3 to 4 Direct, though I see myself as less; when I am working, of course, the Directness is demanded by my function and if I have spent many hours with a strong Direct drive, then I need to relax and restore my balance by being more Flexible, maybe by dancing or listening to music to help me relax and change rhythm.

EXERCISE IN SPATIAL PATHWAYS, FOR A GROUP OF MEN AND WOMEN

In this simple walking exercise one can explore the different feelings that come from using Direct or Flexible spatial pathways; the experience also provides an interesting look at some accepted 'norms' of how men and women interact in social space.

This exercise works best as a group of equal numbers of men and women in as large a room as possible. If there is no teacher, choose a player among you to give the signal to change. Everyone begins to walk at an even pace using Direct spatial pathways. This means having a Direct Aim, using Direct Eye-gaze, knowing where you want to get to in the room, while being aware of the others also moving. Be sure to cover all areas of the room – to avoid moving round in a boring circle, like a prisoner's exercise time, you can imagine that the floor of the room is covered in sand and that you all want to make lines of your footprints in every area.

Don't forget diagonals, neat cornering and clear purpose in your Direct action. Then, at an agreed signal from the teacher and with no break in the group action of walking, change to Flexible pathways, where players will be curving, circling, undulating through the space, with a corresponding flexibility of eye-gaze and no Direct intention to get to a specific point. People nearly always speed up when they change to Flexible pathways, so it is useful to remember, for this exercise, to keep to a walking pace.

If players wish to rest at this point, it's a good time to discuss what feelings they had during the extended Direct walking. How did they feel about other players around them? Was the Direct pathway familiar to them or strange? When would a Direct pathway be used in their daily lives? Which spatial pathway was most familiar or enjoyable for each player?

Direct pathways are connected to cities, places of work, roads, trains, efficiency, planned action, control of the surrounding Space, while Flexible pathways are used when wandering, exploring, discovering, enjoying movement for its own sake, being indecisive, adapting to surroundings. Direct Movement is linear and economic, often using only one or two of the three dimensions (height, width and depth), whereas Flexible movement uses all three.

In the next stage of the exercise, the men use Direct pathways while the women in the group swirl around them in Flexible action, then change (without stopping the walking) to the men being Flexible and the women Direct.

At the signal, the players change from Direct to Flexible pathways and vice versa on eye-contact with any other member of the group. When you have worked through Opening and Closing and are secure in these techniques, you can add consciously controlled Opening and Closing actions. You will find that these rhythmic changes happen instinctively in daily life, so you need to remember and use them in your acting.

NOTES FOR THE TEACHER OF THE SPACE WORKSHOP

There may be too many exercises for one session in this workshop; the teacher needs to decide what and when to present to suit the needs and purposes of the class.

The limbering and stretches exploring Spatial Dimensions, Directions and Extensions can be used as warm-ups or as an energetic movement session; the Six Exercises are best taken in their sequence, but each one can be used separately, as an improv or to support a rehearsal.

When taking any exercise the teacher needs to insist on precise action in response to the two contrasting Space words (Direct or Flexible). Players with little experience can muddle their way through, enjoying the fun, but the rewards come when time and care is taken, and it is for the teacher to decide when to correct and define the work.

You may find that Flexible movement is difficult for some players; often the men need help with the curving action, and women may find it hard too; these people will stay in an imprecise Direct, while believing that they are playing Flexible. Be sure to ask players to stay in their own space in the room and stop anyone who just walks about, through another's territory: walking around is not work! These players need time and help to give them confidence and precision of effort.

I find that a handclap is a useful signal for change within an exercise; I usually prepare the players for a change by saying, as they play the first stage of an exercise, 'When I clap my hands I want the Direct people to change to Flexible and the Flexible to Direct.' Feedback time is useful after these exercises: talking over the experience consolidates the learning.

21 Time

You have now worked through the elements of Flow and Space, during which you were, of course, also using the element of Time, though not with the conscious choice and control that you need for acting. From now on all exercises will involve the two Space words (Direct and Flexible) with the new Time words. Allow the element of Flow to look after itself, as you did when working on Space.

Laban called the two contrasting aspects of Time: 'Sudden' and 'Sustained'. These useful words link Time with Flow in the quality of an action and its emotional content. Sudden action is connected to surprise, shock and/or sharp control, it is a Bound-Flow instant response or impulse; the focus of the action could be in the space behind or to the side of you; it could mean flinching, retreating, escaping, welcoming or attacking. Sustained action has more of a Free-Flow quality, often graceful, gently controlled and fluid, which is why the action can continue for a period. Remember these important aspects of Time and Flow as you work on exercises and on character and emotion.

For actors I find that it is useful to look at the speed of an action and its duration separately: so I call the two contrasting aspects of SPEED: Fast or Slow and the two contrasting aspects of DURATION: Brief or Long-term.

Some words associated with Fast Speed: quick; swift; immediate; lively; instantaneous; prompt; hasty; acceleration; rush; dash; scamper; run; gallop; hustle; bustle; scuttle; scramble; race; impetuous; urgent.

Some words associated with Slow Speed: languor; deliberation; reluctance; caution; deceleration; unhurried; leisurely; patient; tentative; stealthy; imperceptible; ambling; plodding; trudge; shamble; slouch; drag; stagger; chug; limp; hobble; stroll; saunter; dawdle; hesitate.

Do not worry about Duration for the Time exercises. They will obviously be Long-term, because any new exercise needs a long time to learn and work through. This means that actions and speeds which have normally a Brief Duration (such as a fall, a sharp shove or a single handclap) may either have to take a comparatively Long-term Duration or to be played over several times.

This unnatural Duration needed when learning anything is, of course, the stuff of rehearsing and it is useful to consider the process and make friends with it, before you leave it for the Flow of performance. The reverse side of this is that in a play one has to move much more rapidly than in daily life from one situation, crisis or change of thought/feeling to another.

THE SIX EXERCISES APPLIED TO SPACE AND TIME

For the Six Exercises we will work on the Speed aspect, adding this element of Fast or Slow Time to the two Space words, Direct and Flexible. We always start with Slow Time, so that you can get used to the work. So now each stage is doubled in Duration because you will be using:

1 SLOW Time with DIRECT Space movement
2 SLOW Time with FLEXIBLE Space movement

and then the Duration will also be changed because of the Fast Speed of action:

3 FAST Time with DIRECT Space movement
4 FAST Time with FLEXIBLE Space movement

As an exercise in physical/mental control and stamina, and to give you a personal experience of doing without the pauses, stops and rhythmic changes that are an integral part of all natural action, you must establish in the Six Exercises an unchanging speed of Fast or Slow, which you will maintain throughout each stage of the work.

Slow movement **indulges-in** Time and Fast movement **fights-against** Time. Be careful not to get soggy and lethargic when Slow or to rush through Fast in an unfocused scramble. You must maintain the accuracy of your Space words (Direct or Flexible) throughout; if you find that your Space work is getting messy because of your Fast Speed, then slow down a bit and establish the accuracy of your Space word, before speeding it up again.

You also need to practise acceleration and deceleration using both Sudden and Sustained actions, so that you can change speed accurately, knowing exactly what you are doing. This is especially important for comedic timing.

Use the detailed description of each stage of the Six Exercises given in the Space workshop, pp. 214–17.

Exercise one: Working alone with an object

You work with your garment or bag using:

1 Slow Time with Direct Space
2 Slow Time with Flexible Space
3 Fast Time with Direct Space
4 Fast Time with Flexible Space

Exercise two: As one, but with spoken thoughts

Notice the differences that come from a conscious control of two elements, especially the new one of Time.

Exercise three: Improvisation

Play the three improvs, finding the power that comes from conscious variations of speed.

Exercise four: Pure movement alone

Go for the extremes of sustained speed here. It is hard not to speed up during the Slow movement and very hard to maintain the speed you establish, so this needs a lot of practice. When you do Fast movement allow yourself a slightly Briefer Duration for that stage and see how Fast you can be for that period.

This exercise can also be played with a conscious acceleration and deceleration. Remember that you have to play your Space words at the same time, and these must always be under your conscious control. You will notice the connection with Bound Flow when playing Direct and Fast and the connection with Free Flow in Flexible and Fast and in both Slow efforts, though for some people Direct is always close to Bound Flow.

When you are skilled you will be able to play with a Flow which is different to the usual connections; for instance: Fast, Direct with Free Flow; and Flexible and Slow with Bound Flow.

Exercise five: Movement with a partner

Don't get muddled with the four variations of Space and Time. Write down the four combinations if you need to, so that you can look at them. If you have a workshop leader he should make your instructions clear to you as you progress though the four combinations. Give yourself time to monitor and choose what you do, especially when you are working in opposition to your partner.

This means that both your Space and your Time words must be opposed: for instance, when Player A is Direct and Fast, then B must be Flexible and Slow. You can then progress to what happens when ONLY your Time word changes: Player A could be Flexible and Slow, while B is Flexible and Fast or A is Direct and Fast while B is Direct and Slow.

Exercise six: Improvisation using talking in a group

Avoid the dangers of muddle and stereotype as before. When you find you are working thoughtlessly, not listening to others, just stop, think and go back to your two Space and Time words.

It is best at first to keep the same Space word throughout and just change your Time word upon eye-contact with your partner.

Be aware of what Speed is habitual to you in your daily life. Do you eat quickly, make decisions quickly, think and talk quickly? Or do you have a slower breathing rhythm, a more reflective way of thinking and acting? The more you understand about your personal rhythms, the more power you have to change the balances of Space and Time to those of the role you are playing.

Here is a Time Scale. Remember that you are not allowed to be at the perfect balance of zero in the centre, but you can be at ¼ or ½ from it if you wish. First mark where you think you are NOW, at this particular moment on the Time Scale, then mark where you were at a precise moment last night and then where you were early this morning. See the differences and realise that you constantly change rhythm in every aspect of your life.

You might find it useful to mark a place for the beginning of a scene when you rehearse, then progress from that point.

The Time Scale

SLOW										FAST
5	4	3	2	1	0	1	2	3	4	5

PLAYING WITH RHYTHM: PAUSES AND STOPS

The following terms are not Laban's, but mine; I developed this work in class for the purpose of looking at ways that rhythm is used in life and acting.

Pauses and Stops are linked to Free and Bound Flow. A Pause means a temporary break in a thought or action, where the forward drive is interrupted before resuming or adapting its course. It is linked to Free Flow, where the Aim streams onwards, after the interruption. Connecting Flow to Balance, a Pause utilises a shift of balance and a change of breathing, such as a small gasp, a held breath, a little sigh or a new intake of breath.

A Stop is a complete break in a thought or action, marking the end of that subject or movement, before another different thought, action or Aim begins. It is linked to Bound Flow when you Stop in order to change. A Stop is a moment requiring total balance, a moment when time seems to stop for the player, when the heels must be allowed to drop the body-weight onto the floor. The breath deepens (or is held in shock, perhaps) and should be exhaled at each Stop during the exercises, the player waiting until the new breath arrives before moving away from the Stopping place.

In your daily life you may have experienced a Stop when you suddenly remember something as a shock and you need to Stop completely still, wherever you are, to cope with this new knowledge. Your attention is then so concentrated on the intensity of inner thought-discovery that you are, for a moment, quite unaware of whatever is going on around you. An example might be that you suddenly remember that you have left your keys on the table in the cafe . . . or did you? Where did you last see them? Could they have been dropped as you got off the bus? Or, some inner revelation might strike you out of the blue, such as, 'I'm in love', or 'They have been lying to me' or 'What I really want to do is to turn down this job.' Think of an occasion when this happened to you and remember what you did in response. Sometimes you can see a beautiful Stop when a footballer gathers his concentration before a goal-kick.

Going back to aspects of Space, one could say that a Stop can be either a folding-in of attention inwards or an opening-out of attention to an outward event: an example of an Opening Stop is the moment of 'exchange of hearts', when Romeo and Juliet see each other for the first time at the ball, or one can experience an Opening Stop at the sight of a beautiful landscape, a recognition of the wonder of life: I think an Opening Stop is often a memorable and positive experience. Don't get it confused with a Freeze: a Stop is a time of out-of-time reflection or vision, while a Freeze is a momentary cessation of movement, often in a moment of danger or crisis.

Pauses are probably easier to access: they come when you forget a name or an event and are held up in conversation while you remember it; or when you go into a room to fetch something and then forget why you are there – this can be a Stop, too.

A Pause is not a Wait: Waiting has more action and of course can last for some time; Waiting can also have aspects of anxiety and boredom, which Pauses do not have.

Pauses and Stops are tough to do. They need courage and commitment because it feels that they last forever and you worry that 'nothing is happening' and 'I am not doing anything' (that feeling is good; it means that your anxiety is not interfering with your talent – you're fighting the temptation to 'do' something), but if you ask other players to watch you, you will find that they especially rejoice in good complete Stops. These can be thrilling to play and to see when done in the here and now, with no compromise.

You may be surprised to discover how much of your energy is wasted in preparation for your next action during a Pause or a Stop. Do not fool yourself! You cannot fool your audience, because it shares your experience. Persevere until 100 per cent of you is involved in your Pause or Stop. It is helpful to let all your breath out during a Pause or Stop and allow yourself to move onwards only when the new breath is ready to fill your lungs. For Pauses you might want to hold your breath for the moment, but try letting the breath out as well.

The units in a script use both Pauses and Stops to mark the changes of subject in a scene). In speech, a new subject demands a change of pitch and rhythm in the voice and, as a general rule, the slighter changes or shifts of subject or action use a Pause and a comparatively slight change of vocal pitch and rhythm, while the major changes demand a Stop, with a strongly marked change of vocal pitch and rhythm. This is why it is best to unit and re-punctuate a script for the speaking voice, deciding when to breathe and what single stresses you will use, etc., marking the difference between Pauses and Stops.

Acting is easy: just open the door, hit the mark and tell the truth.

(Robert Mitchum)

RUNNING, STOPPING AND PAUSING

Focus: This exercise gives practice to a group in 'hitting the mark' while learning to play Pauses and Stops correctly. Players should allow their Pauses and Stops to be of longer duration than might be normal in daily life, so that they have time to concentrate on their sensations and get them right. The group could play this game without telling their peers whether they are Stopping or Pausing, so that the 'audience' has to guess which one they are doing.

This game requires a large clear space. Mark an X in the centre of the space to indicate the point where the actor must either pause or stop in his run from one corner of the room to the other, on a diagonal pathway.

The actor will learn to 'hit the mark' accurately without looking down, a useful skill for camera and theatre work. Observe your breathing patterns in this game.

For this exercise there are two kinds of running:

1 The actor runs TOWARDS.
2 The actor runs AWAY FROM.

The Space word is Direct, though moments of Flexibility may occur spontaneously in the running. The Time word can be changed to a faster speed once the exercise can be played accurately at a medium speed.

1 To begin with, the actor runs towards the opposing corner, Pausing on the spot marked X and then continuing his run. The whole action is in Free Flow, with the Pause suspending or interrupting the journey, but with the balance tipping freely into the continuing action. The Pause is the 'comma' in the 'sentence' of action.

2 The actor runs Away From his starting corner, into the opposite one; his action is one of leaving, escaping from, rather than arriving as in the first run. He Pauses on the X spot as before.

3 The actor runs Towards the opposite corner, but this time with a Stop on the X spot. The test here is to have no forward planning, no preparation, to be truly in the here and now. Once you have mastered a true, uncompromising Stop you can be proud of that achievement and use it in your acting. It is the answer to playing surprise, shock, crisis and all those difficult moments of high drama or comedy.

4 The actor runs Away From the starting corner, with a Stop on point X. The sequence can be extended by asking for a turn as well as a Pause or Stop on point X. This turn must be planned as a right-hand or left-hand turn before the actor starts his run. This is another test of accuracy and physical memory; we can see the point X as camera position or a spotlight, so that the actor must be 'seen' at that precise spot, and must turn in a certain direction, while

staying within the truth of his running and playing the Pause or the Stop with a sensation of spontaneity. You can then develop the exercise so that the first half of the run (before you reach point X) is an Away From run and the second half is a Towards run, or vice versa.

If each actor plans her runs, Pauses and Stops without telling the rest of the group what they will be, then her audience can judge how clear her 'story' is. Adding Closed and Open responses to Space is also useful (see pp. 209–11). For instance, an Open advance could end with a Closed Stop on meeting a partner; or a Closed advance could change to an Open Stop; also one can extend the exercise so that two or more players, coming from different directions, meet, then pass on or return to their starting places. Later in the training, the game can be played with groups, using the Eight Effort Actions (explained below, p. 241) or individual elements of Space, Time and Force, and the travelling can be in timed sequences so that players can learn to move in precise relation to each other; a useful skill for actors.

> The essence of acting is its apparent spontaneity.
>
> (Henry Irving)[1]

MOVEMENT SENTENCES

I began to use this 'squiggle writing' as an informal shorthand for myself and then found that students enjoyed using it too; the idea is that an actor can use his own informal written shapes to note down any rhythms that he needs to remember in his script or notebook. It in no way attempts to replace or to copy Laban's precise notation of movement.[2]

Actors can devise their own 'movement sentences' using punctuation to indicate Pauses (a comma) and Stops (a full stop) and drawn lines for Direct and Flexible movement and spatial pathways. You can also indicate the Duration of a movement by the line length and the Speeds you require by putting an 'F' for Fast and a 'S' for slow above your Space lines. You will need a large piece of paper and a pencil.

Example:

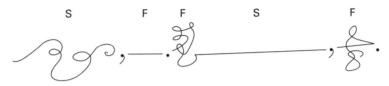

This 'movement sentence' diagram means a Flexible, Slow movement of Medium Duration, followed by a Pause, then a Direct, Fast movement of Brief Duration, followed by a Stop. After that, a Flexible, Fast movement of Brief Duration, followed immediately by a Direct, Slow movement of Long-term Duration, ending with a Pause, and a Flexible, Fast Brief movement, finishing with a Stop.

Try interpreting this 'sentence' yourself, using pure movement. It may be hard to remember, so keep it in front of you until you can play it reliably without forgetting what comes next. Actors need to train their physical memory as much as their line-learning one. An actor who remembers accurately the moves and placements of a scene is treasured by a director and will be employed again and again, while the actor who is physically inept and unreliable holds back the work of the whole company.

Now you can invent a movement sentence of your own – you cannot go wrong. Whatever your choices are, they are right for you, as long as you interpret them accurately.

Play your own sentence on your own in pure movement and ask a partner to call out or to note down, using their own squiggles, what they think you are doing at each point as you move. This is an excellent lesson in observation and accuracy. Then take a partner and teach your friend your movement sentence and learn his from him. So, now you each have two sentences which you can perform in sequence, for a longer duration, to test stamina and memory.

Example of two movement sentences:

PLAYER A:

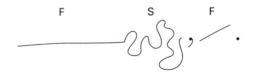

Direct, Fast, Long-term, into Flexible, Slow, Medium Duration, followed by Pause, then Direct, Fast, Brief, ending with Stop.

PLAYER B:

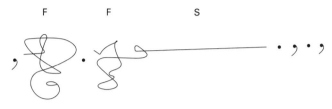

Starting with a Pause, then a Flexible, Fast, Brief action with a Stop, then the Flexible Fast, Brief action again, a direct, Slow Long-term movement, another stop, a Pause, and ending with a Stop followed by another Pause.

The danger here is that you will learn 'choreographically', which is not useful learning for an actor, that is, that you will repeat a pattern of movement in which each element will be represented by a gesture, so that the sequence soon becomes meaningless. The best way round that problem is for each player to read out his movement sentence to his partner, rather than demonstrating it physically: this means that the learning partner interprets the instructions in his own way, rather than copying.

After this, make sure that each time you perform the movement sentence you interpret it in new ways; for instance, you can play it with the whole body in one place. Then play it travelling. Then with hands only (Delsarte[3] said that the hands are the direct agents of the mind); from a sitting position; using only your face; breath; feet; shoulders; and so on. Then with behavioural action, as in a silent scene (not using mime but using real objects, as in putting your shoes and coat on, tidying your bag or writing a letter).

The movement sentence can be extended to an improvised scene with a partner. First, both of you play the same sentence and explore the effect of two people acting with the same rhythmic structure. Then play it again; this time your partner plays his sentence and you play your own, both adapting as necessary to the other player, while keeping your own chosen rhythmic structure. It is interesting to consider the use of shared and opposing rhythms in daily life: to share a rhythm with a partner can be supportive, fun and intimate but also aggressive or miserable, as during a row, or when you are both moaning and wanting sympathy from each other. Think of a time when someone tried to change your rhythm: maybe you were depressed and a friend wanted to cheer you up, or maybe you were being rowdy and someone wanted you to calm down. Any scene can be looked at in terms of the rhythmic transactions between characters.

Once you are friendly with the idea of movement sentences, you may find them useful as little 'maps' of a scene, the dynamic both of outer and inner psychological action.

Make a 'movement sentence' and go through the Six Exercises with it (p. 213). The work is similar to that which you have just been doing above, but uses objects and speech as well.

There are now only two more words, those of the element of Force, to learn before you experience the combination of movement elements that Laban calls the Eight Effort Actions.

A long time devoted to small details exalts us and increases our strength.
(Hermann Hesse)

NOTES FOR THE TEACHER OF THE TIME WORKSHOP

As always, the teacher needs to consolidate one aspect of Time, especially when it is combined with a Space word, before moving on to the next aspect. Students should be secure with the techniques of the Space workshop before moving on to Time; you could remind them of the need to stay in Bound Flow while learning new things; this will ensure precision in their work.

People seem to have no problems in using squiggle writing to build movement sentences, but they do need to keep their sentence with them on a piece of paper while playing it out, so as to remember it accurately. I ask each player to do different unrehearsed actions while they play their movement sentence, such as, 'go to the chair on the left, pick up the coat on the chair and take it over to the table on the right'. This is so that they cannot 'choreograph' their movement sentence in advance, which would take the spontaneity and active learning out of the exercise.

I remind the 'audience' that they are the real workers as they watch and note down in squiggles what they observe of the players' movement sentences, and I give time after each little 'turn' for the audience to check what they observed against what the performer intended to convey. Very often we find that the Time element is unclear . . . was that movement meant to be Slow or Fast? This observation from peers is useful and non-judgemental, pointing out to the player what aspects of action require more work and thought.

It is helpful to practise 'listening' or 'reacting' rhythms, not only the rhythms coming from the more active partner in an improv or pair exercise, but also what happens when people share a rhythm and what happens when one or both change that rhythm.

22 Force

Laban himself found it difficult to choose words to express the complexities of action and I think that the right word for the force of gravity and power in movement is the hardest to fix on. He called it Weight, but I find that many people prefer the words Strength, Power, Energy or Force. I am choosing the word 'Force'. This element can be either Strong or Light. Laban's use of the phrases 'firm touch' and 'fine touch' are helpful.

Some words associated with Strong Force: massive; ponderous; controlling; influence; potent; enduring; authority; firm; compelling; stable; solid; sturdy; hard; dominating; might; muscularity; irresistible; intense; aggressive; active; dynamism; pressure; compulsion; stress; drive; haul; heave; rough; turbulent; savage; resisting; passive; stagnant.

Some words associated with Light Force: buoyant; volatile; fluff; thistledown; levitating; gentle; unresisting; soft; delicate; tender; nimble; changeable; weak; floppy; faint; languorous; quiet; thoughtless; merry.

Force for actors has three aspects:

1 **The pull of gravity**: to be indulged-in or fought-against. An extreme indulging-in gravity has already been experienced through the Falling and Saving game and the fighting-against aspect in the various stages of the Free- and Bound-Flow exercises in the Flow workshop (p. 200). Strong Force, indulging-in gravity, is hard to achieve without a heavy collapsing or a strained muscular tension, so not only the word but the Movement Effort needs careful thought and precise performance. Light Force, fighting-against gravity, though easier to achieve, also needs care if it is not to become flighty, generalised, weak or flimsy. It does not signify a lack of muscle tone.

2 **The kinetic force** (either Weighty or Light): to move the body in space. The actor as artist should be in a state of ease and lightness, Free Flow and freedom from tension. Mastery of movement allows the actor to portray a character in tension without physically tying his voice and body into knots. This is possible with isolation of effort and conscious control: for instance, the character's hands can be tense and anguished, while her voice and breathing remain free and capable. (Lady Macbeth in the sleep-walking scene is an example of this requirement.)

3 **The external force**: to be overcome through an appropriate use of energy – Strong for a heavy object and Light for a light one. The actor might need to endow a prop with the weight that the prop represents, for instance, a 'heavy' box supposedly made of metal might in reality be a lightweight one made of plywood; a 'golden' crown might be papier-mâché and a 'full' suitcase might actually be light and empty. Actors need to have conscious control of their breathing when working with props or in stage fights etc., so that their relationship with Force is believable, while they retain the muscular freedom essential for creativity.

The Force Scale

LIGHT (FINE TOUCH)   STRONG (FIRM TOUCH)

5   4   3   2   1   0   1   2   3   4   5

The central point marked zero in this scale represents the actor's own normal strength or Force level at the moment of the exercise. It is important to be aware of how your energy is as yourself before you attempt to change it for the demands of the exercise or the scene: be sure that you start from a place of truth and do not muddle yourself by pretending, for instance, that you are not tired or that you are physically stronger than you truly are at that moment.

LIFTING THE CHAIR

When we are little children we spend much time experimenting with the appropriate Force effort for handling objects: a toddler lifting a paper cup might use too much Force and crush the cup with his grip;

he will then learn that he needs to use a very Light Force to lift this cup, a grip that is Light but still with enough energy to keep a secure hold as he moves the cup. Having solved this problem, the child may then have to adapt again when the same cup is full of heavy water, when he will also need the skill of balance to avoid spills. Learning appropriate Force requires a lot of practice!

Focus: This exercise plays with differing levels of Force, using an ordinary upright chair so that the actor has an object of static weight against which he can measure his changes of force.

Space, time and numbers: A lot of space is required between each chair. Each player works alone with his chair, there is no interaction between players. Allow 20 minutes for this exercise.

SAFETY NOTE: It is essential that players spread out and that each player, with his or her own chair, stays in his or her own area and does not travel, so that the chairs being lifted never get close to any player or each other. It might be better to divide the group into two parts, so that each player has a partner watching to monitor and remind the player to stay safely in control.

The actor must keep in contact with the chair throughout. There can be the danger of a player throwing or dropping his chair, especially when playing the Stronger Force, which could lead to an accident.

Throughout this exercise, the idea is that the chair remains at its real or 'natural' weight. The changes of force are only within the actor. Start the exercise by lifting the chair, using your own Force as it is at that moment, so that you know your 'neutral' or central point from which you will become Lighter or Stronger.

a. The chair remains at Weight zero, you are at Force 5 Light, so you have no chance of lifting the chair. You only have the power of extremely Fine Touch or Light Force. Your Touch would be appropriate for lifting a feather only. Note: you are not weak; the delicate Touch means that there is control and tone in the muscles being used; you are simply using an inappropriate level of your natural strength for the task of lifting a chair.

Watch out for held breath, clenched mouth, bunched muscles anywhere in the body, frowns, tongues sticking out, or a clenching preparation for action before even the lightest lift. This is an excellent exercise for becoming aware of how you 'prepare to feel' when acting, and how you 'drive with the handbrake on' in your acting when you tense and hold the body even before you start the action.

b. You are now at Force 4 Light. There is a little more Force in the attempted lifting of the chair, but still not enough to get it off the ground, though your hands may be able to grip or hold the chair to some extent.

c. You are now at Force 3 Light; you can probably move the chair, though not yet off the ground. Your Force effort and your adaptation to gravity are becoming more balanced between Heavy and Light.

d. At Force 2 Light, you can now lift the chair with an effort, for a short time and not high. Be careful! The exercise is not about the chair, it is about you. The point of it is that you should understand how you respond to these chosen changes of your strength, so that you have conscious control of those choices.

e. You are now very close to your natural Force in lifting the chair. It is useful to return then to your state of neutrality, lifting it with your natural strength at Force level zero.

f. At Strong Force level 1 you are now deliberately stronger than the chair. You lift it easily, enjoying your natural Firm Touch.

g. Over Strong Force levels 2, 3 and 4 you become progressively stronger, so you feel 'as if' the chair becomes lighter. It is important that this growing power does not show itself in tension or muscular straining. The idea is that you are now so strong that you can easily lift any object, without anxiety or tension.

h. At Strong Force 5 you are Superman/Superwoman! You rejoice in your amazing power and you never let go of that chair or throw it around.

An enjoyable extension of this game is to work as a group of several women and several men (and several chairs), playing it as a speaking improvisation. The women begin at Force 4 to 5 Light, while the men are at Force 4 or 5 Strong. The task, played between a man and a woman in a pair or as part of the group, is for the Strong men to teach the Light women how to lift the chair, without changing their Force number. The 'pay-off' of the game is when you reverse the Force levels and the roles, so that the women, playing at Force 4 to 5 Strong, show the men, who are at Force 4 to 5 Light, how to lift the chair. The reversal of stereotypes pleases everyone.

SIX EXERCISES RELATED TO FORCE

Now you will be combining all four elements of movement as you work on conscious control of your Force in this sequence. Your effort will be either Strong or Light.

Exercise one: Working alone with an object

With a naturally lightweight object, such as the garment you are play-ing with, you will be using an inappropriate amount of Strength when playing Heavy Force. If you imagine that you are ironing the garment, pressing it firmly with a heavy iron, pushing your whole body-weight into the floor, through the garment, this may help to give you a feeling of weightiness through the body. Remember that the exercise is for you, not for your T-shirt. It is you who must be Light or Strong, not the object, which is only there as a means to an end.

Exercise two: As Exercise one, with spoken thoughts

Vocal and mental Force are not manifested only in loud volume or hoarse growling; think of your Strong Force as intensity of voice, emotion and action, and of your Light Force as delicacy, precision and power controlled in Fine Touch.

Exercise three: Improvisations

The improvs might be difficult. Work on Strong Force is not about stamping and tension versus Light, whispery flutterings. Give yourselves plenty of time to find accurate expressions of these two Force words and help each other by observation and advice.

Exercise four: Movement alone

This stage will give you a chance first to feel and indulge-in the pull of gravity, then to feel the lightness and freedom of anti-gravitational action away from the earth. You might like to play this exercise after Exercise one, then to do Exercises two and three later on.

Exercise five: Movement with a partner, without speech

Concentrate on what your partner is doing here and allow it to influence what you do; do not block her off because of the technical details you may be struggling with.

Exercise six: Improvs with a partner or a group

Avoid stereotypes, keep your work accurate and stop at once if you feel trapped or muddled, so that you can sort out what you are doing.

MOVEMENT SENTENCES USING THREE ELEMENTS

The element of Force can now be added to any movement sentence. You can make this clear in your diagram by using Heavy or Light lines.
Example:

A Direct, Fast, Strong, Brief action, then a Pause; a Direct, Slow, Light, Long-term action going into a Flexible, Slow, Light, Long-term movement, ending in a Stop; then a Flexible, Fast, Strong, Brief action followed by a Pause, into a Direct, Fast, Light, Brief action, into a Flexible, Slow, Light Medium Duration action which merges into a Flexible, Slow, Light, Brief action, which finishes the sentence.

To practise your movement sentences combining the element of Force with those of Space and Time, go through the sequence described in the Time workshop (p. 221).

Laban gives us a code word for each of the eight combinations of the elements. These code words, which encapsulate all the detailed work you have done so far, are called 'Effort Actions' and these are worked through in the final Laban workshop (Chapter 23).

NOTES FOR THE TEACHER OF THE FORCE WORKSHOP

I find that the element of Force is the most difficult for students, which is why I leave it to the last; Strong Force seems hardest to play accurately, so it may need more time and correction than Light Force.

In all these exercises, the teacher will need to allow students to go through the clichés (Strong Force always loud and angry, Light Force always weak and ineffective) and then widen the range of expression of the element. The temptation is for the student to play his opinion or judgement of each element and the teacher needs to lead him past that instant interpretation of an element to its actual simplicity and beauty.

23 The Eight Laban Effort Actions

INTRODUCTION

Each of the eight combinations of one Space word (Direct or Flexible) with one Time word (Fast or Slow) and one Force word (Strong or Light) is called an Effort Action. Laban gave a 'code word' for each of these: they serve as useful shorthand when talking about movement rhythms. However, it is important to learn the 'ingredients' for each Effort Action first, carefully, with conscious choice, so that you are aware of its full range, instead of going for a generalised effect aroused by the code word.

When I am teaching this system I keep the code words until the very end of the course and even then do not encourage actors to write them down or to learn them by rote until they can build them one element at a time, through an organic physical experience, which leads to true understanding.

You can see that each Effort Action has its opposite in all three elements of Space, Time and Force. For example, FLOAT (Flexible Space/Slow Time/Light Force) is totally opposed to PUNCH (Direct Space/Fast Time/Strong Force). Each has a pair where two elements are opposed and one element is shared, for example GLIDE (Direct Space/Slow Time/Light Force) and FLICK (Flexible Space/Fast Time/Light Force), where the only similarity is in the Light Force. And each has a pair where two elements are shared and only one is opposed, for example, PRESS (Direct Space/Slow Time/Strong Force) and WRING (Flexible Space/Slow Time/Strong Force) in which only the Space word is different.

When you first perform the Effort Actions you work in a Long-term Duration, as with any new exercise, and there can be a danger that

Chart of the Eight Effort Actions

SPACE	TIME	FORCE	CODE WORD	SYMBOL
Direct	Slow	Light	**Glide**	
Flexible	Fast	Strong	**Slash**	
Direct	Slow	Strong	**Press**	
Flexible	Fast	Light	**Flick**	
Direct	Fast	Strong	**Punch**	
Flexible	Slow	Light	**Float**	
Direct	Fast	Light	**Dab**	
Flexible	Slow	Strong	**Wring**	

they become stereotyped and rather crude in effect. Work carefully against this tendency, mastering one Effort at a time.

A suggested process is for you to:

1 Try the Six Exercises with each Effort Action.
2 Apply each of the Effort Actions to specific tasks.

In opening a door I might push the key into the lock with a sharp Punch, turn it with a Wring if the lock is stiff, then push the door open gently with a Gliding Effort. Picking up a broken glass from the floor I could perform the task Directly, Quickly and Lightly (Dab) or, if I were careless or drunk, Flexibly, Quickly and Strongly (Slash), or with an angry Punch (Direct, Fast, Strong), a fluttery Flick (Flexible, Fast, Light), a neurotic Wring (Flexible, Slow, Strong), an inefficient Float (Flexible, Slow, Light), a calm Glide (Direct, Slow, Light), or a burdened Press (Direct, Slow, Strong). The Effort, or rhythm, would depend on my situation, which is to say my 'character' at that moment. My need is to pick up the glass but my strategy for how I do that varies according to the situation I am in.

Try this with a simple action such as turning the pages of a book, writing your name, putting your shoes on or searching for a pen in your bag and see how your mood, thoughts and attitudes to objects and people (including yourself) change. This is the power that Laban's analysis of movement gives to the actor. It is essential for the Method of Physical Action, as it enables the actor to choose his rhythm and through that to have access to genuine organic feeling and action at all stages of rehearsal and performance.

3   Now, explore a sequence moving from one Effort Action to another in pure movement.

The series should progress smoothly and without stopping from one Effort Action to the next, changing one or possibly two elements at a time, with a smooth flow from one rhythm to the next. Remember that each rhythm creates powerful emotions in you, and do not get exhausted. If you are working by yourself, have the sequence of rhythms written down where you can refer to them; otherwise you could ask a partner to read them out to you, using the following example:

Start with Direct/Slow/Strong (Press)
Change the Force to Light (Glide)
Change the Time to Fast (Dab)
Change the Space to Flexible (Flick)
Change the Force to Strong (Slash)
Change the Space to Direct (Punch)
Change the Space to Flexible and the Time to Slow (Wring)
And end by changing the Force to Light (Float)

It is a good idea to end with a Float as everyone enjoys it and it provides a restful and co-operative feeling for the players.

Laban suggests that each person has a basic rhythm or Effort Action which is closest to their personality and it is helpful to find your own and that of others.

The feeling and effect of each Effort Action changes according to whether it opens or closes: action directed outwards to partners or the surrounding space can be generous, aggressive or grabbing, and so on, depending on the situation of the scene, while actions closing inwards could be neurotic, sensuous, selfish, nurturing, preening or withhold-ing, etc. And each Effort can be experienced at all three extensions, though in early exercises it will be learned probably at the Far extension where the body reaches outwards.

Experienced at the close, inner-space of the body/mind these rhythms can provide the organic emotion needed for truthful acting. Your character will always have a specific Effort for each situation, according to her feelings and the situation of the scene.

ATTENTION, DECISION, INTENTION, PRECISION

Laban says that:

1 Space connects to attention. What is happening now? Is the action in myself or around me Direct or Flexible in nature?
2 Time connects to decision. What is my decision about this situa-tion? How much time is necessary for the activation of my decision? Does my action demand Slow or Fast speed and a Brief or Long-term Duration?
3 Force connects to intention. What is my intention regarding this event? Is my response forceful or light? Am I reacting to this strongly or gently? (Note, a strong inner response to an event can be handled with a comparatively light touch and a trivial event can generate an unexpectedly powerful energy.)
4 Flow is connected to precision. This event is happening (either in me or in my surroundings). So, will my specific response be to limit and control it or to freely allow it to happen?[1]

In Laban's own words

In Laban's 1947 book *Effort: Economy in Body Movement*,[2] in which he records his analyses of the movements of workers in an industrial plant, the chapter entitled 'Psychological Aspects of Effort Control' contains the following useful comments:

TIME: 'People moving with easy Effort seem to be freer than those moving with obviously stressed effort. The latter seem to be struggling against something. [Laban is talking about subjective movements here, that is, those that do not deal with objects and have therefore no outer cause for struggle.] Is this perhaps a fight against Time? [There is] an Effort attitude towards Time. [People can be seen to] swim in an ocean of Time or to race against Time.'

SPACE: 'Easy movers [in Space] might be observed to use a great deal of flexibility and twists in their Efforts. That means they apparently swim, circulate and twist most thoroughly through any possible region of Space, but there are others who deal very sparingly with their moving Space. Such people seem to take careful account of the extension and expansion of their movements which appear to be as Direct as possible; the need of an occasional excursion into Space causes them a clearly visible and highly-stressed effort.'

FORCE: 'We may also distinguish another main characteristic of Effort and this is the presence or lack of bodily Force. Easy effort will show no struggle against time or against Weight, but rather indulgence in each or both of these factors. A person with an entire neglect of speed takes a lot of Time. He or she is, so to speak, bathing, swimming or even submerging in a sea of Time. The person whose bodily energy is lacking seems to enjoy his weightiness and to relax happily in being immersed in the general gravity of nature. Now the strugglers against Weight and the racers against Time are surely different characters; and so also do those differ who are continuously immersed in a lot of Time from those indulging in the experience of their own Weight and in the Weight of their surroundings.'

FLOW: 'People do not move either suddenly or deliberately, weakly or forcefully, flexibly or directly only. We can distinguish the Flow of movement of a person, which can be free or bound, whatever velocity, space expansion or force the movement might have. Some people seem to enjoy letting their movements flow, while others show an obvious reluctance to do so.'

NOTES FOR THE TEACHER OF THE EIGHT EFFORT ACTIONS

The group will only be ready for this workshop if they have absorbed the previous classes on each of the four elements of action. Many teachers of Laban start at the end, using the 'code words' for the Eight Effort Actions and working backwards from there; but I find that many students taught in this way learn the words only, not their meaning or creative uses.

I recommend a thorough Bound-Flow teaching process, using each workshop in sequence and relating this wonderful system of observation and control ('control' meaning in this context 'freedom to choose'), to all aspects of human social behaviour as well as to the craft of acting.

The teacher of the Effort Actions could find music to express the essential quality of each rhythm, or could suggest that students bring a painting, or link an Effort with an aspect of nature or any work of art. During an extended workshop, lasting for some weeks, at the Royal National Theatre Studio, actors from the company enjoyed painting their impressions of the Effort Actions as well as finding pieces of text and music to express them.

It is helpful to spend time on improvs that use shared Efforts or that have one or more partners changing rhythms; this can lead to a practical understanding of the rhythmic needs of a scene in any play and is a great help in acting and directing.

THE LABAN EFFORT ACTIONS: EXAMPLES IN SOUND AND TEXT

Punch

PUNCH (Direct/Fast/Strong) is the strongest and most sudden, dramatic and violent of all the Efforts. In movement it can be a powerful thrust, a stamp, a jump, a kick, a loud clap of hands; in sound a drumbeat, a loud crash, an abrupt chord, a thunderclap; in speech a shout, a cry of triumph, a warning yell, an attack, a big 'No!' or 'Yes!'

Punch is usually of a very brief duration, because of its powerful force, and it is felt to be in Bound Flow because of its Direct spatial quality. However, a Free-Flow, Long-term Punch Effort could be a battle-charge, a horse race or the climax of a speech such as Olivier's

'Once more into the breach, dear friends, once more', in his film of *Henry V*.

The following speech, in which old Capulet attacks his daughter Juliet when she refuses to marry Paris, his choice of a husband for her, exemplifies Punch in text. You can feel the battering force in the series of one-syllable words, sharp consonants and the relentless drive of the verse:

> An you be mine, I'll give you to my friend;
> An you be not, hang, beg, starve, die in the streets,
> For, by my soul, I'll ne'er acknowledge thee,
> Nor what is mine shall never do thee good.
> Trust to 't. Bethink you. I'll not be forsworn.
>
>   (*Romeo and Juliet*, Act 3, Sc. 5)

Some words associated with Punch: stamp; prod; bump; hit; tramp; tread; knock; thump; whack; pummel; batter; bash; sock; cosh; cudgel; club; stun; spank; thrash; beat; flog; spurn; push; shove; throw; jolt.

Float

FLOAT (Indirect/Slow/Light) is the opposite of Punch, being the most wavering, soft, gentle, sustained, buoyant, thistledown, caressing Effort of all. In movement Float is hovering, drifting, roundabout, legato, 'high' or 'spaced-out', etc. In sound it is gentle breathing, humming, singing, light bells ringing. In Speech Float can be delicate, vague, poetic, liquid, beautiful, often where musicality seems more important than immediate sense; it has an insistent Free Flow because of its Flexibility.

In this example the extended vowel sounds, irregular line endings and liquid consonants provide a Floating atmosphere that enhances the story of pagan deities leaving England sadly at the birth of Christ:

> The lonely mountains o'er,
> And the resounding shore,
> A voice of weeping heard, and loud lament;
> From haunted spring and dale,
> Edged with poplar pale,

The parting Genius is with sighing sent,
With flower-enwoven tresses torn
The Nymphs in twilight shade of tangled thickets mourn.
(John Milton, 'Hymn on the Morning of Christ's Nativity')

Words associated with Float: drift; flow; swing; sway; trail; waft; stream; ripple; bubble; levitate; fluctuate.

Slash

SLASH is Flexible, Sudden and Strong, often brief in duration because of its Force, and veering between Bound Flow because of its Speed and Force and Free Flow because of its Flexible Space. In action Slash can be stretching, twisting, spiralling and pleasurably sprawling when it has an Open, Unfolding action, but if it is Closed and Folded Inwards, Slash can become aggressive to the self and to others, whipping, struggling, flinging, throwing and twisting. In sound Slash can be groaning, crying out, moaning loudly or deeply, screaming or yelling, either in pain or in pleasure. In speech Slash is violent, with abrupt or rapidly sliding changes of pitch, volume and rhythm because of its flexibility. Although Strong Force usually means that Slash has Brief Duration, few expressions of feeling can be stronger.

An example in text is this speech by the widowed queen Elizabeth when she hears of her husband's death; she rushes in with her hair 'about her ears' to tell the rest of the court and royal family, including Edward's mother, the Duchess of York.

Flexibility comes from the abrupt changes of subject and the rhetorical questions; the feeling seems to have aspects of both Free and Bound Flow in it – this is experienced in the breathing pattern necessary for the speech. The Force and Speed of the speech are clear and the other characters' reactions to Elizabeth's crisis reinforce the terror of the scene:

ELIZABETH: Ah, who shall hinder me to wail and weep?
To chide my fortune, and torment myself?
I'll join with black despair against my soul
And to myself become an enemy.
DUCHESS: What means this scene of rude impatience?

ELIZABETH: To make an act of tragic violence.
Edward, my lord, thy son, our king, is dead.
Why grow the branches now the root is gone?
Why wither not the leaves that want their sap?
If you will live, lament; if die, be brief,
That our swift-wingèd souls may catch the King's
Or like obedient subjects follow him
To his new kingdom of ne'er changing night.

(*Richard III*, Act 2, Sc. 2)

Some words associated with Slash: wrench; jerk; shake; gash; scythe; grind; crunch; lash out; merciless; unsparing; dashing; contorted; coiled; distorted; convoluted.

Glide

GLIDE is the opposite of Slash. It is Direct/Slow/Light. In movement, Glide's lightness, directness and slow, sustained pace make it calm, thoughtful, soothing and purposeful. It flows outwards freely, rather than being turned introspectively inwards, though it can have a meditative, solitary, self-sufficient peacefulness. The Slow Speed and Light Force give Glide a Free Flow, as in skating, though it could also have a Bound Flow, as in stepping carefully, stopping to make sure that one's tread could not be heard.

In sound, Gliding can be vocalised in a sustained, unwavering noise like humming on one note or like a continuous, soft drum roll. In speech, Glide has a lulling, hushing quality, 'the murmur of innumerable bees', where sound atmosphere is enhancing the sense of the phrase; sometimes in speech Glide can be used to get a clear message across in a calm, smooth and organised manner.

Milton uses lengthened vowels, many of them simple single sounds, rather than diphthongs, with voiced consonants to make them deep and sonorous, as he invokes the spirit of thoughtful meditation:

Come, pensive nun, devout and pure,
Sober, steadfast and demure,
All in a robe of darkest grain,
Flowing with majestic train
And sable stole of Cypress Lawn

Over thy decent shoulders drawn.
Come, but keep thy wonted state,
With even step and musing gait
And looks commercing with the skies,
Thy rapt soul sitting in thine eyes.

(John Milton, 'Il Penseroso')

Some words associated with Glide: roll; slip; slide; frictionless; coast; freewheel; ski; cruise; fly; gentle; smooth; stealth.

Wring

WRING (Flexible/Slow/Strong) can be sustained over a Long-term Duration, especially when it is a sensuous or pleasurable Unfolding action; when turned inwards, however, Wring can be self-centred, tortuous and convoluted, with a feeling of physical, mental or emotional suffering. There is a strong connection with Free Flow because of its Flexibility but it can also be experienced in Bound Flow, when the drive of the action is interrupted by Stops and Pauses.

In sound, Wring can be groaning, moaning, calling or complaining. In speech it can be extended mourning, despairing or protesting, or, when used in pleasure, it can luxuriate in strong sensual feeling. This speech by the Duchess of York in *Richard III* illustrates the qualities of a Wring in text through the twisting changes of images of suffering, the opposing ideas of 'dead life, blind sight', etc., and the long vowels of the first two lines. Here she is addressing Queen Elizabeth, who is now in the same sad situation as her mother-in-law, having lost her children, her crown, her husband and her happiness:

Dead life, blind sight, poor mortal living ghost,
Woe's scene, world's shame, grave's due by life usurp'd,
Brief abstract and record of tedious days,
Rest thy unrest on England's lawful earth
Unlawfully made drunk with innocents' blood.

(*Richard III*, Act 4, Sc. 4)

Some words associated with Wring: knead; ache; pain; writhe; squirm; torment; rack; excruciate; mangle; tangle; twist; shake fervently; distress; afflict; wreathe; coil; extort; distort.

Dab

DAB (Direct/Fast/Light) is the opposite of Wring. Dab's movement is bird-like, darting, crisp, staccato, pattering, efficient, expert at a mechanical task; maybe irritating, bossy or managing in its briskness and precision.

In sound Dab is percussive, tapping, possibly disjointed, with a powerful Bound Flow that comes from the Direct and Fast aspects of the rhythm. A Free-Flow Dab is usually a habitual and expert mechanical or physical skill, where the player's professional art creates a smooth Flow over the Speed of the Dabbing action. The dancing of Fred Astaire is an example of this: while his feet are tapping in an intricate and syncopated Dab, the grace of his head and upper body creates the impression of ease, delight and artistry, which shows itself in an irresistible sensation of freedom.

In Speech Dab is decisive, tidy, sharp, perhaps impatient, with fast-thinking reactions and precise diction, enjoying the clarity of consonants and delivery. Milton achieves this Lightness and Speed by using many unvoiced consonants (such as in the last line here) and short simple vowels, as he invokes the spirit of playfulness:

> Haste thee, nymph, and bring with thee
> Jest and youthful jollity,
> Quips and cranks and wanton wiles
> Nods and becks and wreathed smiles
> Such as hang on Hebe's cheek
> And love to live in dimple sleek;
> Sport that wrinkled Care derides
> And Laughter holding both his sides;
> Come and trip it as ye go,
> On the light fantastic toe.
>
> (John Milton, 'L'Allegro')

Some words associated with Dab: rap; tap; clap; pat; nudge; dig; flip; scratch; lick; pinch; play; jerk; pluck; peck; dabble.

Press

PRESS is Direct, Slow and uses Strong Force, often with a Sustained Duration. It can achieve its Aims by perseverance and sheer force, being firm, sturdy, deliberate and probably reluctant or slow to change course or adapt to others. In movement, Press uses the force of gravity in a slow fall or rise, like ironing a heavy garment, pushing against a wall, lifting a weighty object, or wading through water or snow.

Press can use either Bound or Free Flow, as appropriate. In sound, Press is like a powerful sustained drum roll; an uninflected stream of loud noise. As it is a Slow Punch, you need to be careful to get the Slow Speed when Pressing.

In speech, Press can be pompous, boring, frightening by its force or reassuring by its strength and certainty, with sustained energy and command. This speech of Othello is a sustained and violent Press; it is held back from the Fast Speed of a Punch by the Free Flow demanded by the images and the solemnity of the oath, as by the two breaths needed for the first sentence and the precision needed for the many polysyllabic words:

> OTHELLO: Like to the Pontic sea,
> Whose icy current and compulsive course
> Ne'er knows retiring ebb but keeps due on
> To the Propontic and the Hellespont,
> Even so my bloody thoughts with violent pace
> Shall ne'er look back, ne'er ebb to humble love
> Till that a capable and wide revenge
> Swallow them up. Now by yon marble heaven
> In the due reverence of a sacred vow
> I here engage my words.
>
> (*Othello*, Act 3, Sc. 3)

Some words associated with Press: strive; uncrease; iron; flatten; squeeze; stroke; strain; stress; crush; pull; push; urgent; trundle; heave; clasp; harass; beset; offer urgently or abundantly; entreat.

Flick

FLICK is the opposite of Press, being Flexible, Fast and Light. It shares many qualities with Dab, which is why you must concentrate on the difference in Space between Dab's Directness and Flick's Flexibility. This Flexibility gives Flick a whisking, flickering, scattered, more frivolous movement than the Direct organisation of a Dab.

In sound, Flick can be syncopated, irregular, staccato and percussive in Bound Flow, or rippling inconsequentially in Free Flow. The Flexibility gives a slight edge to the Free-Flow aspect of a Flick Effort. In speech, attention and concentration might be scattered, with sudden leaps of thought from one subject to another and a noticeable Flexibility in vocal inflection.

I have chosen an excerpt from *Loot* by Joe Orton to illustrate the inconsequence and swift changeability of Flick: Fay is advising McLeavy, who has just been made a widower.

> FAY: Realise your potential. Marry at once.
> MCLEAVY: St Kilda's would be in an uproar.
> FAY: The Fraternity of the Little Sisters is on my side. Mother Agnes-Mary feels you're a challenge. She's treating it as a specifically Catholic problem.
> MCLEAVY: She treats washing her feet as a Catholic problem.
> FAY: She has every right to do so.
> MCLEAVY: Don't Protestants have feet then?
> FAY: The Holy Father hasn't given a ruling on the subject and so, as far as I'm concerned, they haven't. Really, I sometimes wonder whether living with that woman hasn't made a free thinker of you. You must marry again after a decent interval of mourning.
>
> (Joe Orton, *Loot*, Act 1)

Some words associated with Flick: flutter; dart; stir; hover; frisk; skitter; flit; flitter; twitch; scatter.

Appendix:
Some suggestions to help
with drama-school auditions

Auditioning for a drama school is an important event in the life of an aspiring actor. The following suggestions come from my many years of being on the audition panel at several different English schools when I often wished that applicants had had some advice to help them do their best before putting their time, effort and money into the audition process.

Each school, of course, has a different system of auditioning, so the first thing to do is to read the information they give you and be sure to follow it. For instance, recently I was talking to a young actor who, in spite of having had the request from the school that applicants should avoid speeches from such characters as fairies or witches in Shakespeare, was happily preparing to do a speech of Puck for his audition. This would not help him …

WHAT ARE THE AUDITION PANEL LOOKING FOR?

It is easy to say 'talent' or 'potential'; this is true, but not precise enough for the anxious applicant. I think there are two things that the panel wants to know about you: the first is who you are – what interests you, what your background is, what it is that makes you want to be an actor, etc.

The second is whether you have the ability to transfer your attention from what I call 'the truth of daily life' – which is, at this point, your awareness of the fact that you are in an audition, that you are nervous, that your focus is on doing well, being accepted and so on – to the 'truth of imagination', which is the imagined situation of the character you are playing for those few precious minutes of the speech.

This shift of attention is hard to make, without the help of the experience of doing the rest of the play up to this point in the action and only an empty chair to talk to. But if you can do this – and most of us can do it to some extent at least – this is evidence of the ability to act. What you need is the courage, determination and intelligence, backed by preparation, to find and sustain your belief in the imagined situation, in spite of the stress of being in an audition. It might be helpful to reread the introduction of this book, to remind yourself of the actor's job description.

Most schools will give you a short interview as well as hearing your two speeches; some will also have asked you to fill in a form about your education and/or previous acting experience (the plays you were in at school, etc.) with a section to write a brief piece about yourself. Some applicants are taught to 'sell' themselves strongly in this written piece: they write and also talk in the interview about how successful they were in a role, how much 'passion' they have for acting, how nothing else will ever satisfy them and so on. For myself, this dazzling presentation is not helpful; I would rather find out the true person beneath. Each one of us is unique and special; let's trust that; it is enough.

When I am nervous I sometimes forget simple facts, such as the names of people or titles of plays I have seen. If this happens to you, prepare some answers to questions that you might be asked in your interview, like 'Have you seen any plays recently that you enjoyed?' 'What was it that you liked/disliked about them?' 'Is there an actor that you particularly admire?' If you want to be a part of the profession (a term which I much prefer to the word 'industry') you need to know as much as possible about the people already working in it and see as many plays (not just musicals!) as you can.

WHAT SHOULD I WEAR?

You don't need to dress up. Wear clothes that you feel comfortable in; be decent, clean and fairly tidy, in your own way. Girls, don't wear too much make-up – we want to see the real you! Be sure that your hair does not obscure your face when you are acting. Shoes are important as they affect the way you move. You don't need different clothes for your two different speeches.

WHAT SPEECHES SHALL I CHOOSE?

A well-written speech that suits you is half the battle! You are usually asked for two speeches – one classical, one modern, with another classical speech as a second choice.

The classical speech

The classical speech is usually taken from Shakespeare – though women, especially, could also look at the Jacobean playwrights – the speech should be in blank verse, rather than prose (see the Shakespeare chapter). Have your second classical speech learned and ready, just in case, as it might be that the panel feel that your first choice did not suit you very well, or that they have heard several other applicants do that speech already that day and would welcome a change.

For men looking through Shakespeare I suggest finding a speech by a less well-known character; this is easy as there are so many lords and messengers, etc. who have great speeches! Avoid characters such as Malvolio or Iago, as they are so strongly individual that you might slip into a formula; choose a young man, someone who you could play today.

Avoid comics! I know it is tempting but such a choice really does you no favours! Those speeches are usually in prose, so we can't hear how you handle the verse rhythm, and the longer speeches are usually directly addressed to the audience, so the main danger is that you will try to be funny, rather than playing the character and situation, and it will be more like an attempt at stand-up comedy, rather than acting in a scene.

For women it is more difficult as there is less choice and in long speeches the female is often pleading or attacking, which can lead to a whining or scolding delivery; look for less well-known speeches, as the obvious ones may well have been done by other applicants already that day! Look at Queen Margaret (*Henry VI*, Parts I, II and III, and *Richard III* (but NOT the 'molehill' speech!)), La Pucelle (Joan of Arc in *Henry VI*) (again NOT the 'conjuring of spirits' speech). Apart from Shakespeare, his colleagues Beaumont and Fletcher and their contemporaries wrote great parts for women; for instance, a play like *The Maid's Tragedy* is full of fine speeches.

With all the speeches you choose, you must read and understand the whole play; if you use one of the many books of audition speeches, find the play that the speech comes from. Other applicants may well choose those recommended speeches, so it is worth reading several plays to find something different. Do not cobble speeches together. On the information sheet that you get from the drama school it will often explicitly state this, but people still do it.

Classical pieces are often soliloquies, addressed to the audience. This can create a problem of delivery in the audition situation: you don't want to make eye-contact with the panel, so where do you focus? If you choose to fix on one point on the wall, behind the heads of the seated panel, there is the danger that you will freeze up and lose belief in the character's function of communication; it is not natural to talk to a wall! Try, instead, being a 'lighthouse': that is, letting the beam of your attention travel to your imaginary audience, behind the heads of the panel, in a sort of slight arc or semicircle, so that your gaze is kept alive. This helps when there is a change of subject or focus within the speech; a turn of the head or switch of attention marks these changes. You could practise this with a group of friends as your audience, so that you know what it feels like.

Alternatively, you could address your soliloquy to an imagined listener in a chair, keeping your focus within the 'stage-space'. If you choose to do this it might be helpful to explain to the panel that you understand that the speech is written as a direct address to the audience, but that you have chosen to play it like this today.

There is no need to announce your speeches, say who the character is or explain the situation of the scene; the panel already knows from the paperwork which speeches you have chosen and the members often know the play too.

If you want to use a chair for yourself or your imagined listener there is no need to ask if you may use one. Just place the chairs where you want them to be, always putting your listener on a downstage diagonal so that the panel can see your face easily as you talk. Listen carefully if you are asked to use a specific area of the room; some people, when asked to play at a little distance, keep coming forwards towards the panel, which makes it difficult to assess what they are doing.

The modern speech

You should select one that was written after the 1950s. You can ask other people for advice about this, but generally avoid playwrights like Noël Coward, Terence Rattigan, George Bernard Shaw, Anton Chekhov, etc., as they are too early.

It is vital to choose a well-written speech; you will know how good it is by seeing if every line is necessary, and there is no padding – not too much 'fine writing', in other words. Look for a strong through-line of intention and connection with the listener and plenty of changes of mood and focus, with a natural feeling that makes it easy to say and understand. Read the whole play.

What sort of noise do you enjoy listening to? If someone is moaning and whining at you, making you feel guilty, perhaps, or bored and embarrassed, or when a person is shouting at and scolding you, do those noises make you want to listen to them and give them what they are asking for? We are talking about the (invisible) scene partner now, as well as the auditioning panel. The character you are playing wants to get what they want from their scene partner/s. They try every Strategy possible through words and action to achieve their Objective by overcoming the Obstacles; the fact that this takes time, effort and many different approaches (we know that because it is a long speech) gives the speaker natural energy and clear connection with the listener. This is the action of your speech.

Dos and don'ts

- In a memory speech, remember that the present intention of the character is the direct communication of their story, rather than a misty reliving of it.
- Avoid victim and bully speeches.
- Choose a clear contrast between your classical and modern speeches. If one is sad the other should be cheerful; look at 'ordinary' life situations – you don't always have to be tense and dramatic!

- Don't set the bar too high! By this I mean avoid speeches that demand actions, situations and emotions which are hard to reach truthfully in an audition. Keep within an area of experience that you can connect with, though you may well not have lived through it yourself.
- AVOID: swearing; sexually explicit or violent language or innuendo. 'Challenging' often means embarrassing and is not helpful.
- Do not try to be funny.
- Do not shout/scream/whine/nag.
- Do not show us what **you** think of the character, i.e. play adjectives like 'silly' / 'posh' / 'ignorant' / 'sly' / 'stupid' / 'sexy' . . . You need to be on the character's side, playing from the inside with the intention / objective flowing out from your inner truth.
- Avoid accents that are not native to you; many applicants choose speeches from American plays and their attempt to master the accent often limits their range of expression. I would suggest choosing speeches that use your own voice and not trying to use 'Received Pronunciation' if that is not your natural accent; always remember that the panel wants to see you, not a pretend version of you.
- Decide on a simple pattern of movement so that you can be seen standing, sitting and moving around. If you don't do this you may well start wandering vaguely, which is a common mistake.
- When sitting, do not hunch forwards, collapsing the upper body.
- Think about gesture and physical expression as well as vocal variety of inflection, pitch, volume, intensity and stress.
- Go through your speeches for unit changes (see pp. 99–102). When the subject changes, a movement will want to happen.
- Find natural changes of rhythm – so many people stay in just one rhythm throughout a speech.
- If you are talking to an invisible listener decide where their face will be and look at that, rather than at the seat of the chair; if you want them to move about, decide in advance where they will go. Try your speech with a real person moving, if that is required by the scene, such as a 'don't go now' speech. Keep it simple.
- Do not used mimed objects. I find that this makes it much more difficult to maintain belief; if you need a prop such as a letter, bring a piece of paper; don't add unnecessary props.

- If the panel offer you any advice, do listen carefully; they want you to succeed. Remember that!
- KEEP BREATHING . . . use the support of the floor to give you stability and freedom of action.
- Enjoy the chance to act to an informed and friendly audience!

Postscript

This book has been hard to finish, because every class and rehearsal brings me new ideas and insights, usually from the achievements and comments of the actors I'm working with. I'd like to feel that your copy, which has helped to give the gift of sight to someone who you will never meet, will help you to understand and practise your craft.

Until one is committed there is hesitancy, the chance to draw back, always ineffectiveness. Concerning all acts of initiative and creation there is one elementary truth, the ignorance of which kills countless ideas and splendid plans: that the moment one definitely commits oneself, Providence moves in too. All sorts of things occur to help one that would otherwise not have occurred. A whole stream of events issues from the decision, raising in one's favour all manner of unforeseen incidents, meetings and material assistance, which no man could have dreamt would come his way. I have learned a deep respect for one of Goethe's couplets:
'Whatever you can do or dream you can, begin it.
Boldness has genius, power and magic in it!'
(W. H. Murray and Johann Wolfgang von Goethe)

Notes

Front matter

1   Joseph Conrad, *The Nigger of the Narcissus* (London: J. M. Dent, 1923)
2   Agnes De Mille, *Dance to the Piper* (London: Hamish Hamilton, 1951), p. 308

Introduction

1   V. O. Toporkov quoting Stanislavski, in *Stanislavski in Rehearsal*, Theatre Arts Books: New York, 1979, 170. The Russian actor tells an absorbing story of Stanislavski's working method in action.
2   As students at Central we were told to read Stanislavski's *An Actor Prepares* (London: Geoffrey Bles, 1937) but I didn't understand it then, as the training we were receiving provided little insight and, as far as I can remember, made very little practical reference to his system. Now that I have the new translations by Jean Benedetti, *An Actor's Work* (London: Routledge, 2007), and his invaluable *Stanislavski: An Introduction* (London: A & C Black, 1982), as well as the great *Stanislavski in Rehearsal: The Final Years*, by Vasily Osipovich Toporkov, I feel supported by Stanislavski's technique, information and inspiration.
3   Stanislavski says that while each actor shares the destination when working on a play, the journey itself varies: sometimes it is swift and direct and other times there are many stops and delays en route.
4   *The Cambridge Companion to Brecht*, Peter Thomson, Glendyr Sacks (eds) (Cambridge: Cambridge University Press, 1994) p. 283
5   Igor Stravinsky, Robert Craft, *Conversations with Igor Stravinsky* [New York: Doubleday, 1959], p. 55

Chapter 2

1 Keith Johnstone, *Impro: Improvisation and the Theatre* (New York: Theatre Arts Books, 1979).
2 Viola Spolin, *Improvisation for the Theater* (Evanston, IL: Northwestern University Press, 1963).

Chapter 3

1 Bertolt Brecht, *Brecht on Theatre*, trans. John Willetts (London: Methuen, 1964), p. 15

Chapter 5

1 There is a similar exercise, together with other mirror games, in Viola Spolin's book, *Improvisation for the Theater* (Evanston, IL: Northwestern University Press, first published in 1963). This useful book is full of exercises and ideas for improvisations.

Chapter 9

1 All quotations from William James' *The Gospel of Relaxation: Selected Papers on Philosophy* (Everyman, 1929), p. 29
2 Ibid.
3 Katya Benjamin, in correspondence with the author, April 2007.

Part Three

1 Published by Oberon in 1995.

Chapter 10

1 George Eliot, *Middlemarch*, eds Margaret Harris and Judith Johnston (London: J. M. Dent, 1997), pp. 189–90

2 Peter Gill has used the Russian patronymics in his translation, where the Christian name of a character is followed by his/her father's name, so Ranevskaya, as a married woman, is called by her husband's name, Ranevsky, with an 'a' added. Her friends call her by her Christian name, Liuba, followed by her father's name Andrey, with the added '-evna' to show that she is Andrey's daughter. Her brother is called Leonid followed by the masculine version of 'son of Andrey', Andreyevich. When I am rehearsing Chekhov plays, I ask my actors to give their own names in the Russian way, so that they can feel at home with this custom: so my name would be 'Brigid Henryevna', as my father was called Henri and my son's name would be Dominic Nicholevich.

Chapter 11

1 This exercise is not the 'word repetition' game used by the American acting teacher Sanford Meisner, as described in Chapter 2 of *Meisner on Acting* (New York: Random House, 1987).

Chapter 12

1 A great book by Caroline Spurgeon, *Shakespeare's Imagery and What It Tells Us* (Cambridge University Press, 1935), explores the central images of each of Shakespeare's plays.
2 Marshall B. Rosenberg, *Nonviolent Communication: A Language of Life* (2nd edition, Encinitas, CA: PuddleDancer Press, 2003), 170.
3 As Colin Cook, a teacher at LAMDA, puts it.

Part 4

1 Joseph Conrad, *Mirror of the Sea*, (London: J. M. Dent, 1923) Chapter 7, p. 32

Chapter 16

1 Harley Granville-Barker, Richard Eyre *Prefaces to Shakespeare: A Midsummer Night's Dream, The Winter's Tale, Twelfth Night* (London: Nick Hern Books, 1993), p. 169.
2 *Prefaces to Shakespeare*, vol. 6 (London: B. T. Batsford, 1974).

3 The play texts used as examples in this chapter are *Hamlet* and *A Midsummer Night's Dream*.

Chapter 18

1 Rudolf von Laban and F. C. Lawrence, *Effort: Economy in Body Movement* (London: Macdonald and Evans, 1947).

Chapter 21

1 Louis Frederic Austin, *Henry Irving in England and America 1838–84* (London: T. F. Unwin, 1884), p. 252.
2 See Rudolf von Laban, *Principles of Dance and Movement Notation* (London: Macdonald and Evans, 1975).
3 François Delsarte (1811–71) was a French music teacher who developed a system that became known as the Delsarte method, by which performers were taught to develop the expressiveness of their bodies.

Chapter 23

1 Rudolf von Laban, *The Mastery of Movement on the Stage* (London: MacDonald and Evans, 1960), pp. 121–2.
2 Rudolf von Laban and F. C. Lawrence, *Effort: Economy in Body Movement* (London: Macdonald and Evans, 1947, pp. 62–75).

Postscript

1 W. H. Murray, *The Scottish Expedition* (London: J. M. Dent, 1951).

Index

Related titles from Routledge

Psychophysical Acting

Phillip B. Zarrilli

"Being taken step-by-step through these highly evocative and fascinating exercises and concepts of actor training by a master such as Zarrilli certainly qualifies as essential reading."

David Zinder

Psychophysical Acting is a direct and vital address to the demands of contemporary theatre on today's actor. Drawing on over thirty years of intercultural experience, Phillip Zarrilli aims to equip actors with practical and conceptual tools with which to approach their work. Areas of focus include:

- A historical overview of a psychophysical approach to acting from Stanislavski to the present
- Acting as an 'energetics' of performance applied to a wide range of playwrights: Samuel Beckett, Martin Crimp, Sarah Kane, Kaite O'Reilly and Ota Shogo
- A system of training though yoga and Asian martial arts that heightens sensory awareness and dynamic energy, and in which body and mind become one
- Practical application of training principles to improvisation exercises.

Psychophysical Acting is accompanied by Peter Hulton's invaluable interactive DVD-ROM featuring exercises, production documentation, interviews and reflection.

ISBN13: 978–0–415–33457–0 (hbk)
ISBN13: 978–0–415–33458–7 (pbk)
ISBN13: 978–0–203–37528–0 (ebk)

Available at all good bookshops
For ordering and further information please visit:
www.routledge.com

Related titles from Routledge

Acting (Re)Considered:
A Theoretical and Practical Guide
2nd Edition
(Worlds of Performance)

Edited by Phillip Zarrilli

Acting (Re)Considered is a challenging and extraordinarily eye-opening collection of seminal essays about intercultural theories of acting, training and the actor's body in performance. *Acting (Re)Considered* is an essential part of every theatre student's repertoire, whether they are studying the history, the theory or the practice of acting.

Included are discussions on acting by or about most of the major figures that have shaped twentieth century performance, such as:

- Meyerhold
- Copeau
- Decroux
- Artaud
- Brecht
- Growtowski
- Barba
- Suzuki
- Fo
- Warrilow
- Rosenthal
- DaFoe

No other volume on acting is as wide-ranging, as comprehensive, or as international as this one. *Acting (Re)Considered* transforms possibilities for teachers and students of acting.

ISBN13: 978-0-415-26299-6 (hbk)
ISBN13: 978-0-415-26300-9 (pbk)

Available at all good bookshops
For ordering and further information please visit:
www.routledge.com